McDONALD INSTITUTE MONOGRAPHS

Archaeoacoustics

Edited by Chris Scarre & Graeme Lawson

Published by:

McDonald Institute for Archaeological Research
University of Cambridge
Downing Street
Cambridge, UK
CB2 3ER
(0)(1223) 339336
(0)(1223) 333538 (General Office)
(0)(1223) 333536 (FAX)
dak12@cam.ac.uk
www.mcdonald.cam.ac.uk

Distributed by Oxbow Books
 United Kingdom: Oxbow Books, Park End Place, Oxford, OX1 1HN, UK.
  Tel: (0)(1865) 241249; Fax: (0)(1865) 794449; www.oxbowbooks.com
 USA: The David Brown Book Company, P.O. Box 511, Oakville, CT 06779, USA.
  Tel: 860-945-9329; Fax: 860-945-9468

ISBN-10: 1-902937-35-X
ISBN-13: 9781-902937-35-9
ISSN: 1363-1349 (McDonald Institute)

© 2006 McDonald Institute for Archaeological Research

Edited for the Institute by Chris Scarre (*Series Editor*) and Dora A. Kemp (*Production Editor*).

Cover illustration: *The Brudevælte lur (see p. 66).*

Printed and bound by Short Run Press, Bittern Rd, Sowton Industrial Estate, Exeter, EX2 7LW, UK.

Contents

CONTRIBUTORS

ELIZABETH C. BLAKE
Department of Archaeology, Downing Street,
University of Cambridge, CB2 3DZ, UK.
Email: ecb46@cam.ac.uk

IAN CROSS
Faculty of Music, University of Cambridge, 11 West
Road, Cambridge, CB3 9DP, UK.
Email: ic108@cam.ac.uk

FRANCESCO D'ERRICO
UMR 5808 du CNRS, Institut de Préhistoire et de
Géologie du Quaternaire, Bâtiment B18 – Géologie,
Avenue des Facultés, 33405 Talence, France.
Email: f.derrico@iquat.u-bordeaux.fr

PAUL DEVEREUX
International Consciousness Research Laboratories,
301 N. Harrison St, Suite 416, Princeton, NJ 08540,
USA.
Email: pd@pauldevereux.co.uk

PETER HOLMES
21 Colin Drive, London, NW9 6ES, UK.
Email: peter@peterholmes.info

GRAEME LAWSON
McDonald Institute for Archaeological Research,
Downing Street, Cambridge, CB2 3ER, UK.
Email: ancientmusic@madasafish.com

IAIN MORLEY
McDonald Institute for Archaeological Research,
Downing Street, Cambridge, CB2 3ER, UK.
Email: irm28@cam.ac.uk

IEGOR REZNIKOFF
Département de Philosophie, Université de Paris X,
92001 Nanterre, France.
Email: dominiqueleconte@yahoo.fr

ELEONORA ROCCONI
Università degli Studi di Pavia, Faculté di
Musicologie, Corso Garibaldi 178, 26100 Cremona,
Italy.
Email: ele.rocconi@tin.it

CHRIS SCARRE
Department of Archaeology, University of Durham,
South Road, Durham, DH1 3LE, UK.
Email: chris.scarre@durham.ac.uk

STEVEN J. WALLER, PhD
5381 Wellesley Street, La Mesa, CA 91942, USA.
Email: wallersj@yahoo.com

AARON WATSON
PO Box 726, Lancaster, LA1 1XS, UK.
Email: a.watson@monumental.uk.com

EZRA B.W. ZUBROW
MFAC 380, PO Box 610005, Department of
Anthropology, University of Buffalo, Buffalo, NY
14261-0005, USA.
Email: zubrow@buffalo.edu

Figures

Tables

Preface

About the subject

Recent calls for an 'archaeology of the senses' have served as a timely, even overdue reminder that the past which we experience — and which others have experienced before us — is multisensory, drawing not only upon the primary field of vision, but also on touch, smell and hearing (Houston & Taube 2000; Cummings 2002; Thomas 1990). When we first enter megalithic tombs, Palaeolithic painted caves or Romanesque churches, the unusual sound qualities of those spaces strike us immediately. Voices resonate, external noises are subdued or eliminated, and a special aural dimension is discerned which complements the evidence of our other senses. Such sounds are intrinsic and indeed prominent elements of such experiences, elements that we ignore at our peril in seeking to understand the human use of places and the construction of buildings and monuments. Yet they are apt to be forgotten when prehistorians discuss such spaces in the abstract.

The growing field of archaeoacoustics focuses on the role of sound in human behaviour, from earliest times up to the development of mechanical detection and recording devices in the nineteenth century. In the British Isles and France archaeological interest in 'site acoustics' has had its origin in the need to unravel the enduring mysteries of Palaeolithic caves and late prehistoric stone monuments — and a growing realization that their acoustics might tell us something useful about the human activities which may or may not have taken place there. In North America, South Africa and Australia, similar concerns surround the interpretation of rock-art panels, where acoustical properties may have drawn people to confer special significance on specific places or features in the landscape.

From this recent beginning the subject has begun to develop its own agenda, primarily prehistoric in scope and architectural or topographical in direction; nevertheless it does not — or should not — exist in isolation from other sound-related enquiry. One of the purposes of the present volume is to bring together studies from separate but related areas of archaeoacoustics to establish more clearly the common ground that exists between the prehistoric acoustics of 'uncertain' places (which is to say, where human activities have gone unrecorded) and those of documented historical structures such as theatres and churches — and finds of musical instruments and sound-tools.

The study of remains of portable sound-producing devices, sometimes termed 'music archaeology', is a long-established and lively one, providing a useful, developed vantage-point from which to view archaeoacoustics. The antiquity of such tool-use behaviours is demonstrated by Upper Palaeolithic bone pipes, from Isturitz in the Pyrenees and from Geissenklösterle in South Germany, dating back some 35,000 years or more. The evolutionary importance of human musical behaviour may take us still further back (Cross 1999; Falk 2000; Mithen 2005). Elite tombs of more recent periods contain many musical grave-goods, sometimes comprising impressive suites of musical instruments; among them the Chinese fifth-century BC tomb of Marquis Yi of Zeng with more than 60 suspended bronze bells, a large rack of stone-chimes and a whole orchestra of stringed instruments, flutes and drums (Falkenhausen 1993). Representations in art (whether figurines or wall paintings) further assist the interpretation of musical traditions, especially elite traditions, in these more recent centuries. But it is through the routine processing of archaeological small-finds that we obtain the broadest, most coherent view of music's social prehistory. Following the pioneering example of Vincent Megaw (e.g. Megaw 1961; 1968a,b; 1981), work in this area at first followed a broadly organological and music-historical direction: focusing on specific artefact classes such as pipes or stringed instruments, and developing museum survey and cataloguing programmes in the search for new pieces — a process which still continues.

Interest in music archaeology in Cambridge goes back to the work of John Coles on Bronze Age horns (Coles 1963; 1973), and subsequently that of his PhD students who are amongst the contributors to the present volume (Holmes 1976; 1986; Lawson 1978 *et seq.*) In 1982, one of us (GL) hosted in Cambridge the first international conference of the 'Study Group on Music Archaeology', in association with the International Council for Traditional Music.

Since the mid-1980s these organological and socio-cultural approaches have matured considerably, leading in turn to increasing awareness of the need to address also the cognitive and behavioural implications which underlie 'music archaeology'; in particular seeking to elicit those elements which may characterize musical purpose and musical tradition in the archaeological record. It is to re-frame these wider and deeper questions in a way that embraces both tool-based and environmental phenomena that we have lately begun advocating the establishment of what might be called 'cognitive archaeoacoustics' (Lawson *et al.* 1998; Lawson & d'Errico 2002; 2003; Lawson 2004).

About the volume

The attentive reader will identify two interwoven approaches to archaeoacoustics in the contributions to the present volume. In the first, tools such as musical instruments and simple sound-makers offer an important alternative viewpoint in the study of ancient acoustic architectures, through consideration of the abilities of ancient peoples to generate and manipulate sound using portable objects, either natural or fabricated. Alongside this is set the study of the spaces themselves: from natural enclosures such as caves and ravines to chambers or other structures whose built forms would have served — whether by accident or design — to contain or exclude sound. In between is that large category of places and spaces where sound may or indeed must have played a role, but which are inherently difficult to assess.

But throughout the volume the primary focus of the contributors is, for want of a better word, *intention*. Hitherto we have tended in archaeoacoustics to employ commonsense arguments to allow us to assert the probability that ancient people — like ourselves — would have responded to and even engineered acoustic space. Such arguments risk becoming circular, however, as we attempt to peer further back into our human past. In the present volume, therefore, the contributors consider aspects of their own observations or methodologies which might enable us to convert data drawn from measurement of the ancient phenomena we study into admissible evidence of behavioural connexion; 'admissible', that is, in the sense that they are based on compelling arguments derived from specific evidence. The establishment of such arguments is in our view essential to the future of archaeoacoustics as a disciplinary endeavour, whether considering the properties of structures or of natural settings; and undoubtedly it represents a considerable challenge to our ingenuity.

The multi-period nature of 'music archaeology' may help us: for example, the sheer quantities of finds of Roman, medieval and even later date can offer an epistemological proving-ground and therefore inform our interpretation of still older material. Crucial insights are also afforded by ethnography, which not only illustrates the diversity of ways in which instruments and music can be made around the world today, but also reveals contrasting, non-western attitudes to 'sound' and 'music' and the different meanings attached to them by different cultures. Furthermore, the inherent interest of particular kinds of instruments or monuments should not obscure the fact that the most obvious and most ancient sound-producer of all is the human body: feet, hands and voice. The ubiquity of rhythmic and other musical behaviours in human populations today and the evident deep-rootedness of some of them in the archaeological record is indeed one of the most exciting aspects of archaeoacoustics, and is touched upon in several of the contributions to this volume.

The original papers from which the volume has developed were first presented at a workshop held at the McDonald Institute in Cambridge in June 2003. Although the purpose of the meeting was primarily to address methodological issues, it was also our aim in bringing together a broad range of specialists who were operating in this field to help give archaeoacoustics the prominence in archaeology that it most surely deserves. For, whatever difficulties we may encounter in trying to establish the specifics of prehistoric sound-use behaviours, no-one who has witnessed the phenomena for themselves can fail to appreciate their potential significance.

References

Coles, J.M., 1963. Irish Bronze Age horns and their relations with northern Europe. *Proceedings of the Prehistoric Society* 11, 326–56.

Coles, J.M., 1973. *Archaeology by Experiment*. London: Hutchinson University Library.

Cross, I., 1999. Is music the most important thing we ever did? Music, development and evolution, in *Music, Mind and Science*, ed. W.-Y. Suk. Seoul: Seoul National University Press 10–39.

Cummings, V., 2002. Experiencing texture and transformation in the British Neolithic. *Oxford Journal of Archaeology* 21, 249–61.

Falk, D., 2000. L'Australopithèque gracile: était-il musicien? La Recherche. *Hors-série* 4, Novembre 2000, 79–81.

Falkenhausen, L. von, 1993. *Suspended Music: Chime-bells in the Culture of Bronze Age China*. Berkeley (CA) & Oxford: University of California Press.

Holmes, P., 1976. The Evolution of Player-voiced Aerophones Prior to AD 500. Unpublished PhD thesis, University of London.

Holmes, P., 1986. The Scandinavian bronze lurs, in *The Bronze Lurs: Second Conference of the ICTM Study Group on Music Archaeology, Stockholm*, vol. II, ed. C.S. Lund. (Publications of the Royal Swedish Academy of Music 53.) Stockholm: Royal Swedish Academy of Music, 51–125.

Houston, S. & K. Taube, 2000. An archaeology of the senses: perception and cultural expression in ancient Mesoamerica. *Cambridge Archaeological Journal* 10(2), 261–94.

Lawson, G., 1978. The lyre from Grave 22, in *The Anglo-Saxon Cemetery at Bergh Apton, Norfolk*, eds. B. Green & A. Rogerson. (East Anglian Archaeology 7.) Gressenhall: Norfolk Museums Service, 87–97.

Lawson, G., 1999. Getting to grips with music's prehistory: experimental approaches to function, design and operational wear in excavated musical instruments, in *Experiment and Design: Archaeological Studies in Honour of John Coles*, ed. A. Harding. Oxford: Oxbow Books, 133–8.

Lawson, G., 2004. Music, intentionality and tradition: identifying purpose, and continuity of purpose, in the music-archaeological record, in *Studien zur Musikarchäologie IV*, eds. E. Hickmann & R. Eichmann. Rahden, Westf.: Verlag Marie Leidorf, 61–97.

Lawson, G. & F. d'Errico, 2002. Microscopic, experimental and theoretical re-assessment of Upper Palaeolithic bird-bone pipes from Isturitz, France: ergonomics of design, systems of notation and the origins of musical traditions, in *Studien zur Musikarchäologie III. Archäologie früher Klangerzeugung und Tonordnung*, eds. E. Hickmann, A.D. Kilmer & R. Eichmann. Rahden, Westf.: Verlag Marie Leidorf, 119–42.

Lawson, G. (with F. d'Errico), 2003. Origin of musical tradi-tions, 33–48, in The emergence of language, symbolism and music — an alternative multidisciplinary perspective, by F. d'Errico, C. Henshilwood, G. Lawson, M. Vanhaeren, A.-M. Tillier, M. Soressi, F. Bresson, B. Maureille, A. Nowell, J.A. Lakarra, L. Backwell & M. Julien. *Journal of World Prehistory* 17, 1–70.

Lawson, G., C. Scarre, I. Cross & C. Hills, 1998. Mounds, megaliths, music and mind: some thoughts on the acoustical properties *and purposes* of archaeological spaces. *Archaeological Review from Cambridge* 15, 111–34.

Megaw, J.V.S., 1961. Penny whistles and prehistory: further notes. *Antiquity* 35, 55–7.

Megaw, J.V.S., 1968a. Problems and non-problems in pal-aeo-organology: a musical miscellany, in *Studies in Ancient Europe: Essays Presented to Stuart Piggott*, eds. J.M. Coles & D.D.A. Simpson. Leicester: Leicester University Press, 333–58.

Megaw, J.V.S., 1968b. The earliest musical instruments in Europe. *Archaeology* 231, 124–32.

Megaw, J.V.S., 1981. The archaeology of musical instruments. *World Archaeology* 12.

Mithen, S., 2005. *The Singing Neanderthals: the Origins of Music, Language, Mind and Body.* London: Weidenfeld & Nicolson.

Thomas, J., 1990. Monuments from the inside: the case of the Irish megalithic tombs. *World Archaeology* 22, 168–78.

Chapter 1

Sound, Place and Space:
Towards an Archaeology of Acoustics

Chris Scarre

All spaces, both natural and cultural, have acoustical properties that would have been readily perceived by prehistoric and early historic societies. Some of these spaces may furthermore have been intentionally designed, or explicitly chosen, for rituals, ceremonies or other performances in which sound, and sound quality, was a crucial ingredient. They range from 'natural spaces' such as rock-art sites on the seashore or deep within caves, to sophisticated temples, churches and theatres. Whereas the built-in acoustical properties of the latter categories are well established, for many prehistoric structures and spaces it is difficult to determine that any given acoustical effect is the result of design and intention rather than simply an accidental by-product. Here archaeoacoustics shares the methodological difficulties encountered in archaeoastronomy, but two specific principles may be proposed: recurrent patterning, and closeness of fit. The former relies on the identification of homologies or similarities among different structures within a class: for example, that all vaulted churches or megalithic circles display similar acoustical properties. Closeness of fit, by contrast, applies to individual sites or structures that possess design features that are difficult to explain save by human intention. That design intentions are frequently complex is illustrated by European Romanesque churches where vaulting may have been introduced as much to reduce fire risk as to provide an enhanced acoustic for religious observances.

The study of sound and acoustics is an essential element in the development of an archaeology of the senses. Given the fundamental muteness of monuments and materials, it is also one of the most difficult aspects of prehistoric experience that we might seek to address. Symbolically-structured sound has an especially important role in human behaviour, in the form both of language and music. The structure of the throat and the position and morphology of the hyoid bone indicate that the potential for producing sophisticated vocalizations may already have been present in *Homo heidelbergensis* (300–400,000 years ago). There is then a considerable delay before the first evidence for musical instruments appears, at *c.* 35,000 years ago, but rhythm, music and vocalizations may have played a significant part in enhancing social bonding and group cohesiveness in early hominins (e.g. Morley 2002;

d'Errico *et al.* 2003; Mithen 2005). Humans also often attribute symbolic significance to naturally-occurring sounds; identifying thunder as the voice of a deity, for example, is one manifestation of the inherent tendency of humans to anthropomorphize their experience of natural phenomena (Guthrie 1993).

One approach to the study of sounds in prehistoric contexts is to consider the acoustics of archaeological spaces. This approach has been employed with success in the study of decorated Palaeolithic caves in France, where images were shown to have been positioned preferentially in those specific locations within the caves that present a high degree of resonance (Reznikoff & Dauvois 1988; Scarre 1989). Ethnographic evidence demonstrates that the attribution of special or sacred status to natural features such as caves, coasts and waterfalls frequently draws upon the acoustic effects associated with them (e.g. Colson 1997).

Armed with the appropriate specialist equipment, it is a relatively straightforward exercise for the researcher to demonstrate that certain spaces possess a particular acoustic. It is much less easy, where the context is a prehistoric site or feature, to interpret the human response to such properties. Interpretation in such circumstances is necessarily heavily dependent on criteria such as modification (the placement of rock art, the deposition of special artefacts) or design (the specific morphology of a built structure). Secure knowledge will necessarily be very difficult to achieve. A key methodological difficulty will be to determine whether those spaces were *designed* to have certain acoustical properties, or used in special ways because of those properties; or conversely whether those properties were simply an *incidental feature* of an enclosed or partially enclosed space. This is not, indeed, the whole of the enquiry, since unintended acoustic effects may themselves have played an important role in the activities carried out in a specific structure or location. But what we must seek to avoid is the fallacy of argument by assertion: that those acoustical properties which are an integral and unavoidable part of any space or structure must inevitably have been sought out and given salient significance by the prehistoric communities who created or encountered them.

It may be argued that this approach implies a narrow understanding of the behaviour and understanding of past societies, not many of whom will have shared concepts of causation and intention that are familiar in modern Western societies. It may be observed that in some ethnographic contexts, the makers and players of musical instruments do not consciously express the connection between design and manufacture, on the one hand, and the sounds produced, on the other. Such criticism — that in seeking evidence of intention we are failing to see these prehistoric artefacts, structures, or behaviours in ways that they would have been understood by those prehistoric, non-Western societies — is well taken. But it does not overcome the fundamental problem, that *any* structure, space or artefact, along with any natural feature or setting, will have acoustical properties. The argument can be reversed: sound may have been an important element at archaeological sites that display no evidence of acoustical intent. Hence the absence of a specific acoustic does not demonstrate that sound played no part in the activities carried out there. Equally, however, it is not sufficient to demonstrate that a site or structure (or a natural location) possesses acoustic properties for the argument to be made that sound was or must have been an important part of the

activities and beliefs associated with that place. The problem with such an assumption is very simply the observation that every setting or structure will possess acoustic properties. When studying the physical remains the archaeologist may hence expect to encounter a range of circumstances, from sites with very specific acoustic effects, so specific that they appear to have been carefully designed; to places or structures where patterns are less clear and greater ambiguity of interpretation remains.

My intention, therefore, is not to impose a twenty-first-century understanding of causation and intention on prehistoric or other non-Western societies, but to ask how archaeologists may seek to identify places and structures where sound and sound properties were of special significance. Sound will of course have played a significant part in the human comprehension and use of virtually all spaces and places. Acoustics are present both in humanly-built structures and unmodified nature. The sounds of the waves may have played a part in making coastal boulders a preferred location for Saami rock art in northern Europe (Helskog 1999). The silence and sensory deprivation experienced in deep Palaeolithic caves in France and Spain are essential to understanding the significance of the art produced there, though whether such deprivation is directly related to trance and hallucination and whether those experiences were among the sources of the art remains controversial (Helvenston & Bahn 2003; 2004; Clottes 2004). The implication of acoustics have also been explored in the case of prehistoric structures such as stone circles, where sounds will naturally be modified and deflected by the monolithic uprights (Watson & Keating 1999; 2000). Finally of course we may cite the very intentional acoustics of specially-designed structures such as Romanesque churches and Graeco-Roman theatres (Reznikoff this volume; Rocconi this volume).

All of these have the potential for either natural ambient sounds or special humanly-produced sounds to have played a significant part in any human practices associated with them. That is perhaps very clear in the case of structures such as theatres and (to a lesser extent) churches; but becomes progressively less clear as our evidence for the activities carried out in those locations becomes less secure, because more remote from our own experience.

Mesoamerica

In some instances, direct evidence for activities involving sound survives in the form of musical instruments or other sound producers. These allow specific acoustical properties to be explored and documented, and may enable the relationship between sound producers and the physical settings in which they were used (such as particular buildings) to be investigated. One such instance is the discovery of Danish Bronze Age horns, known as lurs, close to reverberant rock faces (Goldhahn pers. comm.). Another is the cave of Isturitz, where it may be no coincidence that a large assemblage of Palaeolithic bone pipes came from a large cave with a powerful natural acoustic (Lawson & d'Errico 2002).

Useful though this is, however, the analysis of preserved instruments can never be more than a small part of the total sound story. On the one hand, preserved instruments from most periods of prehistory remain relatively rare. Some categories, such as ceramic vessels that may have been covered in hide to serve as drums (Malinowski 1981, 267), might still be lying unrecognized in museum collections, but it is clear that musical instruments have not survived in significant numbers from the more distant periods of the human past.

The second obstacle in studying sounds from the remains of musical instruments is that the most important of all sound producers will have been the human voice. Here our principal source of information is both relatively recent and also very uneven in its geographical and chronological distribution: the survival of notations or depictions. In recent European traditions, the use of written musical notations has become commonplace since their origins in the ninth century AD (Lawson forthcoming). Depictions of musicians or musical performances are more common and many of these are relatively well known, such as the tomb paintings of second-millennium Egypt or the models from Chinese tombs of the Zhou, Han and Tang periods (e.g. Manniche 1991; Caroselli 1987). These rarely include any representation of the sounds or music that was produced. In Mesoamerican art, however, actual sounds were portrayed in a number of ways:

- 'sound scrolls', as in the Codex Borbonicus (Fig. 1.1a) where the Aztec god of music Xochipilli is shown with an elaborate song scroll marked with a jewelled flower (Houston & Taube 2000, 276). Flowers were closely associated with rulers and gods in Aztec belief; the souls of Aztec warriors were thought to go to a flowery celestial paradise. The flower might also, however, be intended to convey something of the special quality or beauty of the sounds emanating from the gods. Murals from the Tepantitla compound at Teotihuacan (Fig. 1.1b) take this a stage further, indicating the content of the sounds by the addition of adjectival hieroglyphs describing what is being said (Houston & Taube 2000, 278).

- 'speech scrolls', common in Classic Maya art, where the scroll ends in or contains a hieroglyphic text. The text conveys the content of the speech, but it is interesting to note that additional meaning may be encoded in the form of the scrolls themselves. There are also Zapotec examples (Fig. 1.1c). As Houston & Taube observe

  > Speech scrolls, although often faint and easily undetected, loop about in whiplash motions in Late Classic Maya art. This may indicate the modulated tone or oscillating volume expected in rhetoric. Truly the glyphs talk: in most cases the speech scrolls loop from open mouths to glyphic captions. (Houston & Taube 2000, 280)

- what we may term 'modified sound scrolls' take this further and seek to depict sound effects. These include 'echo effects in architectural spaces through the expedient of stray speech scrolls detached from human lips' (Fig. 1.6d) and 'thunderous reverberations from the mouth of the rain and lightning god Chaak or similar deities' where the 'undulating or jagged lines seem to denote powerful, rumbling sound' (Figs. 1.6e & 1.6f) (Houston & Taube 2000, 280).

For Houston & Taube, one implication of these depictions is to draw attention to the acoustical properties of Maya architecture:

> The analytic implications of an emphasis on spaces filled with speech are that archaeologists need to pay more attention to the acoustics of buildings, especially palaces. For example, most visitors to Maya sites comment anecdotally on whisper effects or the astonishing distances that sound can travel over plazas, and up or down staircases ... It is improbable that the Maya were unaware of such qualities and that, as master builders, they failed to manipulate the interplay of sound and speech (Houston & Taube 2000, 280–81).

This conveniently brings us back to the material evidence of buildings and spaces, and the question as to whether we can ascertain from their morphology that they were designed with particular effects of sound or acoustics in mind.

Chavín

The ambiguity that so often arises from examining buildings for their acoustic properties may be illustrated by another American example: the temple of Chavín de Huántar in Peru.

The ceremonial centre of Chavín de Huántar was founded in around 900 BC in the late Initial Period of the Peruvian Highland zone. It is located in dramatic terrain, in the lowland basin close to where the deeply entrenched Huachecsa River flows into the broader

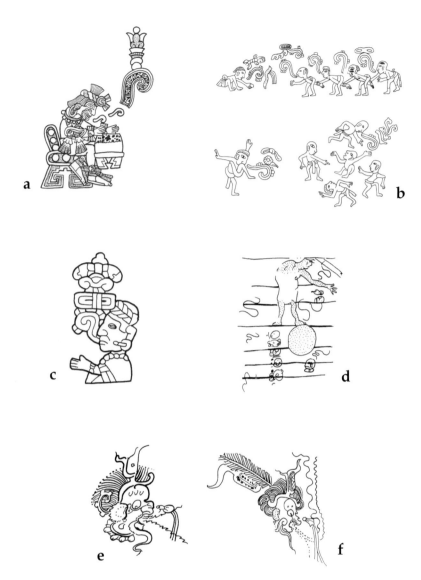

Figure 1.1. *Representations of sound in Mesoamerican art: (a) the Aztec god Xochipilli with elaborate song scroll topped by a jewelled flower sign; (b) dancing figures from the Tepantitla compound at Teotihuacan with sound scrolls; (c) Zapotec figure from Lápida de Matatlan with speech scroll containing hieroglyphic signs; (d) Maya ballcourt scene with stray speech scrolls that may represent echoes; (e) and (f) Maya rain and lightning god Chaak with jagged lines perhaps depicting the sound of thunder. (After Houston & Taube 2000.)*

in the rituals performed at Chavín: the use of psychotropic snuffs such as ground vilca or epena seeds (containing tryptamine) is suggested by carved reliefs depicting nasal discharges. One seventeenth-century missionary described the taking of such snuffs among people of Colombia. A stone frieze in the circular plaza at Chavín also includes representations of the San Pedro cactus, a plant containing mescaline, an infusion of which was apparently drunk as a beverage. These hallucinogens were associated with the belief that the priests could transform themselves into jaguars, and stages in the process of transformation were also carved in the stone sculptures at the temple (Burger 1992, 157).

The taking of hallucinogens may have been restricted to priests but particular features of the architecture indicate that special sound effects were also created, and that these were directed not towards the ritual specialists but towards a wider audience of onlookers. The monumental structures at Chavín are divided into the chronological groups labelled the 'Old Temple' and 'New Temple'. The Old Temple was a U-shaped structure with the projecting wings surrounding a sunken circular court. The temple faces east, towards the rising sun. Behind the circular court, in the heart of the temple, a hidden gallery leads to a tall chamber containing a sculptured granite monolith known as the Lanzón (lance), standing at the centre of a cruciform gallery (Fig. 1.2). In symbolic terms, the Lanzón constitutes an *axis mundi*, with its top set into the roof of the chamber and its base deeply embedded in the floor.

Mosna (Fig. 1.2) (Burger 1992, 128). The remains of the temple lie on slightly raised ground within the confluence of the two rivers, but are overlooked by the high mountains of the Cordillera Blanca. The site itself probably had cosmological significance. The junction of the two rivers was regarded by traditional Quechua communities as a place of the harmonious meeting of opposing forces; the name Chavín may itself derive from Quechua *chawpin* meaning 'in the centre' (Burger 1992, 128, 130). Hallucinogens may have played a part

Access to this chamber was probably carefully restricted, and it is thought that visitors or worshippers stood in the circular plaza below the temple (Von Hagen & Morris 1998, 211). Here they may have experienced a series of auditory effects generated by special structures built into the foundations of the Old Temple. Beneath the platforms and courts was a series of subterranean galleries. These lacked windows and had constantly to be supplied with fresh air by hundreds of air ducts that allowed air flow both from gallery to gallery and between the galleries and the outside world. Air flow was driven by temperature differences:

> The ventilation ducts brought all the passages and chambers of the Old Temple together into a single system of air circulation whose outlets were in the masonry facing of the parament and the roof the pyramid ... The thermal difference between the two environments generated a continual flow of fresh air throughout the subterranean galleries (Burger 1992, 141).

In addition to these ventilation ducts, an extensive series of conduits runs under the building. These were intended for drainage in the wet season, to prevent the temple being weakened by water seepage. The principal conduits measure up to 60–70 cm square in section and are stone-lined, with stepped floors and sometimes sinuous courses. They run over the Lanzón and under the central staircase and Circular Plaza, channelling rainwater safely away into the River Mosna (Burger 1992, 141).

The objectives of these air shafts and water conduits were to keep the interior dry. The relatively low temperature, constant humidity, and good air circulation of the internal chambers of the Old Temple may also have made them suitable for the storage of perishables. Lumbreras, however, has argued that the profusion of air ducts and water conduits exceeds practical needs and was designed and built to create acoustic effects: whose source may have appeared mysterious and perhaps supernatural to worshippers gathered in the central Court (Burger 1992, 143). In an experiment, water was poured into the conduits running under the central staircase. As Burger describes it, 'The noise made by the water rushing through stone-lined canals, over steps and around right-angled corners was surprisingly loud, and closer to the sound of pulsating applause than flowing water' (Burger 1992, 143). Furthermore, the resulting sound was projected from the temple onto the plazas and terraces below. Lumbreras was able to amplify the sound of the rushing water by opening and closing different vents. As one commentator has noted, by virtue of these carefully-designed structures, 'Chavín's temple

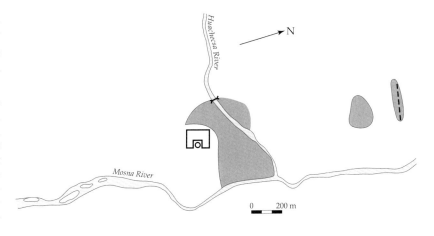

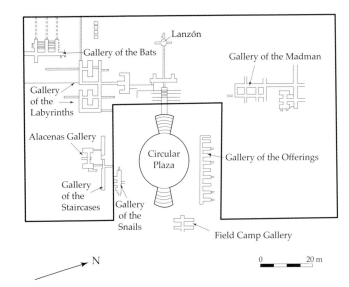

Figure 1.2. *Chavín de Huántar, Peru: (above) location of the temple site at the junction of two river valleys; (below) plan of the Old Temple showing some of its internal galleries. (After Burger 1992.)*

may have literally roared, thunder-like, with the voice of its oracle' (Von Hagen & Morris 1998, 212).

The Whispering Gallery

Chavín provides an excellent example of a structure that may have incorporated special sound effects — indeed we may positively assert that it did incorporate such effects. Yet there remains the issue of intentionality. Were the subterranean galleries and conduits built specifically from the outset to create sound effects? Or was that simply an accidental by-product of a construction that was designed for other purposes? Of course, even should the latter have been the case, that does not necessarily mean that the builders — or the priests — may not have exploited the acoustics in the performance of ceremonies and rituals where mysterious sounds would have added to the supernatural effects. And here indeed we may have an elision between built structures which accidentally incorporate specific acoustic properties, and places in the natural landscape which offer echoes and reverberations that may have drawn human attention and made them the locus of mythological explanations and ritual practices. The placement of art in Palaeolithic caves has also been shown to relate to the natural acoustical properties of particular locations within those caves (Reznikoff & Dauvois 1988; Scarre 1989). The location of open-air rock art of Horseshoe Canyon in Utah has also been shown to correlate exactly with the five locations within the canyon possessing the greatest intensity of echoing (Waller 2000; this volume).

In the case of built structures, therefore, the presence of specific acoustical effects can be subject to at least three alternative interpretations:

a) that they were an integral part of the design, intended from the very outset;
b) that they were an accidental by-product of the design, but were recognized and exploited to enhance rituals and ceremonies;
c) that they were an accidental by-product of the design, and were never used in an intentional way.

That striking acoustic effects can arise completely by accident is illustrated by a number of famous examples, including St Paul's Cathedral in London. This was designed by Sir Christopher Wren in the late seventeenth century and built between 1695 and 1710. It is the only baroque cathedral in Britain and is particularly famous for its dome, which is second in size only that to that of St Peter's in Rome.

At the base of the dome, a circular gallery runs around its interior, some 30 metres above the floor. This has become known as the Whispering Gallery, a name which derives from what has been called a 'charming quirk' in its design, on account of which a whisper against the wall of the gallery becomes audible on the opposite side. The internal diameter of the dome at this point is 42 metres, which makes the phenomenon particularly striking, and much loved by tourists. Yet despite contemporary interest in whispering galleries and similar acoustical effects (discussed for example by Athanasius Kircher in his *Neue Hall- und Tonkunst* of 1684) it is generally considered that the Whispering Gallery of St Paul's Cathedral is an accidental by-product of the shape of the dome, and not an intended feature (Downes 1988, 115). There is no suggestion that it played any part in ceremonies or performances within the cathedral. It might be argued that such an isolated example of a striking but accidental (and unexploited) acoustical

effect has little significant bearing on the archaeological study of the acoustics of prehistoric structures. On the contrary, it has an important methodological implication, to which we shall return below. And it provides a caution that not all acoustic affects are intended; and furthermore some that are detected by modern analysis may neither have been recognized nor exploited in the past.

Archaeoastronomy

It may be objected that the Whispering Gallery of St Paul's is of limited general relevance since it is an isolated case. It is clear that reliable interpretations will emerge best where patterns can be detected in the evidence. The discovery of a particular acoustical property at a single site or building may be difficult to assess in isolation, as it could have arisen by chance. To discover the same or a similar effect across a whole range of sites, by contrast, allows a more powerful argument to be presented.

A close analogy may here be drawn with the problems of validation facing another branch of archaeology: the study of archaeoastronomy. Historical records make clear that many structures — from traditional houses to Christian churches — are set out in accordance with the cardinal directions or the movements of the sun at particular times of year. It may safely be assumed that similar considerations governed the laying-out and location of prehistoric structures. The challenge for archaeologists lies in devising a methodology on the basis of which robust arguments can be made for associating particular sites or monuments with specific astronomical events. The position is significantly complicated by attempts to associate prehistoric structures not only with the movements of the sun, but also with those of the moon and certain stars and planets.

Archaeoastronomy has gained rather a bad name in many areas of archaeology owing to the methodological weakness and wishful thinking that has accompanied some of the more famous attempts. Part of the problem lies in the statistics. Alexander Thom believed he had identified patterns of 8 or 16 months in the orientations of stone circles in western Scotland (Thom 1967). Clive Ruggles has recently re-analyzed this body of information and has indicated a number of serious weaknesses (Ruggles 1999, 49ff., 142). These relate both to the claimed precision of the observations and to ethnographic information which indicates, for example, that the concept of the equinox (mid-way between the summer and winter solstices) appears to hold little significance outside the Western scientific tradition (Ruggles 1999, 148).

Principle 1: patterned repetition

Recent reassessments of orientation observations on west European prehistoric monuments have sought to establish methodological principles which can support more robust arguments than those of Alexander Thom and earlier pioneers. The most significant methodological principle is that of establishing repeated trends or patterns (Ruggles 1999). An astronomical alignment observed at a single site may be no more than accidental; one that is repeated across whole series of sites of a similar kind and date may however be attributed to something more than chance.

This can be illustrated by a contrasting pair of examples. The chambered cairn of Carn Ban on the Isle of Arran appears to show a striking orientation on the midsummer solstice sunrise. When we place this single example within its immediate context, however, a very different pattern emerges: of 21 chambered tombs on Arran, only one other approaches Carn Ban in its midsummer sunrise orientation; the others have orientations which are scattered around the compass (Fig. 1.3) (Burl 1981). It is hard to make a case that the orientation of Carn Ban on the midsummer sunrise was the result of intention rather than chance; though equally we cannot rule that out.

A very different level of confidence attaches to the orientations of passage graves in Brittany: here a whole series of tombs displays the same orientation, clustering between east and south (L'Helgouach 1965, 76–9). Studies of tomb orientations in southern France and Iberia have revealed a similar range of values which may have been associated with particular sets of funerary practice and belief (Hoskin 2001). In this case, the repeated nature of the orientation creates a strong argument that it was an intended outcome on the part of the builders.

Principle 2: closeness of fit

It is important, however, not to dismiss isolated cases without further consideration. For if one principle of a

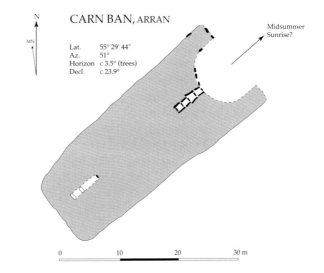

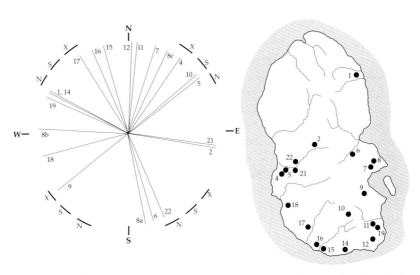

Figure 1.3. *Neolithic chambered tomb orientations on the Scottish island of Arran: (above) Carn Ban, showing its apparent alignment on the midsummer solstice sunrise; (below) alignments of 21 chambered tombs on Arran illustrating the absence of any predominant orientation. (Carn Ban = tomb no. 10.) (After Burl 1981.)*

secure knowledge of the past is patterned repetition, another must be closeness of fit.

Stonehenge may serve as an appropriate if somewhat contentious illustration of this second methodological principle. This major Neolithic monument developed through a series of stages over a period of several hundred years, beginning as a simple bank and ditch with timber structures, and ending with the complex stone settings that we see today.

It was William Stukeley in 1723 who first noted that at dawn on the midsummer solstice the rising sun shines directly along the axis of Stonehenge. This axis is set by the Heel Stone and its now vanished neighbour, by the midline of the avenue in its final approach to Stonehenge, and by the layout of the trilithon horseshoe at the centre of the monument. The alignment of these features is so precise that it must have been intentional. Whether Stukeley and later observers have correctly read the direction of the alignment has recently been called into question; there are grounds for believing that it was the midwinter sunset, rather than the midsummer sunrise, that was the true focus of the phase 3 monument (Chippindale 2004, 236–7).Whichever interpretation is preferred, this orientation is a feature only of the third phase of Stonehenge, and the earlier phases do not appear to have followed the same axis. Thus the original northeastern entrance, defined by the break in the bank and ditch, frames a segment of the sky between 30° and 24°N, centred on 27°N. The midsummer solstice orientation of 24°N barely fits within this window, and leads us to conclude that the original Stonehenge was not aligned on either midsummer sunrise or midwinter sunset. It may have been aligned on lunar events, or may have had no astronomical reference at all (Ruggles 1999, 136–8).

Thus solar symbolism appears only to have become important during the later modification of the monument, and it is the evidence that the monument was modified so as to incorporate the midsummer sunrise/midwinter sunset orientation that provides the strongest argument that this orientation was knowingly and intentionally created. Even were Stonehenge the only prehistoric monument in southern Britain to incorporate this orientation, it would be difficult to argue that it had arisen by chance alone. Intention on the part of the builders appears the inescapable conclusion. Hence in this case, the argument is not based on repeated patterning but on 'closeness of fit'. This principle may be applicable to features of acoustical design that are difficult to explain as being other than the product of a careful planning or manipulation of the building or structure.

Monastic vaults

We have argued that the quest for a secure knowledge of the creation and use of acoustic effects in prehistoric and early historic structures rests essentially on two methodological bases: the recognition of repeated patterns in the evidence; and striking closeness of fit in specific individual cases. Unique cases that do not form parts of a pattern may nonetheless provide evidence for a convincing argument, as in the case of the solar alignment at Stonehenge. The apparently accidental yet pronounced acoustics of many structures, such as the Whispering Gallery at St Paul's, urge that

considerable caution be exercised in the interpretation of such isolated examples. Patterns of evidence hence provide the strongest argument for the intentional creation of acoustic effects in prehistoric and early historic structures. They are amenable to archaeological analysis, and hence provide a positive basis from which to proceed. It would be misleading to conclude, however, that such approaches allow us to 'read off' the aims and experiences of those who built and used prehistoric structures. The ambiguity of architectural design may be illustrated by historically-documented examples, such as the widespread introduction of vaulting in major West European churches during the central Middle Ages.

Stone vaulting became a regular feature of church design in western Europe during the tenth and eleventh centuries AD. Vaulting appears in most of the wealthy monastic or cathedral churches from the mid-tenth century onwards. This innovation may in part be associated with the foundation in the early tenth century of the Cluniac monastic order (Conant 1974). The monks of Cluny and its daughter houses placed great emphasis on impressive religious ceremonies accompanied by music, and above all by the singing or chanting of monastic choirs. As one architectural historian has written 'the Cluniac psalmody, admired and imitated throughout western Europe, was most beautiful when sung in vaulted — especially tunnel-vaulted — churches' (Conant 1974, 187). Hence eleventh-century Cluniac churches had groined vaults over aisles and tunnel vaults over naves.

The employment of stone vaulting, however, not only had acoustic properties but was also a method of fire-proofing. Thus vaulting was used in castles, even in basement storage areas where no acoustic purpose seems likely. The history of churches with timber roofs also makes clear how vulnerable they were to fire. The cathedral of Chartres, for example, was subject to recurrent fires: the church built in AD 743 was burned in 858 and rebuilt; this in turn was burned in 1020 and replaced by a grandiose but still wooden-roofed church, whose completion was delayed by a fire during the works in 1030. This building was completed in 1037, only to be destroyed in turn by another fire, exactly a century later, in 1137. The early twelfth-century church had an even shorter life than its predecessor, meeting its end in the 'wonderful and miserable fire' of 1194, after which the current Gothic cathedral, with stone vault, was built (Conant 1974, 155). Even the stone vault, did not render the cathedral completely immune to fire risk, though the fire of 1836 resulted only in the loss of its outer wooden roof.

Hence stone vaulting may have been considered by the builders of these churches to create a particular and desired acoustic that was associated with a new emphasis on music in ritual. Tunnel vaults in Cluniac churches would be the clearest expression of this relationship. Yet vaulting in itself does not serve only as an acoustic device, but also as fire protection. This documented mixture of possible motives is an important reminder that simple explanations will rarely provide an adequate understanding or interpretation, and it also helps to situate acoustical concerns within a broader framework of human activities and intentions. The advantage of these historical examples is that comparison can be made between structural design and the specific practices carried out within or adjacent to buildings or structures. The results may often be amibiguous, but they provide further foundations upon which secure methodologies for the interpretation of prehistoric sound spaces can be built.

Conclusion

The archaeoacoustics of prehistoric contexts is potentially a vital part of the understanding of the lived experience of past societies. When visiting prehistoric sites — or indeed when handling and observing prehistoric artefacts — the practice of privileging the visual is deeply entrenched in archaeological method. Very few archaeologists have thought to record the auditory experience of entering a tomb or temple, or standing in front of a panel of rock art. The sound-producing properties of prehistoric remains have all too often been only tacitly recognized. Yet sound would have been an integral part of many of the activities performed at or associated with these sites and objects. This may include the sounds of their creation. Goldhahn has very pertinently observed that pecking the carvings into the rocks at Nåmforsen would itself have had an auditory accompaniment, the hammering of rock against rock creating a particular acoustic effect against the background sound of the roaring rapids (Goldhahn 2002). The Shoshoni of North America believed that the rock art represented spirits, and that those spirits were steadily adding new depictions of themselves, an activity associated with its characteristic sound: 'one can hear the spirits chiselling their pictures if one comes near these places in the wintertime' (Hultkrantz 1986, 54). In Scandinavian Bronze Age rock art, the noise made by pecking of the images may also have been a form of ritual communication with the various spirits that were thought to dwell in the rocks. Nordström suggests that the echo might have been interpreted as a carrier of messages between the world of the living and the dead: the ancestor's answer and participation in rituals (Nordström 1999, 134; quoted in Goldhahn 2002). Nor are such acoustic

effects limited to the sounds of rock-art creation. Several rock-art sites are associated with 'ringing rocks' that when struck emit a particular sound. At Kupgal in southern India, 'ringing rocks' were marked by multiple small groove-like depressions which indicated where the stone should be struck to produce the sound. The associated rock art included cattle depictions probably of Neolithic date, and while the practice of striking the rocks could not itself be dated, it may be of considerable antiquity (Boivin 2004). The 'ringing rocks' of Kupgal appear to be analogous to the 'gong rocks' of southern Namibia, which emit a harsh metallic sound when struck in certain places with the palm of a hand, a piece of wood or a cloth-wrapped rock (Ouzman 2001, 241). Waller suggests that the striking of rocks to create a sound similar to hoof beats may have been practised in the decorated caves of south-western France during the Upper Palaeolithic (Waller 1993; this volume).

Such direct evidence of acoustic behaviour in prehistoric contexts is rare. In most cases it is left to the archaeologist to infer from the characteristics of the space or place, drawing also on appropriate ethnography, whether acoustics and sound may have played a special or prominent role. Careful assessment of the available evidence does however open a rich field of possibilities. The methodological frameworks outlined above are offered as a contribution to debate, as a way of setting inferences on a more secure footing. As the contributions to this volume show, however, the diversity of the evidence from prehistoric and early historic periods remains at present a largely untapped resource. The study of archaeoacoustics has much to offer, and has scarcely begun.

Acknowledgements

I am grateful to Graeme Lawson for reading and commenting on an earlier version of this paper, and to Dora Kemp for preparing the illustrations.

References

Boivin, N., 2004. Rock art and rock music: petroglyphs of the south Indian Neolithic. *Antiquity* 78, 38–53.
Burger, R.L., 1992. *Chavín and the Origins of Andean Civilization.* London: Thames & Hudson.
Burl, A., 1981. 'By the light of the cinerary moon': chambered tombs and the astronomy of death, in *Astronomy and Society in Britain during the period 4000–1500 BC*, eds. C.L.N. Ruggles & A.W.R. Whittle. (British Archaeological Reports, British Series 88.) Oxford: BAR, 243–74.
Caroselli, S.L. (ed.), 1987. *The Quest for Eternity: Chinese Ceramic Sculptures from the People's Republic of China.* London: Thames & Hudson.

Chippindale, C., 2004. *Stonehenge Complete*. 3rd edition. London: Thames & Hudson.

Clottes, J., 2004. Hallucinations in caves. *Cambridge Archaeological Journal* 14(1), 81.

Colson, E., 1997. Places of power and shrines of the land. *Paideuma* 43, 47–57.

Conant, K.J., 1974. *Carolingian and Romanesque Architecture 800–1200*. Harmondsworth: Penguin Books.

d'Errico, F., C. Henshilwood, G.Lawson, M. Vanhaeren, A.-M. Tillier, M. Soressi, F. Bresson, B. Maureille, A. Nowell, J. Lakarra, L. Backwell & M. Julien, 2003. Archaeological evidence for the emergence of language, symbolism and music — an alternative multidisciplinary perspective. *Journal of World Prehistory* 17, 1–70.

Downes, K., 1988. *The Architecture of Wren*. Reading: Redhedge.

Goldhahn, J., 2002. Roaring rocks: an audio-visual perspective on hunter-gatherer engravings in northern Sweden and Scandinavia. *Norwegian Archaeological Review* 35, 29–60.

Guthrie, S.E., 1993. *Faces in the Clouds: a New Theory of Religion*. New York (NY): Oxford University Press.

Helskog, K., 1999. The shore connection: cognitive landscape and communication with rock carvings in northernmost Europe. *Norwegian Archaeological Review* 32, 73–94.

Helvenston, P.A. & P.G. Bahn, 2003. Testing the 'three stages of trance' model (with comments by J.L. Bradshaw & C. Chippindale). *Cambridge Archaeological Journal* 14(2), 213–24.

Helvenston, P.A. & P.G. Bahn, 2004. Waking the trance-fixed. *Cambridge Archaeological Journal* 14(1), 90–98.

Hoskin, M., 2001. *Tombs, Temples and their Orientations: a New Perspective on Mediterranean Prehistory*. Bognor Regis: Ocarina Books.

Houston, S. & K. Taube, 2000. An archaeology of the senses: perception and cultural expression in ancient Mesoamerica. *Cambridge Archaeological Journal* 10(2), 261–94.

Hultkrantz, A., 1986. Rock drawings as evidence of religion: some principal points of view, in *Words and Objects. Towards a Dialogue between Archaeology and History of Religion*. ed. G. Steinsland. Oslo: Norwegian University Press, 42–56.

Lawson, G. & F. d'Errico, 2002. Microscopic, experimental and theoretical re-assessment of Upper Palaeolithic bird-bone pipes from Isturitz, France: ergonomics of design, systems of notation and the origins of musical traditions, in *Studien zur Musikarchäologie III. Archäologie früher Klangerzeugung und Tonordnung*, eds. E. Hickmann, A.D. Kilmer & R. Eichmann. (Orient-Archäologie Band 10.) Rahden: Verlag Marie Leidorf, 119–42.

L'Helgouach, J., 1965. *Les Sépultures Mégalithiques en Armorique*. Rennes: Travaux du Laboratoire d'Anthropologie Préhistorique de la Faculté des Sciences.

Malinowski, T., 1981. Archaeology and musical instruments in Poland. *World Archaeology* 12, 266–72.

Manniche, L., 1991. *Music and Musicians in Ancient Egypt*. London: British Museum Press.

Mithen, S., 2005. *The Singing Neanderthals: the Origins of Music, Language, Mind and Body*. London: Weidenfeld & Nicolson.

Morley, I., 2002. Evolution of the physiological and neurological capacities for music. *Cambridge Archaeological Journal* 12(2), 195–216.

Nordström, P., 1999. Ristningarnas rytm. Om hällristningar och lanskap — exemplet Boglösa i Uppland, in *Aktuell Arkeologi 7*, eds. P. Nordström & M. Svedin. Stockholm, 127–36.

Ouzman, S., 2001. Seeing is deceiving: rock art and the non-visual. *World Archaeology* 33, 237–56.

Reznikoff, I. & M. Dauvois, 1988. La dimension sonore des grottes ornées. *Bulletin de la Société Préhistorique Française* 85, 238–46.

Ruggles, C., 1999. *Astronomy in Prehistoric Britain and Ireland*. New Haven (CT) & London: Yale University Press.

Scarre, C., 1989. Painting by resonance. *Nature* 338, 382.

Thom, A., 1967. *Megalithic Sites in Britain*. Oxford: Oxford University Press.

Von Hagen, A. & C. Morris, 1998. *The Cities of the Ancient Andes*. London: Thames & Hudson.

Waller, S.J., 1993. Sound and rock art. *Nature* 363, 501.

Waller, S.J., 2000. Spatial correlation of acoustics and rock art exemplified in Horseshoe Canyon. *American Indian Rock Art* 24, 85–94.

Watson, A. & D. Keating, 1999. Architecture and sound: an acoustic analysis of megalithic monuments in prehistoric Britain. *Antiquity* 73, 325–36.

Watson, A. & D. Keating, 2000. The architecture of sound in Neolithic Orkney, in *Neolithic Orkney in its European Context*, ed. A. Ritchie. (McDonald Institute Monographs.) Cambridge: McDonald Institute for Archaeological Research, 259–63.

Chapter 2

(Un)intentional Sound?
Acoustics and Neolithic Monuments

Aaron Watson

Were the acoustics of Neolithic monuments intentional or fortuitous? Recent research has suggested that structures as diverse as Maeshowe and Stonehenge have the potential to create extraordinary sounds, yet it remains extremely difficult to prove whether such effects were deliberately intended by their builders and users. This paper discusses the broader implications of demonstrating 'intentionality' in the archaeological record and questions whether it is a useful concept to assist interpretation. Sound itself cannot be recovered from the archaeological record, and evidence to support its use is often ambiguous. Rather than seeing such subjectivity as inherently problematic, however, the paper suggests that an emphasis upon ephemeral sensory experiences might ultimately encourage new, and unexpected, interpretations of the Neolithic.

Recent research at Neolithic chambered cairns and stone circles has suggested that many possess acoustic properties that could have been utilized in prehistory. While such theories challenge the emphasis on vision in archaeological research, a major critique is their inherent subjectivity. Unlike other regions of Europe, few musical instruments or other sound producing devices are known from the British Neolithic (see Lund 1981; Megaw 1960; 1968; 1984), and acoustic interpretations have largely been deduced through experimental research at well-preserved sites (e.g. Devereux & Jahn 1996; Watson & Keating 1999; 2000; Watson 2001a; Devereux 2001, ch. 7). Is it possible, therefore, to demonstrate the extent to which Neolithic monuments were constructed for their acoustics? Given that any standing structure, whether ancient or modern, will influence the behaviour of sound, might the acoustic properties of monuments be best explained as fortuitous modern discoveries?

This paper will discuss this critique with reference to case studies from archaeological and ethnographic literature. One of the greatest challenges to our interpretations of the Neolithic is the imposition of modern values onto the past, and it is critical to explore the possibility that past conceptions of sensory experience were very different to our own. The question of intentionality will be considered generally, alongside specific references to the acoustics of Neolithic monuments.

To begin, I shall consider the implications of modernist tendencies to separate nature and culture.

The (un)intentionality of humans and non-humans

'Intentionality' describes the deliberate investment of purpose or meaning. One example is the manufacture of artefacts to fulfil some kind of role or function. Traditionally, the 'artifice' of the archaeological record has been its defining characteristic, enabling it to be separated from the domain of geology or other natural sciences. Indeed, the historical development of archaeology has, to a significant extent, been a process by which its practitioners have learnt to separate things made by people from those that result from 'natural' processes (Bradley 1997; 1998). For this reason, archaeology tends to favour objects or places that display clear evidence of having been altered or used in order to serve a particular purpose, and a central role ascribed to the archaeologist is to determine precisely what that purpose might have been.

There are problems with this diagnosis, however. The clear-cut separation of 'culture' and the 'nature' is not a universal philosophy, being bound within a way of rationalizing the world that has predominantly arisen in the West since the Enlightenment (Thomas 1996, ch. 1; Ingold 2000). Archaeologists state with confidence that a pot or monument has been intentionally constructed, but the same attributes are never extended to a river or a mountain.

Archaeological practice has typically been concerned with defining the boundaries of monuments, a perspective adopted and reinforced by legislation that affords protection to those sites. Such perimeters could be said to contain *the archaeology of intention*, while that which is outside their margins is a natural, unintentional, seemingly disposable, *other*. Are we correct to assume, however, that this conscious separation and polarization of 'intentional archaeology' and 'unintentional other', bound within the dichotomy drawn between nature and culture, was a perception shared by Neolithic people? This seems unlikely given ethnographic accounts of living societies who do not share this perspective. Indeed, the concept of 'nature' would be quite meaningless to people who, for example, conceive the world to be the result of supernatural forces, and even to have been intentionally created by their ancestors (e.g. Taçon 1991; Tilley 1994, 37–54). To deny the possibility that Neolithic understandings might differ from our own only serves to promote archaeology as a colonial project. After all, it is equally possible that Neolithic people conceived of natural (and therefore 'unintentional') landscapes in ways that Western archaeologists would ordinarily attribute to 'intentional' monuments. Failure to acknowledge this possibility results in the frequent disturbance of landscapes conventionally conceived to be *in-between* monuments, thereby imposing our own expectations directly upon the past.

Henge monuments, circular enclosures constructed in the later Neolithic (*c.* 3000–2500 BC), can be ambiguous in this respect. At the Ring of Brodgar in Orkney, a ring of standing stones were set within a waterlogged ditch, itself surrounded by natural lochs and a circuit of hills. It appears that the monument was built as a microcosm of that elemental landscape, a place that was the centre of the world (Richards 1996). By extension, however, might it be misleading to categorize this place as a 'site' at all? The Ring of Brodgar actually blurs the boundary between (unintentional/geological) landscape and the (intentional/archaeological) 'site' by creating an experience that arises from the interaction between them (Watson 2001b; 2004a). Like ourselves, a Neolithic observer at the Ring of Brodgar would have seen the standing stones, ditch, lochs and the hills, but they would not have understood, categorized and objectified them in the ways we do today. To suggest that the Ring of Brodgar was constructed with the specific intent of creating a particular effect in the landscape is to assume that it was conceived like a modern construction project. Perhaps sites like this need not have been solely conceived in the abstract, but were also *gathered* from the land (see Ingold 2000, 192).

In 1996 a team of environmental scientists visited Northeastern Arnhem Land, Australia, to learn Aboriginal techniques for starting bush fires that encourage vegetation regeneration (Verran 2002). The scientists were dismayed to discover, however, that Aboriginal conceptions of intent were largely unintelligible to them. The spoken guidelines for fire-setting appeared both disconcerting and irrelevant, involving sessions of hunting and gathering, the naming of plants, animals, ancestors and people, alongside the recitation of complex kin relations. When asked why a specific location was chosen, reasons were given in terms of animals and plants, including seemingly unimportant species such as shellfish and yams. The scientists found it impossible to make sense of these instructions, partly because their understandings of topography, and therefore the places to set fires, did not accommodate the inextricable relations drawn between land, humans and non-humans by their Aboriginal instructors (Verran 2002, 739). Likewise, an archaeologist studying this phenomenon might explain the intent behind fire-setting on the basis of logical deductions based upon measured environmental factors: factors that actually appear to have been of little relevance to the perceptions of the society concerned.

A comparable acoustic example emerges from a study of the Ilahita Arapesh in Papua New Guinea who use large bamboo pipes to create the highly theatrical voices of dangerous cult spirits (Tuzin 1980; 1984). While the ends of these instruments are deliberately inserted into large hourglass drums, creating an illusory and distorted effect, those permitted to 'play' the pipes did not rationalize a connection between their actions and the sounds that were produced (Tuzin 1984, 580), confounding our Western sense of cause and effect. Rather, the otherworldly sounds remained mysterious and it was the players who were said to have assumed god-like powers (Tuzin 1980, 57). Again, the sense of intent is rather indirect. From a Western perspective, the Arapesh pipes appear to have been deliberately constructed to generate unusual sounds, and this might well be the interpretation offered if such artefacts were recovered from an archaeological context. Such a view would not, however, reflect the ways in which they were perceived by members of the society who used them.

Given that contemporary societies can challenge the concept of intent, is it appropriate to apply it so uncritically to the actions of past societies? While it may be contrary to our modern sensibilities to ascribe intentionality to a natural place, a plant or an animal, this predilection imposes a narrow and specific ideology upon the Neolithic. Likewise, it is easy to impose our own preconceptions regarding the causality of musical instruments or acoustic spaces. In the instance of the Arapesh spirit voices, there appeared to be evidence for the deliberate construction of instruments, yet this was denied by their users. Therefore, if the architecture of an archaeological site appears to have been enhanced to improve its acoustics, to what extent can we label this as intentionality? In the Aboriginal case there was intent to set fires but the reasons for choosing one location over another were incomprehensible to Western scientists and appeared to bear little relation to environmental factors in the Western sense. Therefore, if an archaeological site displays no evidence of acoustic intent, is this safe ground for assuming that sound did not play a role in its conception or use? At the Ring of Brodgar, modern visitors can hear distinct echoes ricochet around the interior of the circle (Watson & Keating 2000, 260), yet there is no evidence that the site was constructed to facilitate this effect. This perspective, however, is founded upon conceptions of acoustics which presume that physical phenomena such as architecture and soundwaves are passive and therefore 'silent' actors. Alternatively, might echoes rebounding from the stones be understood as 'voices', supernatural powers or ancestors that possess their own agency? Furthermore, I have suggested that monuments might have been *gathered* from the land and were not separated from it in the ways traditionally perpetrated by archaeology. At Midhowe, a chambered cairn on the Atlantic coast of Orkney, the sounds of the sea would have entered the tomb, creating an nearly constant sound that is as much a part of the built architecture as the stones and earth. Sounds made at the Dwarfie Stane, also in Orkney, resound around both the monument and the surrounding mountains (Watson & Keating 2000, 261), while loud noises made within the Ring of Brodgar are transmitted out across the surrounding lochs. In short,

Figure 2.1. *Precise stone walling inside Maeshowe. Acoustic feature or visual effect?*

the acoustics of these monuments could not only indicate relations of agency that are unfamiliar, dissolving the boundaries traditionally deemed to separate them from the wider world, but were actively gathered into the fabric of monumental architecture.

The (un)intentionality of design

Can we presuppose that the acoustic properties of Neolithic monuments would be optimized in their design? Were the filtering or resonant effects that have been heard within monuments intended by their builders? Might sound even have been the sole purpose of these structures? These questions test the ability of archaeology to demonstrate that something has been optimized to perform a particular purpose. This might seem to be clear-cut when artefacts appear suited to a purpose — an arrowhead, for instance — yet such an appraisal might itself be superficial. Even in the modern Western world, is technology optimized to perform its purpose? It is often assumed, for example, that the intention underlying modern aeroplane design is driven solely by the desire to maximize safety and economic efficiency, yet investigations by Pierre Lemonnier have suggested that this is not strictly the case (Lemonnier 1992, ch. 3). The design of civil jet airliners actually appears to be determined by a complex web of social relations that complicate and diffuse so-called 'rational' intent. Indeed, if issues of safety and fuel efficiency were foregrounded in the design process, airliners might look rather different. First designed in 1910, the 'flying wing' has greater speed, stability and efficiency than current designs, but it has never been commercially adopted. Aircraft retain their conventional appearance, Lemonnier argues, as the result of a complex network of competing interests in the airline industry, including fashions and preconceptions about what aircraft are 'supposed' to look like (Lemonnier 1992, 70).

This example illustrates that an uncritical search for intentionality might neglect the complex, fluid and dynamic set of relationships that are involved in the creation of a material artefact, whether it is a jet airliner or chambered cairn. Drawing upon the example from hi-tech industry, it is plausible that any acoustic intentionality in the design of Neolithic monuments was bound up with a multitude of contrasting intentions, rather than being rationally optimized. Indeed, these places could have served a multitude of purposes, some of which may have compromised one-another. The megalithic passage grave of Maeshowe in Orkney could act as an acoustic space (Watson 2001a), yet there are also aspects of its design which appear to be largely visual. Precision dry-stone walling creates good sound reflections yet is also impressive to look at (Fig. 2.1). The entrance is aligned upon the midwinter sunset, allowing a beam of light to illuminate the chamber (MacKie 1997; Ruggles & Barclay 2000), and a profusion of abstract patterns are scratched into the walls (Bradley *et al.* 2001). The format of the passage grave has parallels elsewhere, ranging from houses in the settlements of Barnhouse and Skara Brae (Richards 1993) to the even more massive site of Newgrange in Ireland. It appears that Maeshowe could not be concerned purely to propagate sound, but served to assimilate varied and multisensory elements of an elaborate ideological scheme that included references to far-away places, traditions of rock art and the movements of the sun.

Just as an archaeologist in the future might not identify safety or efficiency as particular concerns of aircraft design in the late twentieth century, so we might find the acoustic intentionality of Neolithic monuments enormously difficult to recognize. The airline industry claims safety and cost to be central to its business, but the significant element here is that these aims appear not to be optimized in the material culture that is produced. Likewise, acoustic intent might not be clearly evidenced in the remains of Neolithic monuments, but this does not necessarily mean that these aspects were unimportant to their builders and users.

The (un)intentional lives of artefacts

The acoustic intentionality of Neolithic monuments might be further compromised if we acknowledge that the intentions which determine the creation of an artefact may be quite unrelated to the ways in which it ultimately comes to be used and understood at later stages in its life. There are numerous instances from the archaeological and ethnographic record that illustrate how the consumption of artefacts can diverge from their original purpose, whether they be portable artefacts or buildings (e.g. Hingley 1996; Bradley 2002). This is clearly illustrated when Western material culture has been adopted by people elsewhere in the world to fulfil roles unimagined by its designers. For instance, the Kellogg company almost certainly never envisaged that their packaging would be used as a decorative head-dress in Papua New Guinea, yet this is exactly what happened when a biscuit container was removed from its anticipated pattern of circulation and introduced into another (Verhart & Wansleeben 1997, fig. 3b). In this instance, our sense of intent becomes blurred because the container is no longer performing the role for which it was designed, yet has been adopted for an entirely new purpose that is no less significant or meaningful.

During the two millennia that span the British Neolithic, both artefacts and ideas were moved or transmitted through space and time, and between contrasting social and environmental contexts. Many portable artefacts and monuments had lives that extended long beyond those of their makers, and it seems that their roles and meanings evolved accordingly. For this reason, distinctive echoes that have been heard and measured within the recumbent stone circle of Easter Aquorthies in northeast Scotland (Watson & Keating 1999, 326–7) need *not* have been integral to the initial design in order to be significant. Indeed, excavations at nearby sites have shown that recumbent stone circles are unlikely to have been unitary monuments (Bradley 2005). In their first phase they appear to be pyre or beacon sites where fires burnt at the centre of a low platform. Only later were the platforms enclosed by standing stones, introducing the potential to create intricate echoes. Likewise, we cannot discount the possibility that basic acoustic effects were not original aspects of passage graves, but became important *during* their use. Their architecture need, therefore, display no evidence for acoustic intent, even though sound may have become a central facet of their subsequent use. This would be difficult to demonstrate given the paucity of evidence for musical instruments across Britain, although many objects found at these sites, including pottery, could have been utilized to produce sound in ways that we might not anticipate. Bronze Age 'food' vessels have been successfully utilized as effective drums (Purser 1997), and there is no reason to suggest that the same

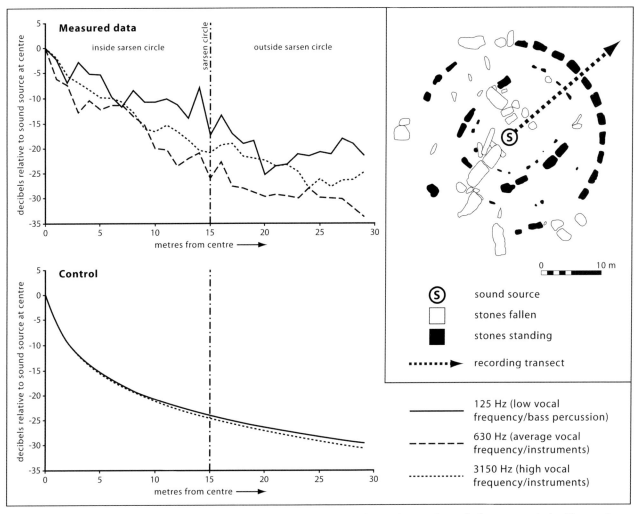

Figure 2.2. *Data collected along a transect leading from the centre of Stonehenge through the sarsen circle, illustrating the increased volume within the stone circle as compared with the control. All measurements are relative to the recorded volume of sound at the source. (Plan after Cleal et al. 1995.)*

need not be true of styles such as Grooved Ware. Vocalizing, hand clapping and foot stamping can also introduce dynamic sounds, yet leave no evidence at all. We should not forget that many effects are simple to create inside monuments, and it seems unlikely that they would not have been noticed in prehistory. Perhaps the unusual audio properties, which could not be recreated at more ephemeral structures in the wider landscape, might ultimately have been perceived as an integral part of the significance and experience of megalithic buildings.

The (un)intentionality of the senses

Sound in the modern Western world is considered to be one of five bodily senses, but this is not a universal perception. In the ethnographic literature, there are many instances of societies using their senses in ways

that we would not expect and might find difficult to comprehend (e.g. Howes & Classen 1991). The Javanese have five senses, but they substitute tasting for talking. The Hausa of Nigeria conceive of only two senses, while the Dogon of Mali 'hear' odours and classify words according to how they smell. The Batek Negrito of Malaysia classify their world according to smell, while the Tsimshian of the Northwest Coast hear with their eyes, drawing pictures of the way things sound (Howes & Classen 1991, 257–83). As part of healing rituals, shamans of the Shipibo-Conibo of eastern Peru use intricate geometric designs that are 'seen' acoustically and transformed into vocalization. The images also have a powerful olfactory dimension and are perceived to be fragrant (Gebhart-Sayer 1985). In addition, it is important to question the rather crude contrasts sometimes drawn between the sensory experiences of Western and non-Western societies. It

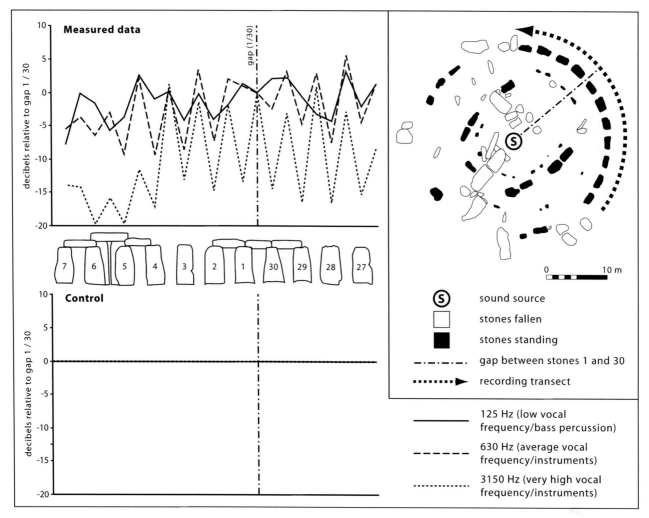

Figure 2.3. *Data collected along a transect around the outside of the sarsen circle at Stonehenge, emphasizing how the stones differentially filter high- and low-frequency sound. The notable trough in the high-frequency range between stones 4 and 7 corresponds to the presence of additional stones in the Trilithon Horseshoe that lie between the listener and the sound source. All measurements are relative to the recorded volume of sound at the gap between stones 1 and 30. Plan and stone elevations are shown schematically. (After Cleal* et al. *1995.)*

is often assumed that the Western sensorium is predominantly visual, even though many experiences, such as eating, inextricably merge multiple sensations. Secondly, there has been a tendency to 'map' the sensory balance of a society at the expense of the abilities of individuals (Howes 1991, 167–8; Ingold 2000, ch. 14). Rather than attempting to characterize a society's sensorium in isolation from personal experience, Tim Ingold has encouraged anthropologists to adopt a greater awareness of the 'lived experience of individuals', and in particular 'the involvement of whole persons with one another, and with their environment, in the ongoing process of social life' (Ingold 2000, 285).

The ethnographic literature warns us that it is problematic to compartmentalize the senses in order to study each in isolation. Rather, we need to foreground pluri-sensorial or synaesthetic possibilities when considering the intentionality of archaeological materials and places. Perhaps certain shapes or forms — natural textures, rock art or buildings — could have been perceived to possess a sound dimension in the Neolithic. The possibility that the perceived sound properties of a site or artefact may owe little to its abilities to reflect sound in a strictly acoustic way would create difficulties for diagnosing their intent from archaeological evidence. Furthermore, sensory acuity and meaning can reflect the gender, age, status and profession of a person (Howes & Classen 1991, 257–83), and be impacted by the activity they are conducting, from sensory deprivation to the ingestion of mind-altering substances (e.g. Dronfield 1995a,b; 1996). Among the

Approaching the Heel Stone along the Avenue. Open landscape, natural ambient sounds; wind, rain, animals.

Approaching the Slaughter Stone, passing through the earthwork. Distant, barely audible sounds emanate from activities within the circle.

Inside the earthwork, approaching the outer sarsen circle. Only lower frequency sounds (drums?) discernable. Indistinct, distorted and unintelligible vocals.

Approaching the entrance. Louder sounds emerge, continued distortion. Distinct changes to sounds are heard while moving past stones and apertures.

Passing through the entrance, moving towards the centre. Dramatic increase in sound intensity. Higher frequencies, including vocals discernable, echoes and standing waves clearly audible - participants immersed in a dynamic soundscape.

Figure 2.4. *Approaching the Stonehenge soundscape.*

Figure 2.5. *Two sarsen stones at Stonehenge, showing how the inner surfaces (on the left) tend to be flat or concave relative to the outer surfaces, improving their ability to reflect sound.*

were taken around the best-preserved sectors. Figure 2.2 shows the relative amplitude of three sound frequencies at one-metre intervals along a transect leading from the loudspeaker out towards the Heel Stone, passing through the outer sarsen circle. Despite its ruinous condition, the surviving stones of Stonehenge contain higher frequency sounds within the interior, amplifying them, while a series of peaks and troughs on the graph indicate standing waves. Standing waves cause the volume and nature of sounds to change unexpectedly as listeners move around (for a full account of the methodology and standing waves see Watson & Keating 1999). Outside the sarsen circle, the amplitude of the higher frequencies is abruptly attenuated as they are blocked by the large stones of the outer circle, while lower frequencies pass around these sarsens and travel some distance. To some extent, the severity of this effect relates to the position of the listener relative to the gaps in the outer sarsen circle. This is best illustrated by a set of measurements taken around the perimeter of the northeastern sector of the outer sarsen circle (Fig. 2.3), illustrating how higher frequencies only emerge through gaps between the stones.

One interpretation of these results is that the contrasting acoustic experiences between the interior and exterior could have served to create a sense of exclusion, or differential access to knowledge, in the Neolithic/Early Bronze Age. In other words, an audience occupying the confined centre of Stonehenge would have heard enhanced sound, including a range of effects such as standing waves and echoes, while anyone outside heard only a distorted and largely unintelligible impression of activities within. The impact of moving towards, and entering, Stonehenge would also have been striking, entailing a theatrical transition between ambient sounds in the world to those controlled and contained by the monument itself (Fig. 2.4).

But were the acoustics of Stonehenge intentional? The results from the data collection are unsatisfactory. Figures 2.2 and 2.3 show how sound moves around, but there is little to indicate that this is not simply the

Shipibo-Conibo, it is exclusively the shaman who enacts the synaesthetic transformation between vision, sound and fragrance (Gebhart-Sayer 1985, 161); while in Western society, a musician is said to have a more sensitive 'ear' (Howes 1991, 168).

The first half of this paper has highlighted some questions about the concept of intentionality. In the next section, I will discuss how such ideas might be constructively applied within archaeological research.

Stonehenge: intentional sound?

Over the past few years, a pilot project to explore the acoustics of Stonehenge has been conducted as part of a wider investigation of the audio properties of Neolithic monuments by the author and David Keating (Watson & Keating 1999; 2000; Watson 2001a). Stonehenge is known to have been constructed and reconstructed in many phases, and the study was intended to explore Phase 3 (*c.* 2500–1600 BC), when the monument took on its final form (Cleal *et al.* 1995). The following account is intended only as a preliminary report.

An omni-directional loudspeaker emitting pink noise was located at the centre of Stonehenge, and sound pressure and frequency measurements fortuitous result of large stones being arranged in close proximity. Perhaps the most compelling evidence is the shaping of the stones. Observations by the author and David Keating within Stonehenge suggest that the inner faces of many stones were dressed to be flat or concave, which improves their ability to reflect sound, while their outer surfaces are irregular or even convex (Fig. 2.5). The enormous effort invested in dressing sarsens and bluestones into subtle and barely visible shapes is difficult to explain, but it certainly lends credibility to their possible acoustic role.

So far, my account of Stonehenge research has followed specific traditions of scientific analysis and represents the results using established conventions (Figs. 2.2 & 2.3). Is this a satisfactory approach? Problems and concerns immediately arise. For example, Figures 2.2 and 2.3 purport to represent sound, yet they are silent and static graphics which simultaneously depict sound in many different locations. This implies a significant disjuncture between the measured acoustics and the embodied experience of the monument: Figures 2.2 and 2.3 can be visually consumed as representations of the acoustics of Stonehenge, but in the process they effectively disguise how the recording apparatus had to be physically moved to collect data in each location (Fig. 2.6). In other words, these graphics deny one of the most striking aspects of being at Stonehenge, namely the experience of hearing dynamic transformations and changes in sound that occur as the listener moves about. Might it even be the adoption of an objective approach that ultimately leads us to consider the 'intentionality' of acoustics in the first place?

Western science seeks to apply neutral and empirical method to reveal universal truths that lie beyond the subjective social world of 'power and politics' (Thomas 1996, 14), yet it can only support hypotheses that it is able to articulate and measure (Woolgar 1988). Throughout this paper I have highlighted social practices from the ethnographic literature that would not be possible to quantify in this way, or even identify in the archaeological record. The search for intentionality, it seems, might actually be bound up within the practice of science itself, and is therefore historically situated in the modern era. For example, principles of acoustic physics are largely built upon nineteenth- and twentieth-century concepts of sound waves, and the mathematical principles that underlie them (e.g. Rayleigh 1896), and would be largely meaningless to people living outside the Western and modernist paradigm upon which science is itself founded. Stonehenge was constructed by people who did not objectify the world in this way and it is, therefore, unlikely that they shared a similar sense of intentionality.

Figure 2.6. *David Keating (left) and the author conducting acoustic measurements at Stonehenge.*

Just as science is unable to tell us whether the results of acoustic tests at Stonehenge are significant, or what their meaning might be, so the uncritical application of its methods in understanding the Neolithic might have misleading consequences. Indeed, the application of scientific principles to demonstrate intentionality in the past might ultimately reveal rather more about *our own* understandings of the world than those of Neolithic people. I do not, however, suggest that we simply reject such analyses (see Cross & Watson this volume), but emphasize the need to recognize that science is itself constrained and structured by the social and material 'conditions' under which it is produced (Jones 2002). One possibility for the future is to situate scientific knowledge and empirical research alongside rather more reflexive approaches, ranging from archaeological theory and ethnographic case studies, to fieldwork experiences and even experimental and imaginative representations of monuments (Watson 2004b,c). Rather than simply questioning whether Stonehenge was built as an intentional soundscape, we need to also explore a multi-sensory Stonehenge that is rather more dynamic and ambiguous, a Stonehenge that is both measured and experienced (Fig. 2.7).

Figure 2.7. *Stonehenge as a gathering of people, places, memories and measurements: mythical origins among the bluestone outcrops in Wales, the ambiguity of built and natural places, empirically-measured sound during recent research, ambiguous multisensory experiences and, ultimately, interpretation.*

Conclusions

At the end of the day we should remember that no interpretation can ever be proven to be *the* single Neolithic 'truth'. Perhaps the question of intentionality should not be about imposing modern preconceptions on the Neolithic; rather, we need to find ways of identifying the potential of archaeological sites to generate diverse experiences, leading to *multiple* interpretations. Indeed, I hope to have emphasized that archaeology may actually be constraining its scope for interpretation by insisting that the intentions underlying the use of a place or artefact have to be empirically demonstrated. To uncritically investigate the acoustic intentionality of a Neolithic building might be to impose a tradition of analytical research that is not always appropriate and which may provide only a modernist and possibly misleading account. Using a series of case studies, I hope to have shown that the past might not always furnish data that are stable or easily quantified. If we account for the possibility that Neolithic people might not have shared our distinction between 'culture' and 'nature', the concept of a 'site' or 'monument' might itself need to be rethought in our interpretations. Sounds of the sea might be considered as part of the architecture of a monument, or create tangible interconnections between places and events. Likewise, we cannot be certain how people in the past would conceive of the relationship between cause and effect; they may attribute agency and intentionality to supernatural entities, non-humans, places or objects. An echo might be the voice of an ancestor rather than a sound wave, while people might not associate their playing of an instrument with the sounds that are produced. Nor can we infer that a building would be designed to optimize acoustics; intent may reflect complex webs of social and material relations rather than function, and the role or meaning of a place might change over time. The architecture of a structure need exhibit no evidence of acoustic functionality for sound to have played a significant role there. Sensory perception in the Neolithic might have been strange and unfamiliar to us, including synaesthetic relations to places and objects, or the evocation of memories, people or relationships through the sensorium.

Ultimately, archaeology need not view such perspectives negatively, but as opportunities to broaden and diversify its method. In order to realize and explore the different ways in which Neolithic monuments might be interpreted, many different approaches need to be taken. Thus it is critical to pursue detailed empirical assessments of monuments *alongside* alternative kinds of analysis, whilst also acknowledging that we might find such understandings to be unfamiliar, fluid and confusing. For these reasons, experimental approaches to the acoustics of monuments have the potential not only to challenge expectations, but to uncover new and unexpected experiences of the Neolithic.

Acknowledgements

Many thanks to Graeme Lawson and Chris Scarre for inviting me to present at the 'Acoustics, Space and Intentionality' symposium, and to all of the participants for their lively and constructive discussion. Thanks also to Richard Bradley for commenting upon a draft of the text and to David Keating for his invaluable advice and assistance with fieldwork. The research at Stonehenge was made possible in association with English Heritage, Yorkshire Television and BBC Science Radio.

References

Bradley, R., 1997. 'To see is to have seen'. Craft traditions in archaeology, in *The Cultural Life of Images: Visual Representation in Archaeology*, ed. B.L. Molyneaux. London: Routledge, 62–72.

Bradley, R., 1998. Ruined buildings, ruined stones: enclosures, tombs and natural places in the Neolithic of south-west England. *World Archaeology* 30, 13–22.

Bradley, R., 2002. *The Past in Prehistoric Societies*. London: Routledge.

Bradley, R., 2005. *The Moon and the Bonfire*. Edinburgh: Society of Antiquaries of Scotland.

Bradley, R., T. Phillips, C. Richards & M. Webb, 2001. Decorating the houses of the dead: incised and pecked motifs in Orkney chambered tombs. *Cambridge Archaeological Journal* 11(1), 45–67.

Cleal, R., K. Walker & R. Montague, 1995. *Stonehenge in its Landscape: Twentieth Century Excavations*. London: English Heritage.

Devereux, P., 2001. *Stone Age Soundtracks*. London: Vega.

Devereux, P. & R. Jahn, 1996. Preliminary investigations and cognitive considerations of the acoustical resonances of selected archaeological sites. *Antiquity* 70, 665–6.

Dronfield, J., 1995a. Subjective vision and the source of Irish megalithic art. *Antiquity* 69, 539–49.

Dronfield, J., 1995b. Migraine, light and hallucinogens: the neurocognitive basis of Irish megalithic art. *Oxford Journal of Archaeology* 14, 261–75.

Dronfield, J., 1996. Entering alternative realities: cognition, art and architecture in Irish passage-tombs. *Cambridge Archaeological Journal* 6(1), 37–72.

Gebhart-Sayer, A., 1985. The geometric designs of the Shipibo-Conibo in ritual context. *Journal of Latin American Lore* 11, 143–75.

Hingley, R., 1996. Ancestors and identity in the later prehistory of Atlantic Scotland: the reuse and reinvention of Neolithic monuments and material culture. *World Archaeology* 28, 231–43.

Howes, D., 1991. 'To summon all the senses', in *The Varieties of Sensory Experience*, ed. D. Howes. Toronto: University of Toronto Press, 3–21.

Howes, D. & C. Classen, 1991. Sounding sensory profiles, in *The Varieties of Sensory Experience*, ed. D. Howes. Toronto: University of Toronto Press, 257–88.

Ingold, T., 2000. *The Perception of the Environment*. London: Routledge.

Jones, A., 2002. *Archaeological Theory and Scientific Practice*. Cambridge: Cambridge University Press.

Lemonnier, P., 1992. *Elements for an Anthropology of Technology*. Ann Arbor (MI).

Lund, C., 1981. The archaeomusicology of Scandinavia. *World Archaeology* 12, 246–65.

MacKie, E.W., 1997. Maeshowe and the winter solstice: ceremonial aspects of the Orkney Grooved Ware culture. *Antiquity* 71, 338–59.

Megaw, J., 1960. Penny whistles and prehistory. *Antiquity* 35, 6–13.

Megaw, J., 1968. Problems and non-problems in palaeo-organology: a musical miscellany, in *Studies in Ancient Europe*, eds. J. Coles & D. Simpson. Leicester: Leicester University Press, 333–58.

Megaw, J., 1984. The bone ?flute, in *Gwernvale and Penywyrlod: Two Neolithic Long Cairns in the Black Mountains of Brecknock*, eds. W.J. Britnell & H.N. Savory. (Cambrian Archaeological Monographs 2.) Cardiff: Cambrian Archaeological Association, 27–8.

Purser, J., 1997. *The Kilmartin Sessions: the Sounds of Ancient Scotland*. Audio CD produced by the Kilmartin House Trust: KHT CD1.

Rayleigh (Strutt, J.W.), 1896. *The Theory of Sound*, vol. 1. London: Macmillan.

Richards, C., 1993. Monumental choreography: architecture and spatial representation in late Neolithic Orkney, in *Interpretative Archaeology*, ed. C. Tilley. Oxford: Berg, 143–78.

Richards, C., 1996. Monuments as landscape: creating the centre of the world in late Neolithic Orkney. *World Archaeology* 28, 190–208.

Ruggles, C. & G. Barclay, 2000. Cosmology, calendars and society in Neolithic Orkney: a rejoinder to Euan MacKie. *Antiquity* 74, 62–74.

Taçon, P., 1991. The power of stone: symbolic aspects of stone use and tool development in Western Arnhem Land, Australia. *Antiquity* 65, 192–207.

Thomas, J., 1996. *Time, Culture and Identity*. London: Routledge.

Tilley, C., 1994. *A Phenomenology of Landscape*. Oxford: Berg.

Tuzin, D., 1980. *The Voice of the Tambaran*. Berkeley (CA): University of California Press.

Tuzin, D., 1984. Miraculous voices: the auditory experience of numinous objects. *Current Anthropology* 25, 579–96.

Verhart, L. & M. Wansleeben, 1997. Waste and prestige: the Mesolithic–Neolithic transition in the Netherlands from a social perspective. *Analecta Praehistorica Leidensia* 29, 65–73.

Verran, H., 2002. A postcolonial moment in science studies: alternative firing regimes of environmental scientists and Aboriginal landowners. *Social Studies of Science* 32, 729–61.

Watson, A., 2001a. The sounds of transformation: acoustics, monuments and ritual in the British Neolithic, in *The Archaeology of Shamanism*, ed. N. Price. London: Routledge, 178–92.

Watson, A., 2001b. Composing Avebury. *World Archaeology* 33, 296–314.

Watson, A., 2004a. Monuments that made the world: performing the henge, in *Monuments and Material Culture: Papers on Neolithic and Bronze Age Britain in Honour of Isobel Smith*, eds. R. Cleal & J. Pollard. East Knoyle: Hobnob Press.

Watson, A., 2004b. Fluid horizons, in *The Neolithic of the Irish Sea*, eds. V. Cummings & C. Fowler. Oxford: Oxbow.

Watson, A., 2004c. Making space for monuments: notes on the representation of experience, in *Substance, Memory, Display: Archaeology and Art*, eds. C. Renfrew, C. Gosden & E. DeMarrais. (McDonald Institute Monographs.) Cambridge: McDonald Institute for

Archaeological Research, 79–96.

Watson, A. & D. Keating, 1999. Architecture and sound: an acoustic analysis of megalithic monuments in prehistoric Britain. *Antiquity* 73, 325–36.

Watson, A. & D. Keating, 2000. The architecture of sound in Neolithic Orkney, in *Neolithic Orkney in its European Context*, ed. A. Ritchie. (McDonald Institute Monographs.) Cambridge: McDonald Institute for Archaeological Research, 259–63.

Woolgar, S., 1988. *Science: the Very Idea*. London: Routledge.

Chapter 3

Ears & Years:
Aspects of Acoustics and Intentionality in Antiquity

Paul Devereux

In our visually-oriented modern world we often forget '(overlook') the simple fact that ancient people had ears. Even today some tribal cultures find hearing to be more important to them than sight. While arguing that the intentional awareness and use of sound in antiquity can thus already be reasonably assumed, this paper describes four avenues of research that could potentially prove fruitful in the garnering of information enabling the more robust assessment of such intentionality. One of these suggested research approaches is the use of EEG monitoring to determine brain responses to acoustic effects discovered at ceremonial and ritual archaeological sites; this references a recent and unexpected finding that a frequency band around 110 Hz — the primary or natural resonance frequency found by the present writer and colleagues to occur in a sample selection of megalithic chambered monuments — has significant and specific effects on the brain.

The title of this paper might seem trivial or jocular, but the human ear is no joke. It is a remarkable instrument and has been attached to people's heads throughout human history and prehistory. This absurdly simple fact is too often forgotten, owing in large part to the strong visual bias of our modern world. This can subtly affect how modern people, even scholars, think about the remote past.

While we often try to minimize the din of the modern world around us, people in early cultures would have found the act of listening to the sounds in their quieter world to be of key importance. This had to be true of hunters and those travelling through primordial forests, where listening for quarry, or sounds indicating danger, would have been of major importance. It would also have been the case that to ancient people (which means those without a wave-based model of acoustics) sound would have seemed magical: wind in foliage was the utterance of gods, echoes were spirits calling, and the roar of waterfalls and the babble of streams contained prophetic voices from the Otherworld.

We know that environmental sound was consciously appreciated at least as far back as the Classical world. We can glean this from authors such as Vitruvius, who wrote about architectural features, locations and devices relating to the acoustics of Roman and Greek theatres (Rowland & Howe 1999) or Pausanias telling us of a stone that made a lyre-like sound at Megara. There is no reason to doubt that such awareness went back into deep prehistory — how could Stone Age ears have failed to register the exquisite echoes and resonant rumblings of cavern systems? And in any case we have evidence of the musical use of stalactites (Dams 1985) and the creation of bone whistles from Upper Palaeolithic times (Lawson *et al.* 1998; Palmer & Pettit 2001). Wherever there was acoustic awareness there would have been manipulation, for it is a deeply-ingrained human impulse to explore, copy and then to 'improve on' nature.

To fail to accept the probability of acoustic intentionality in the remote past is in effect to doubt the human ear. Nevertheless, scholarly rigour demands harder evidence than assumptions, no matter how logical and obvious they may be. In that spirit, a few (by no means exhaustive) suggestions are offered concerning certain lines of research that may be able to provide information helping in the assessment of intentionality when studying acoustics in archaeological contexts.

Knock on rock: an acoustic census

First and most simply, the excellent work already being undertaken by numerous investigators who are using prehistoric rock art to confirm acoustic intent (Reznikoff 1995; Waller 1993) needs to be continued and extended. Interesting work in this regard has been conducted at Lake Onega in Russia (Lauhakangas 1999). There, on the Karetski Peninsula, a slab of rock over a deep crack in the bedrock at the water's edge issues a deep, resonant sound when struck with a piece of wood. The sound reverberates down the crack and propagates out onto the surface of the lake which then acts as a kind of amplifier so that the sound can be heard for approximately four kilometres around. The important point is that the Karetski Peninsula is a major focus of Neolithic or Bronze Age petroglyphs, and they surround this resonant slab of rock that is itself not carved. A second such rock, also at the centre of a focus of rock art, has now reportedly been identified elsewhere on the shores of the lake (R. Lauhakangas pers. comm.). Another example where rock art appears to mark natural acoustic features occurs in the United States where boulders incised with petroglyphs have been found to be 'ringing rocks', producing bell- or gong-like sounds when subjected to percussive impacts (Hedges 1990). It is also the case that boulders elsewhere marked with rock art have been found to be naturally musical — in Scotland, for instance. A cup-marked, naturally-musical glacial erratic on the island of Tiree provides one Scottish example.

It is suggested that a more complete acoustic census than currently exists be undertaken of a worldwide sample of individual natural rock features — boulders, prominent outcrops, rock projections, or isolated slabs — embellished or otherwise associated with rock art to see just how many produce natural musical sounds. This would provide a fuller picture of the extent of such coincidences and so give a basis for a better measure of intentionality.

Variations on this approach, in which natural rock formations in potentially significant non-rock art locations are also tested for acoustic properties, could yield unexpected research dividends in specific cases. Take, for example, the Stonehenge bluestones. Their source has been identified as the Preseli Mountains of southwest Wales (Thomas 1923) and much intellectual energy has been expended on how they made the long journey from that source to Salisbury Plain — whether by natural or human agency. Less thought has been applied to why they were identified as special by the builders of Stonehenge. Was it because, when wet, their colour was distinct from the local sarsen stone? Was it because they were considered to possess *mana* from the Preseli region, which, judging by the number of Neolithic monuments there, was considered to be sacred land? It is possible that another (perhaps complementary) answer involves acoustics. One hamlet in the Preseli area is called Maenclochog, a Welsh name meaning 'ringing rocks', in reference to two locally famous natural rock gongs that were unfortunately broken up during roadworks in the eighteenth century. But it has long been noted that a number of outcropping rocks in the Preseli range produce musical notes when struck (Fagg 1957). Furthermore, there are reportedly specific outdoor areas there called 'anathoths' where echoes are said to be particularly strong.[1] It could be that it was the acoustic properties of the Preseli Mountains that made them a sanctified location in prehistoric times. It would therefore be useful to check the acoustic properties of Carn Menyn, reputedly the specific origin point of the Stonehenge bluestones, as well as other selected outcrops on the Preseli range.[2]

Acoustic symbolism

A second approach to seeking indicators of acoustic intentionality would be to recognize the existence of acoustic symbolism: it is known that ancient societies used visual symbolism, and they would have indulged their ears as well as their eyes. The following are just two examples where visual symbolism is accompanied by an apparent acoustic dimension.

One of the most significant structures at Chichen Itza in Mexico is the Mayan-Toltec stepped pyramid temple called the Castillo (Fig. 3.1). It was dedicated to Kukulcan, the feathered serpent. It displays visual symbolism in that the setting sun at the equinoxes causes a stepped corner of the pyramid to cast a serrated light-and-shadow display reminiscent of a diamond-back snake onto the balustrade of the stairway on the northern face of the pyramid; the alternating triangles of light and shade connect with a carved stone serpent's head at the lower end of the balustrade to complete the illusion (Krupp 1997). Less well-known generally (though long known to the local Maya) is the fact that a percussive sound such as a handclap made in a certain area to the north of the Castillo results in a curious 'chirped echo' rebounding off the pyramid's northern face. This has been closely studied by acoustician David Lubman, who identifies it as a 'remarkable picket-fence echo' (Lubman 1998). The effect is produced by the design of the staircase on the north side of the pyramid causing it to act as an acoustical diffraction grating. At least two steps are needed to produce a perceptible tone, and with additional steps the tone becomes stronger. The frequency of the tone is determined by the height and length of the individual steps; its duration by the height of the staircase. Because the northern staircase on the Castillo is so tall, the echo lasts for more than a tenth of a second. The possible symbolic aspect to all this revolves around the fact that the Castillo's picket fence echo sounds just like the call of the quetzal, a bird of colourful plumage sacred to the Maya. In fact, present-day Maya actually call the echo *la cola del Quetzal* (the quetzal's tail). Lubman has made an acoustical analysis of the echo and compared it to the quetzal bird's primary call: the two are a very close match. The starting frequency of the echo is about 1300 Hz, ending in 922 Hz — a high note followed by a lower note. This is because the time between successive echoes gradually lengthens for the upper steps, as the ray path becomes nearly parallel to the angle of rise of the staircase.

The prefix 'Kuk' in Kukulcan has roots in the Maya name for the quetzal bird, viewed by the ancient Maya as the messenger of the gods. There is also evidence that Maya kings made use of quetzal feathers in their ceremonies at Chichen Itza and elsewhere. Potential further support for the symbolic interpretation of this acoustic phenomenon comes from the Temple of the Feathered Serpent at Teotihuacan: the present writer

Figure 3.1. *North side of the Castillo, Chichen Itza, Yucatan.*

Figure 3.2. *Entrance to the Treasury of Atreus, Mycenae.*

has found that it, too, produces a similar quetzal bird chirped echo, while other temples in the large complex so far tested do not.[3]

A second example of possible acoustic symbolism involves the so-called Treasury of Atreus in Mycenae (Fig. 3.2). The interior of this tholos tomb forms an intriguing acoustic space: there is an acoustic 'dead spot' in the middle of the floor directly beneath the 13.5-metre-high apex of the beehive-shaped ceiling, while around the curved walls at head height there can be heard a distinct buzzing sound, very similar to that of a swarm of bees. The buzzing is caused by the distortion of ambient sound coming in through the great portal of the tomb, a variant on the well-known

'whispering gallery' effect (Fig. 3.3). This may have been symbolic, since in ancient Greece bees were associated with immortality — it was thought the spirits of the dead could enter bees. Bees were also known in Greece as the 'birds of the Muses', doubtless because of the sound they made. The origin of the beehive shape of tholos tombs is unknown, but a reference to the associations of immortality and spirits with bees cannot be dismissed. The buzzing sound would have added an acoustic dimension to the visual symbolism that might possibly have had an oracular function, involving the voices of the ancestral dead interred in the tomb.

Other instances of possible acoustic symbolism have been noted at other sites, such as the ancient

Figure 3.3. *Interior of the Treasury of Atreus. The doorway is 5.4 m tall.*

Peruvian pilgrimage centre and oracular temple of Chavín de Huantar (Von Hagen & Morris 1998) or the Akapana pyramid at Tiahuanaco, Bolivia, where elaborate rainwater drainage systems and use of imported materials seem visually to have symbolized the course of water draining through distant though visible sacred mountains, while the cascading water made sounds resembling the thunder reverberating through those peaks (Kolata 1996).

The automatic dismissal of all such effects as mere coincidence is an inadequate response and could unnecessarily close off access to potentially valuable information present in ancient ceremonial architecture. Correct answers can only be forthcoming if the right questions are posed, and the concept of acoustic symbolism clearly provides an appropriate platform for such questions.

The testimony of anthropology

The third research avenue involves a greater use of anthropology in archaeoacoustic investigation. The study of surviving traditional societies where hearing is at least as important as seeing can teach us much about the use of sound in earlier societies. For example, peoples living in rainforests or other visually-restricted territories can be expected to rely a great deal on sound in their everyday life, and that will spill over into their language, their music and their ritual.

This is supported by observations among tribal peoples of Papua New Guinea. Alfred Gell conducted fieldwork with the Umeda people there in 1969–70, but later realized that there was much about his study that he wanted substantially to revise. He came to understand that he had approached the Umeda in a characteristically Western visual way rather than paying appropriate attention to the acoustic dimension of their culture. During his fieldwork, Gell had become frustrated at not being able to obtain complete views of anything — he never saw a complete native village, for instance. For 14 months the extent of his vision was limited to tens of metres, or half a kilometre at most. He now knew, as more recent anthropological studies were revealing, that the intimate environment inhabited by forest peoples made hearing their prime sense, not sight. Indeed, sight came only third in the sensory pecking order after hearing and smell. To properly understand these people and their worldview, one has to enter their 'auditory domain' (to use Gell's phrase). Gell also conducted fieldwork with the Kaluli, another tribal people of Papua New Guinea. The Kaluli consider the birdsong emanating from the dense foliage around them to be the voices of the dead, or, more accurately, that the living birds embody the spirit voices. Bird classification is based not on what birds look like, but on the kind of songs they have. Birdsong, however, as Gell informs us, is only one category of the 'acoustic coding of the environment' by the Kaluli. The sounds produced by rivers, streams and waterfalls also enter their language and poetics: 'The descending movement of Kaluli song is the sung equivalent of a waterfall, and particular streams and falls are perpetually evoked in the texts of Kaluli songs . . . Place, sound and social memory are fused together in Kaluli poetics' (Gell 1995).

In another example, the Arapesh people of Papua New Guinea introduced Donald Tuzin to their secret cult instruments, among which were amplifying pipes: four-metre-long open-ended bamboo tubes. The operator sings into one end while the other is inserted into a slit-gong. When several of the tubes are used in unison, the awesome sound produced supposedly manifests the voice of Nggwal, the most powerful forest spirit. Rituals using such cult instruments take place during the season when thunderstorms occur over distant hills to the south of Arapesh territory. The storms are too far away for the thunder to be audible, but infrasound (3–15 Hz) from electrical storms can travel some 20 kilometres and can be sensed, if not directly heard. Tuzin came to the conclusion that the ritual instruments also produced infrasound which he suspected augmented the storm-generated infrasound washing through the area, thus maximizing their powerful effects which Tuzin confessed he found to be eerie and 'stunning' (Tuzin 1984).

Knowing about the factors that encourage societies to be acoustically sensitive can help the investigator to be particularly alert to evidence of acoustic use, or to be more confident in ascribing intentionality to such evidence where found. So, for instance, the ancient Maya, being a rainforest people, can be expected to have employed sound in ceremonial and ritual structures and contexts to a greater extent than a society living in an open environment.

Another example of anthropological input to archaeoacoustics is the tantalizing anecdotal evidence concerning the way in which the highly specialized percussion, whistling, chanting and rattle sounds produced by shamans conducting rituals with people who have ingested hallucinogenic plants can seemingly control visionary experience in the participants (Wasson 1965; Katz & Dobkin de Rios 1971; Dobkin de Rios & Katz 1975; Shah 2001). A better understanding of the basis on which such sounds were used on people in highly suggestive and sensitized states of consciousness could teach us much about the role of acoustics in ritual contexts.

Monitoring brain responses

Fourth, and finally, it is suggested that the use of EEG monitoring would be a desirable adjunct to archaeoacoustic investigations. It could determine if there are specific brain responses to those acoustic effects discovered in ancient architectural structures that might have ritual significance. This may seem a rather desperate research initiative were it not that the potential value of this approach has already been illustrated by a recent finding resulting from initial fieldwork conducted by Robert Jahn and the present writer in 1994.[4]

Full details of this 1994 archaeoacoustic investigation and relevant technical information have been presented elsewhere (Jahn et al. 1995; 1996; Devereux & Jahn 1996; Devereux 2001). Here it need only be noted that acoustic investigations of a small but representative sample of prehistoric megalithic chambered structures in England and Ireland were conducted using an omni-directional loudspeaker driven by a variable-frequency sine-wave oscillator and a 20-watt amplifier, the sound frequency verified by an external, hand-held, digital multimeter. The sound source was placed (with the acoustic axis oriented vertically) on the ground or on a short tripod in the centre of the chamber being investigated (Fig. 3.4); the amplitude

Figure 3.4. *Robert Jahn setting up acoustic equipment in Wayland's Smithy passage grave, 1994.*

of the soundwaves that were broadcast was mapped with a portable sound-level meter sensitive to between 55 and 105 decibels.[5]

The sites studied were a Neolithic chambered tomb (Chûn Quoit, Cornwall: Fig. 3.5), an Iron Age 'beehive' structure of unknown purpose adjoining a souterrain (Carn Euny, Cornwall), and four Neolithic passage graves, some of which are multi-chambered (Wayland's Smithy, England; Loughcrew Cairns I and L and Newgrange, Ireland). The sole aim of the investigation was to establish the primary (natural) resonance frequencies of the chambers. Unexpectedly, it was found that the resonance frequencies of the chambers, which vary in size, shape and constructional details, fall into a very narrow frequency band of 95–120 Hz, with the majority clustering around 110 Hz. The primary resonance of the chamber at Newgrange, for example, the largest and most architecturally sophisticated of all the monuments tested, is almost exactly 110 Hz (Fig. 3.6). This frequency band

Figure 3.5. *At Chûn Quoit during the 1994 ICRL archaeoacoustic fieldwork.*

is in the lower baritone range of the human voice.

The repetitive nature of these results was one indication of intentionality on the part of the monuments' builders. Another was the evidence of 'retro-fitting' in some cases, in which bays in the walls of some of the main chambers and individual stones set at points on chamber floors had the effect of tuning the chamber to the frequency range described. But there was a third piece of evidence indicating intentionality which has only very recently come to light. Jahn and the present writer asked Ian Cook of the Neuropsychiatric Institute at UCLA to conduct EEG monitoring to test the effects (if any) of the 110 Hz audio frequency on the human brain. The results, described in Cook's internal ICRL report, are noteworthy and are summarized by the following excerpts:

Subjects: 30 healthy individuals (16 females:14 males) participated in this program; it was part of a larger project on brain function and cognition in healthy aging (Cook *et al*. 2002a).

Stimuli: Subjects were instructed to listen to tones at each of five frequencies (90, 100, 110, 120, and 130 Hz) as they rested with eyes closed. The duration of the each tone was approximately 1 minute and the stimuli were presented through speakers positioned near the subjects' ears.

EEG Recording: Quantitative EEG (QEEG) recordings were performed using the QND digital EEG system (Neurodata, Inc., Pasadena CA) and surface EEG activity was recording with 35 scalp electrodes, positioned with a lycra cap (ElectroCap, Inc., Eaton OH) in accordance with the International 10–20 system of electrode placement. Signals were recorded at 256 samples/channel/second (filter passband 0.3–70 Hz).

Cordance Measure: Cordance values were calculated using 20–30 seconds of artifact-free QEEG data for each tone frequency. Cordance is a transformation of QEEG spectral power; it offers an advantage over conventional power because it is more highly correlated with regional brain perfusion (Leuchter *et al*. 1999). Cordance values in the theta band (4–8 Hz) have been used to detect differences in regional brain activity during treatment for depression (Cook *et al.* 2002b) and may reflect cortically projected rhythms from the activity in deeper limbic structures that are related to emotional experience.

Figure 3.6. *Entrance to the passage at Newgrange, Ireland.*

Preliminary Findings: Cordance values at 110 Hz differed from values at other frequencies in the left temporal region and over the prefrontal cortex. In the left temporal region, cordance values were significantly lower at 110 Hz compared with 90 Hz ($p = 0.04$), and 130 Hz ($p = 0.01$), with a trend value at 100 Hz ($p = 0.07$). In the prefrontal region, a trend was noted; average cordance values in channels over the left hemisphere were lower than the right at 90, 100, 120, and 130 Hz, but this asymmetry reversed at 110 Hz.

Comment: Listening to tones at 110 Hz was associated with patterns of regional brain activity that differed from listening to tones at neighboring frequencies; differences were particularly noted in left temporal and prefrontal asymmetries. The meaning of these changes is open to speculation. The left temporal region has been implicated in the cognitive processing of spoken language; lower cordance values at 110 Hz would be consistent with reduced activation under that condition, which might be interpreted as a relative silencing of language centers to allow other processes to become more prominent. Studies of prefrontal asymmetry have suggested that patterns of shifting asymmetry are related to emotional states, so the inversion of the asymmetric pattern we observed may reflect some differences in activation in neural networks in response to that specific tone. (Cook 2003)

The theta band of brain electrical activity implicated in these findings is associated with the onset of sleep, specifically the half-awake/half-asleep hypnogogic state, which is prone to the irruption of transient but vivid mental imagery and auditory hallucinations. It also appears accompanied by other frequencies in deep meditation and trance states. In other words, it is the ideal brain frequency to be encouraged if one is conducting ritual activity. That one of the stone-built chambers should be able to produce acoustic frequencies that cause changes in patterns of activity in the prefrontal and the left temporal cortex with effectively the precision of a switch being thrown would be an interesting coincidence. The fact that *all six* sites tested did so makes it a remarkable feature. It is at least as likely that these findings indicate an empirical discovery by the prehistoric builders that was deliberately employed in at least some of their chambered monuments.

The use of EEG monitoring to determine the effects (or otherwise) on the human brain of acoustic properties found at ancient ceremonial monuments could open up a fruitful area of cognitive research, especially if the EEG data were collected by portable instrumentation on site.

Summary

Four areas of research development have been suggested that may provide valuable new information on archaeoacoustics that will allow intentionality to be assessed. The suggested areas are: (i) conducting studies worldwide to extend our knowledge of the coincidence of musical natural features and rock art, and cataloguing the results; (ii) recognition that acoustic symbolism may be expressed at a site, so that archaeoacoustic findings can be evaluated for meaning (and thus intentionality) against a range of appropriate factors; (iii) broader use of anthropological data to help identify (a) environmental and other factors characterizing cultures likely to have been disposed toward the intentional use of sound, and (b) the range of such use that may have been involved; (iv) use of EEG monitoring to determine what effects, if any, archaeoacoustic phenomena might have on the human brain. Examples of all four suggested approaches have been given above.

Acknowledgements

The writer is particularly grateful to Robert G. Jahn and Ian Cook for their input to parts of this paper.

Notes

1. D. Bowen, personal communication citing a conversation with the late John Richards, a folklore museum curator local to Preseli. If Richards wrote about this observation, his notes have not yet been found.
2. Since this paper was written, the present writer has tested selected outcrops on Carn Menyn for acoustic properties (in October 2005), and has confirmed the presence of ringing rocks there. Of the sample tested (by percussion), approximately 10 per cent of rocks were found to produce ringing sounds. A more thorough survey is required and is planned. Other types of possible acoustic properties were also noted, and these will also be further investigated. The bluestones at Stonehenge should also be tested for acoustic properties.
3. This research is incomplete so definite conclusions cannot yet be drawn.
4. This work was conducted under the aegis of the International Consciousness Research Laboratories (ICRL) group, an informal multi-disciplinary consortium of researchers based in Princeton.
5. The frequency coming from the sound source was manually swept through the lower audible range until the lowest natural resonance of the chamber became clearly discernible. When this was established, the loudness was adjusted to the highest comfortable level, and a measured grid or measuring tape laid on the ground from the sound source out to the walls of the chamber. This enabled radial

horizontal surveys of the acoustic standing waves within the chamber to be made with the sound-level meter. If the frequency of the sound was set accurately at whatever the natural resonance of each chamber was, it was to be expected that there would be a series of antinodes and nodes, with a primary antinode at the wall of the chamber, because a standing wave within a chamber is created by the sound reflecting off the wall back towards the source, thus causing two soundwave patterns to be superimposed one on the other.

References

Cook, I.A., 2003. *Ancient Acoustic Resonance Patterns Influence Regional Brain Activity.* (Internal Report). Princeton (NJ): International Consciousness Research Laboratories.

Cook, I.A., A.F. Leuchter, M. Morgan, E. Witte, S.David, R. Lufkin, A. Babaie, J. Dunkin, R. O'Hara, S. Simon, A. Lightner, S. Thomas, D. Broumandi, N. Badjatia, L. Mickes, R. Mody, S. Arroyo, Z. Zheng, M. Abrams & S. Rosenberg, 2002a. Cognitive and physiologic correlates of subclinical structural brain disease in elderly healthy control subjects. *Archives of Neurology* 59, 1612–20.

Cook, I.A., A.F. Leuchter, M. Morgan, E. Witte, W.F. Stubbeman, M. Abrams, S. Rosenberg & S.H. Uijtdehaage, 2002b. Early changes in prefrontal activity characterize clinical responders to antidepressants. *Neuropsychopharmacology* 27, 120–31.

Dams, L., 1985. Palaeolithic lithophones: descriptions and comparisons. *Oxford Journal of Archaeology* 4, 31–46.

Devereux, P., 2001. *Stone Age Soundtracks: the Acoustic Archaeology of Ancient Sites.* London: Vega.

Devereux, P. & R.G. Jahn, 1996. Preliminary investigations and cognitive considerations of the acoustical resonances of selected archaeological sites. *Antiquity* 70, 665–6.

Dobkin de Rios, M. & F. Katz, 1975. Some relationships between music and hallucinogenic ritual: the 'jungle gym' in consciousness. *Ethos* 3, 64–76.

Fagg, B., 1957. Rock gongs and slides. *Man* 57, 30–32.

Gell, A., 1995. The language of the forest: landscape and phonological iconism in Umeda, in *The Anthropology of Landscape*, eds. E. Hirsch & M. O'Hanlon. Oxford: Oxford University Press, 232–54.

Hedges, K., 1990. Petroglyphs in Menifee Valley. *Rock Art Papers* 7, 75–82.

Jahn, R.G, P. Devereux & M. Ibison, 1995. *Acoustical Resonances of Assorted Ancient Structures.* (Technical Report PEAR 9500.) Princeton (NJ): University of Princeton.

Jahn, R.G., P. Devereux & M. Ibison, 1996. Acoustic resonances of assorted ancient structures. *Journal of the Acoustical Society of America* 99, 649–58.

Katz, F. & M. Dobkin De Rios, 1971. Whistling in Peruvian ayahuasca healing sessions. *Journal of American Folklore* 84, 320–27.

Kolata, A., 1996. *Valley of the Spirits.* New York (NY): John Wiley.

Krupp, E.C., 1997. *Skywatchers, Shamans and Kings.* New York (NY): John Wiley.

Lauhakangas, R., 1999. A lithophonic drum in Lake Onega. *Adoranten (Scandinavian Society for Prehistoric Art)*, 42–3.

Lawson, G., C. Scarre, I. Cross & C. Hills, 1998. Mounds, megaliths, music and mind: some thoughts on the acoustical properties and purposes of archaeological spaces. *Archaeological Review from Cambridge* 15, 111–34.

Leuchter, A.F., S.H.J. Uijtdehaage, I.A. Cook, R. O'Hara & M. Mandelkern, 1999. Relationship between brain electrical activity and cortical perfusion in normal subjects. *Psychiatry Research: Neuroimaging* 90, 125–40.

Lubman, D., 1998. An archaeological study of a chirped echo from the Mayan pyramid of Kukulcan at Chichen Itza. Paper presented to the Conference of the Acoustical Society of America, 12–16 October 1998.

Palmer, D. & P. Pettitt, 2001. In search of our musical roots. *Focus* 105, 80–84.

Reznikoff, I., 1995. On the sound dimension of prehistoric painted caves and rocks, in *Musical Signification* (ed. E. Taratsi). Berlin: Mouton de Gruyter, 541–55.

Rowland, I. & T.N. Howe (eds.), 1999. *Vitruvius: Ten Books on Architecture.* Cambridge: Cambridge University Press.

Shah, T., 2001. *Trail of Feathers.* London: Weidenfeld & Nicolson.

Thomas, H.H., 1923. The source of the stones of Stonehenge. *Antiquaries Journal* 3, 239–60.

Tuzin, D., 1984. Miraculous voices: the auditory experience of numinous objects. *Current Anthropology* 25, 579–96.

Von Hagen, A. & C. Morris, 1998. *The Cities of the Andes.* London: Thames & Hudson.

Waller, S., 1993. Sound reflection as an explanation for the content and context of rock art. *Rock Art Research* 10, 91–101.

Wasson, G., 1965. The hallucinogenic fungi of Mexico, in *The Psychedelic Reader*, eds. G. Weil, R. Metzner & T. Leary. New York (NY): University Books, 23–38.

Chapter 4

Intentionality of Rock-art Placement Deduced from Acoustical Measurements and Echo Myths

Steven J. Waller

The motivation for the global production of prehistoric rock art has long resisted explanation. Not only is the subject matter depicted puzzling, but the unusual locations chosen by the artists are perplexing. Pictographs and petroglyphs are typically found deep in caves, or high on canyon walls and cliff faces, often crowded onto particular surfaces while other apparently suitable and more convenient surfaces remained blank. A clue to these unusual locations may be found in the observation that hundreds of rock-art sites are associated with unusual acoustic phenomena such as echoes, reverberation, resonance, and sound carrying unexpectedly far. Systematic measurements at some of these sites have shown that sound reflections at decorated locations are at significantly greater decibel levels than at nearby non-decorated locations. The cultural significance of this can be found in the numerous ethnographically-recorded myths from around the world that attribute the phenomenon of echoing to supernatural spirits. These ancient myths show that echoes were actively worshipped as divine, were considered to be the 'earliest of all existence', and were systematically sought out. Together with this cultural information, quantitative acoustical data leads to the conclusion that the artists intentionally selected the most strongly sound-reflecting surfaces to decorate. It is theorized that a substantial proportion of rock art is a physical manifestation of locally-focused ritualistic behaviour that expressed common belief systems in which acoustical phenomena such as echoes were perceived in a spiritual context. This acoustic theory harmonizes with other rock-art theories such as structuralism and shamanism. Although it is not possible unequivocally to prove that the artists purposely chose to decorate echoing places with the images evoked upon hearing echoes, the corollary that rock art occurs preferentially at echoing locations is scientifically testable. From this follows the need to preserve the acoustical properties of rock-art sites.

The impetus for the production of images on rock surfaces is among the least well understood behaviours exhibited by ancient humans. The motivation for the creation of prehistoric cave paintings and rock engravings (Fig. 4.1), found throughout the world, is a key question in the emerging discipline (Odak 1991) of rock-art studies. The enormous effort exerted by the artists over many thousands of years is an indication that the production of rock art held a high degree of significance to ancient peoples. The legacy of rock art

produced by diverse cultures on different continents displays unexplained similarities in both the restricted subject-matter of the art, and the unusual locations selected for decoration. The subject matter of the art is quite narrow. For example, more than ninety per cent of the recognizable figures in Upper Palaeolithic European cave art consist of hoofed animals (Leroi-Gourhan 1967; 1981; Waller 1993b). The locations that were selected for artistic decoration are even more baffling to modern scientists, as the art was often pro-

Figure 4.1. *Prehistoric rock art at echoing locations: a) pictographs at the Great Gallery in Horseshoe Canyon, Utah; b) petroglyphs from the main concentration of rock art in Hieroglyphic Canyon, Arizona. (Photos: S. Waller.)*

there is poor agreement with species hunted and eaten (Hadingham 1979, 97). Furthermore, the hunting-magic theory is incomplete in that it does not explain the art's unusual locations. Structuralist theories that attempted to explain the patterns of decoration based on cave shape (Laming-Empéraire 1962; Leroi-Gourhan 1967; 1981) revolutionized the study of cave art, but have not been well accepted owing to vagueness and the inconsistencies found in subsequently discovered caves. Theories of totemism (Ucko & Rosenfeld 1967) are based on very tenuous ethnological analogies. Recent explanations invoking shamanism (Lewis-Williams & Dowson 1990) have attracted much attention and controversy.

Acoustics

In 1957 Giedion mentioned the notion of 'acoustic space' in caverns. Ringing rocks, gong rocks, bell rocks, and lithophones, as well as the related but distinct category of sounding stones, were found by a number of researchers in association with rock art (Bean 1975; Dams 1985; B. Fagg 1956; Glory 1968; Heizer 1953; Knight 1979; Nissen & Ritter 1986; True & Baumhoff 1981). Although those reports suggested a possible relationship between acoustics and location, there was no theory plausibly relating acoustics to the subject matter of the art, leaving the motivation for the art unknown.

The author independently became aware in 1987 of startlingly strong echo effects at the mouth of the Palaeolithic decorated cave of Bédeilhac in southern France. These echoes could be perceived as sounds 'mysteriously' emanating from the cave in answer to sounds made outside. It is clear that early societies had supernatural explanations of sound reflection (see Appendix). Thus, before the discovery of an acoustical theory of sound reflection, echoes and reverberation phenomena gave the illusion of being spontaneously-generated noises produced by certain surfaces. This would have lent a magical aura to such locations as caves and canyons that reflect sound.

duced on surfaces relatively difficult to reach, such as high on canyon walls or deep within caves, and was usually concentrated in certain spots, while nearby surfaces were ignored. There has thus been a failure to understand the motivation for the choice of both the content and context of rock art.

Explanations (reviewed by Ucko & Rosenfeld 1967; Bahn & Vertut 1988) for rock art have proved unsatisfactory. 'Art for art's sake' (Halverson 1987) is useless as a theory to explain either the restricted subject matter or the unusual locations. It has been proposed that the animal subjects were related to sympathetic hunting magic (Breuil 1952), although

Experimentation with different types of noises performed in a variety of acoustic environments led to the discovery that when rocks are struck together in the manner of making stone tools, the echoes sound remarkably like hoof-beats (Waller 1993a). This was realized to be particularly relevant since statistical studies of Upper Paleolithic art (Leroi-Gourhan 1967, 1981) can be reinterpreted to show that more than ninety per cent of parietal European figurative art is composed of hoofed animals (Waller 1993b). Ungulates such as sheep and deer are also very numerous in the rock art of the Americas. The observation that sound-reflecting places such as caves and canyons can give rise to hoof beat-like echoes that mimic the ungulates depicted there by prehistoric artists provides a scientifically testable theoretical connection between the context and content of rock art.

It has been suggested that the location of deep cave art may correspond to places in those caves where particular musical notes resonate (Reznikoff & Dauvois 1988). While this does not explain open-air sites nor the content of the art, that study continues a chain of observations in the literature about acoustics and rock art. Evidence is accumulating to suggest that acoustics may have been a motivating influence for the production of a substantial proportion of the

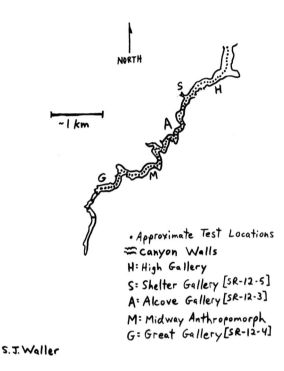

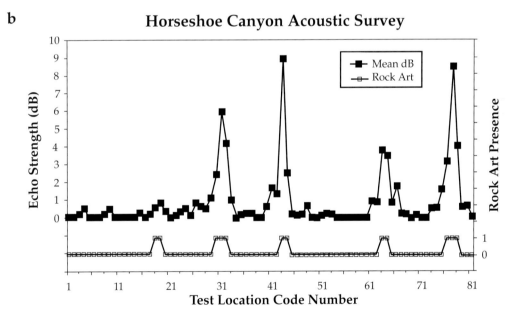

Figure 4.2. *Sound reflection at locations in Horseshoe Canyon, including locations decorated with rock art: a) plan of canyon showing approximate locations of sound tests relative to rock art; b) echo strength in dB plotted against test location, numbered from the mouth of Horseshoe Canyon. Presence (1) or absence (0) of rock art at each test location is indicated by the lower line. Note how test locations with rock art present significantly stronger echoes than those where rock art is absent. Abbreviations for rock-art sites: H = High Gallery; S = Shelter; A = Alcove; M = Midway anthropomorph (approximate location); G = Great Gallery.*

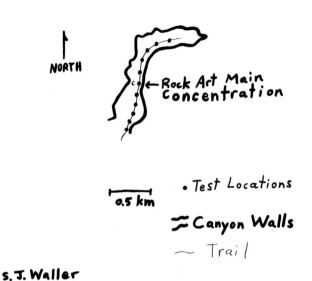

a

HIEROGLYPHIC CANYON
ACOUSTIC TESTING

↑
NORTH

←Rock Art Main
Concentration

•Test Locations

⇒ Canyon Walls

~ Trail

0.5 km

S. J. Waller

rock art found around the world. Sound — in the form of echoing, reverberation and resonance (Bjork 1997; M.C. Fagg 1997; Hedges 1990; 1993; Dauvois 1989; 1996; Ouzman 1997; 2001; Parkman 1990; 1992; Reznikoff 1995; Reznikoff & Dauvois 1988; Steinbring 1992; Waller 1993a,b; 1994; 2000; 2004) — appears to have been a determinant in the selection of location and/or subject matter in a large number of cases.

The cultural relevance of echoes and their mythology

It is known through numerous ethnographically-documented legends that most ancient cultures held the belief that certain natural phenomena were caused by supernatural beings. This type of belief is categorized as 'animism', a form of personification. One complex natural phenomenon that was personified by ancient cultures is the echo, which has been explained only in modern times by invisible sound wave reflections. Legends documented from around the world show that echoes were perceived as emanating from spirits or were considered spiritually important (see Appendix for list of echo myths).

Since echoes appear to originate from rock surfaces such as those found in canyons and caves, the spirits that were perceived as making these sounds were probably thought to dwell within those rocks. There are many recorded examples of rock-art sites from around the world that have unusual acoustical properties such as echoes, supporting the theory of a connection between rock art and sound reflection (Waller 1993a,b; 1994; 2000; 2001). This acoustical theory of rock-art motivation enriches, rather than competes with, other theories of rock-art motivation. Although it is not possible unequivocally to prove that the artists purposely chose to decorate echoing places with the images evoked upon hearing echoes, the corollary that rock art occurs preferentially at echoing locations is scientifically testable. Acoustical testing of rock-art sites has progressed from subjectively listening for the existence of echoes, to performing objective measurements to determine whether rock art occurs specifically at locations with the better echoes than those of the non-decorated surroundings. An analysis of acoustic data systematically collected in a portion of Horseshoe Canyon in Utah

b

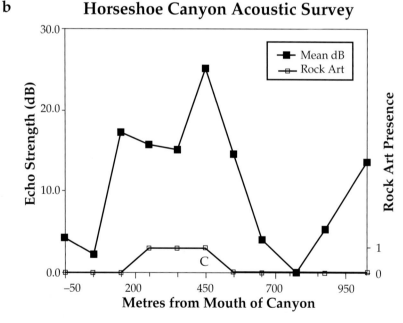

Horseshoe Canyon Acoustic Survey

Figure 4.3. *Sound reflection at locations in Hieroglyphic Canyon including locations decorated with rock art: plan of canyon showing approximate locations of sound tests relative to rock art; a few isolated rock-art motifs occur at an estimated 250–400 metres from the mouth of the canyon, and the main concentration of rock art (C) is at approximately 450 metres from the canyon mouth; b) echo strength in dB plotted against estimated distance from canyon mouth. Presence (1) or absence (0) of rock art near each test location is indicated by the lower line. Note how the principal concentration of rock art (C) coincides with the location with the strongest echo measurements, at c. 450 metres from the canyon mouth.*

showed that the five art sites within the study area correlate exactly with the five locations within the canyon that possess the greatest intensity of echoing (Waller 2000) (Fig. 4.2). Subsequent results from a similar study conducted in Hieroglyphic Canyon, Arizona, also showed a correspondence of art locations with echo intensity (Waller 2002) (Fig. 4.3).

A possible connection has also been proposed (Waller 2001) between sound and the San supernatural belief that the rock surface acts as a veil that separates the outer world from a spirit world within the rock. The veil concept is highly relevant to rock-art studies since evidence from South Africa indicates that the rock surface was decorated because of the belief in the spirit world behind (Lewis-Williams & Dowson 1990). A close analogy to this concept can be found in *Through the Looking Glass* by Lewis Carroll (1871). In this tale, Alice sees objects reflected in the mirror's surface, and concludes there is another world on the other side of the glass, deep within the mirror. In a similar fashion, modern acoustical physics describes how sound waves can be reflected by the boundary between air and a denser material such as rock. Under the proper conditions, reflected sound is perceived as what is called in modern terms an echo: a duplicated, delayed sound that appears to come from the direction of the rock (Fig. 4.4). This applies to sound-wave reflection in the same way as to light-wave reflection. The auditory illusion produced is that of sound emerging from within the rock — behind the veil of the rock surface. As an example of how real the experience can seem, one researcher said he first noticed rock-art acoustics when he 'heard a car "drive" out of the Buckhorn panel' (William Biesele pers. comm. 1997).

The observation that echoes can be experienced as voices calling out from the rock, together with the illusion of depth due to sound reflection, may have inspired the belief in a spirit world within the rock. From our knowledge of cultures worldwide that explain natural phenomena in terms of animism, this belief in a spirit world behind the veil of the rock surface would be a quite understandable response to sound reflection. Since echoes appear to originate from behind certain specific rock surfaces, the spirits conceived as making the sounds were probably thought to dwell within those rocks. The rock surface would consequently have been regarded as a veil between the spirits and the listener.

A quotation from South African Bushman (San or /Xam) folklore dictated in 1878 by /Han=kass'o lends credence to this hypothesis: 'O beast of prey! Thou art the one who hearest the place behind, it is resonant with sound' (Bleek & Lloyd 1911). In this cultural context, the 'beast of prey' has been interpreted as a

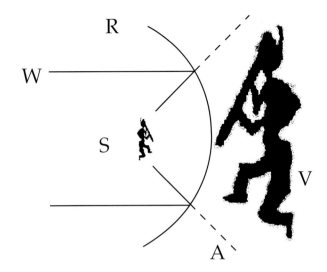

Figure 4.4. *Diagram of light- or sound-wave reflection resulting in a virtual image apparently behind the reflecting plane. Owing to bending, the source waves of this visual or acoustic image are perceived to be coming through the reflecting plane, giving the illusion of permeability and depth. R: reflecting surface (concave in this example); W: waves of light or sound; S: source; V: virtual image (magnified/amplified in this example); A: apparent waves of light or sound.*

term of respect for a shaman, and 'the place behind' as the spirit world (Ouzman 2001). The belief in the spirit world within the rock has been considered very important and relevant to rock-art images that decorate the rock surface veil (Lewis-Williams & Dowson 1990). Evidence presented by Lewis-Williams & Dowson that San rock art relates to San belief in a spirit world beyond the rock surface includes many examples of painted images emerging from cracks or holes within the rocks. Painted San rock shelters have been found to produce echoes, as for example at Rose Cottage Cave (Ouzman 1997), and to exhibit other unusual acoustics (Sven Ouzman pers. comm. 2000).

In North America, recorded Ojibway and Matagaming legends are remarkably similar. Parallels include the belief in a spirit world within the rock, and that spirit beings inside the rock produce many sounds such as heartbeat drumming and songs that echo. Furthermore, here again the rock wall is thought to appear like a magic transparent window when viewed from within, as if the paintings hung in the air, and sounds of voices are heard around the paintings (Conway 1993).

This evidence indicates an indirect connection between sound and rock art that supplements direct observations of an association between sound reflection and rock-art locations. It is possible to speculate that the rock-art subject matter represents the images of the spirits that the artists envisioned to be causing the mysterious echoed sounds from behind the veil. Anthropomorphic figures, for example, may have been inspired by echoes of voices, and zoomorphic figures by percussive echoes perceived as hoof-beats. Might therianthropes represent the spirits imagined upon hearing both hoof beat-like percussion echoes and voices emanating from the same place? In a fashion similar to the conventions of modern cartoonists, abstract symbols such as circles, zigzag lines and starbursts may be the result of attempts to represent the sounds themselves. Thus, acoustics may explain not only the perplexing locations of rock art, but its unusual subject matter as well (Waller 1993a).

Intentionality

In summary, although the thoughts of the artists were lost thousands of years ago, there remains today solid evidence that can be studied in order to deduce the general nature of the motivation of rock art. This evidence includes the art itself and the subject matter depicted, the locations of the rock surfaces that are decorated as compared with those that are not (although some may have been in the past), the echoes and other acoustic phenomena that can be produced by various surfaces, and the related myths. Since much art is located at places that have unusual acoustics, and since echoes were widely considered a supernatural phenomenon, it is reasonable to conclude that the artists intentionally selected sound-reflecting surfaces to decorate.

A practical implication of the theoretical advances and experimental research results in rock-art acoustics is that rock-art conservation efforts should be expanded to preserve (Waller 2003) and record (Berrier 2000) not just the images themselves, but also the acoustical properties of the sites.

Acknowledgements

The author thanks the many people who have helped and encouraged him in this research over the years.

References

Antoninus Liberalis 26 http://www.theoi.com/Okeanos/ Saggarios.html.

Bahn, P.G. & J. Vertut, 1988. *Images of the Ice Age*. New York (NY): Facts on File.

Bean, L.J., 1975. Power and its application in native California. *Journal of California Anthropology* 2, 25–33.

Berrier, M., 2000. Proposed documentation and storage of data related to acoustic phenomena at rock art sites. *1999 IRAC Proceedings* 1, 718.

Bjork, C., 1997. Why here? *Bay Area Rock Art News* 15, 1–7.

Bleek, W.H.I. & L.C. Lloyd, 1911. Doings of the Springbok VII – 121, in *Specimens of Bushman Folklore*, ed. W.H.I. Bleek. London: George Allen, 245–7.

Bonnefoy, Y., 1992. *Greek and Egyptian Mythologies*. Chicago (IL): University of Chicago Press.

Breuil, H., 1952. *Four Hundred Centuries of Cave Art*. Montignac: Centre d'Etudes et de Documentation Préhistoriques.

Bulfinch, T., 1855. *The Age of Fable or Stories of Gods and Heroes*. Boston (MA): S.W. Tilton & Co.

Carroll, L., 1871 (1971). Through the looking glass and what Alice found there, in *Alice in Wonderland*, ed. D.J. Gray. New York (NY): W.W. Norton.

Conway, T., 1993. *Painted Dreams: Native American Rock Art*. Minocqua: Northword.

Cushing, F.H., 1901. *Zuñi Folk Tales*. New York (NY): Putnam.

Dams, L., 1985. Palaeolithic lithophones: descriptions and comparisons. *Oxford Journal of Archaeology* 4, 31–46.

Dauvois, M., 1989. Sons et musique paléolithiques. *Dossiers de l'Archéologie* 142, 2–11.

Dauvois, M., 1996. Evidence of sound-making and the acoustic character of the decorated caves of the western Paleolithic world. *International Newsletter on Rock Art* 13, 23–5.

Dionysiaca 6.257 http://www.theoi.com/Kronos/Pan. html.

Dixon, R.B. 1916. *Oceanic Mythology*. Boston (MA): Marshall Jones.

Fagg, B., 1956. The rock gong complex today and in prehistoric times. *Journal of the Historical Society of Nigeria* 1, 27–42.

Fagg, M.C., 1997. *Rock Music*. (Pitt Rivers Museum Occasional Paper on Technology 14.) Oxford: Pitt Rivers Museum.

Giedion, S., 1957. *The Eternal Present: the Beginnings of Art*. New York (NY): Pantheon.

Gill, S.D. & I.F. Sullivan, 1992. *Dictionary of Native American Mythology*. Oxford: Oxford University Press.

Glory, A., 1968. L'énigme de l'art quaternaire peut-elle être resolue par la théorie du culte des ongones? *Simposio de Arte Rupestre, Barcelona 1966*, 25–60.

Hadingham, E., 1979. *Secrets of the Ice Age*. New York (NY): Walker & Co.

Halverson, J., 1987. Art for art's sake in the Paleolithic. *Current Anthropology* 28, 63–89.

Hedges, K., 1990. Petroglyphs in Menifee County. *Rock Art Papers* 7, 75–83.

Hedges, K., 1993. Places to see and places to hear: rock art and features of the sacred landscape, in *Time and Space: Dating and Spatial Considerations in Rock Art Research*, eds. J. Steinbring, A. Watchamn, P. Faulitsch & P. Taçon. (AURA Occasional Publication 8.) Melbourne: Australian Rock Art Research Association, 121–7.

Heizer, R.F., 1953. Sacred rain rocks of northern California. *University of California Archaeological Survey Reports* 22, 33–58.

Highwater, J., 1984. *Ritual of the Wind*. Toronto: Methuen.

Jobes, G., 1961. *Dictionary of Mythology, Folklore and Symbols*. New York (NY): Scarecrow Press.

Judson, K.B., 1912. *Myths and Legends of California and the Old Southwest*. Chicago (IL): A.C. McClurg & Co.

Knight, L., 1979. Bell Rock and Indian Maze Rock of Orange County. *Pacific Coast Archaeological Society Quarterly* 15, 25–32.

Laming-Empéraire, A., 1962. *La Signification de l'Art Rupestre Paléolithique*. Paris: Picard.

Leroi-Gourhan, A., 1967. *Treasures of Prehistoric Art*. New York (NY): Abrams.

Leroi-Gourhan, A., 1981. *The Dawn of European Art*. Cambridge: Cambridge University Press.

Lewis-Williams, J.D. & T.A. Dowson, 1990. Through the veil: San rock paintings and the rock face. *South African Archaeological Bulletin* 45, 5–16.

Mooney, J., 1900. Myths of the Cherokee. *Nineteenth Annual Report of the Bureau of American Ethnology 1897–98*, part I, 125.

Neapu, A., 1983. Wenewene Temane (Echo Story). *Oral History* 11, 42–5.

Nissen, K.M. & E.W. Ritter, 1986. Cupped rock art in North Central California: hypothesis regarding age and social/ecological context. *American Indian Rock Art* 2, 59–75.

Odak, O., 1991. A new name for a new discipline. *Rock Art Research* 8, 3–12.

Ouzman, S., 1997. Hidden in the common gaze: collective and idiosyncratic rock paintings at Rose Cottage Cave, South Africa. *Navorsinge van die Nasionale Museum, Bloemfontein* 13, 225–56.

Ouzman, S., 2001. Seeing is Deceiving: rock-art and the non-visual. *World Archaeology* 33, 237–56.

Parkman, E.B., 1990. Toward a Proto-Hokan Ideology. Paper presented at the 23rd Annual Chacmool Archaeology Conference.

Parkman, E.B., 1992. Creating Thunder: a California Rain-making Tradition. Paper presented to the California Indian Conference.

Reznikoff, I., 1995. On the sound dimension of prehistoric painted Caves and rocks, in *Musical Signification: Essays on the Semiotic Theory and Analysis of Music*, ed. E. Tarasti. (Approaches to Semiotics 121.) New York (NY): Mouton de Gruyter, 541–57.

Reznikoff, I. & M. Dauvois, 1988. La dimension sonore des grottes ornées. *Bulletin de la Société Préhistorique Française* 85, 238–46.

Spence, L., 1913. *The Myths of Mexico and Peru*. London: Harrap.

Steinbring, J., 1992. Phenomenal attributes: site selection factors in rock art. *American Indian Rock Art* 17, 102–13.

Thompson, S., 1929. *Tales of the North American Indians*. Cambridge (MA): Harvard University Press.

True, D.L. & M.A. Baumhoff, 1981. Pitted rock petroglyphs in southern California. *Journal of California and Great Basin Anthropology* 2, 257–68.

Ucko, P.J. & A. Rosenfeld, 1967. *Palaeolithic Cave Art*. New York (NY): McGraw-Hill.

Waller, S.J., 1993a. Sound and rock art. *Nature* 363, 501.

Waller, S.J., 1993b. Sound reflection as an explanation for the content and context of rock art. *Rock Art Research* 10, 91–101.

Waller, S.J., 1994. Taphonomic considerations of rock art acoustics. *Rock Art Research* 11, 120–21.

Waller, S.J., 2000. Spatial correlation of acoustics and rock art exemplified in Horseshoe Canyon. *American Indian Rock Art* 24, 85–94.

Waller, S.J., 2001. Sounds of the spirit world: auditory perceptions of depth at rock art sites. *American Indian Rock Art* 28, 53–6.

Waller, S.J., 2002. Rock art acoustics in the past, present and future, in *1999 IRAC Proceedings (American Indian Rock Art* 26 (Part 2), 11–20), vol. 2, eds. P. Whitehead, W. Whitehead, L. Loendorf & W. Breen Murray. Tucson (AZ): American Rock Art Research Association, 11–20.

Waller, S.J., 2003. Conservation of rock art acoustics: 'unexpected' echoes at Petroglyph National Monument. *Rock Art Papers* 16, 31–8.

Waller, S.J., 2004. Rock art acoustics. http://www.geocities.com/CapeCanaveral/9461.

Waller, S.J., D. Lubman & B. Kiser, 1999. Digital acoustic recording techniques applied to rock art sites. *American Indian Rock Art* 25, 179–90.

Werner, A., 1933. *Myths and Legends of the Bantu*. London: Harrap.

Westerveld, W.D., 1915. *Hawaiian Legends of Old Honolulu*. Boston (MA): G.H. Ellis Press.

Williamson, R.A., 1984. *Living Sky: the Cosmos of the American Indian*. Boston (MA): Houghton Mifflin.

Winstedt, R.O., 1925. *Shaman, Saiva and Sufi: a Study of the Evolution of Malay Magic*. Glasgow: University Press.

Appendix

Myths documented from around the world show that echoes were perceived as emanating from spirits or were considered spiritually important. Examples include the following:

Greece:

a) the nymph Echo was thought to be responsible for repeated words (Bonnefoy 1992).

b) 'After Hylas had disappeared, Herakles saw that he was not coming back to him and deserted the heroes, searching everywhere in the thickets, calling "Hylas" again and again. The nymphs, fearing that Herakles might discover that they had hidden the lad among them, changed him into an echo which again and again echoed back the cries of Herakles.' (Antoninus Liberalis 26).

c) 'and Selene's turning-mark received the creaking echo from Kronos' starting-point' (Dionysiaca 2.170)

Iceland:

'The black or Night Elves' . . . language was the echo of solitudes, and their dwelling-places subterranean caves and clefts. . . They were particularly distinguished for a knowledge of the mysterious powers of nature, and for the runes which they carved and explained . . . Gray's ode on the "Descent of Odin" contains an allusion to the use of Runic letters for incantation:

> Facing to the northern clime,
> Thrice he traced the Runic rhyme;
> Thrice pronounced, in accents dread
> The thrilling verse that wakes the dead,
> Till from out the hollow ground
> Slowly breathed a sullen sound. (Bulfinch 1855)

South Pacific:

a) 'Echo as the bodiless voice, is the earliest of all existence' (Jobes 1961).

b) 'the deity Tu-mute-anaoa = "Echo"' (Dixon 1916)

c) 'Tiki was the first man, and Ma-riko-riko ("Glimmer") the first woman, the latter being created by Arohi-rohi ("Mirage") from the warmth of the Sun and Echo' (Dixon 1916)

d) Hawaii '. . . became the echo-god and lived in "the hollow gray rocks" (Westerveld 1915)

d) Papua New Guinea; the Hagen people's 'Wenewene Temane (Echo Story)' (Neapu 1983).

North America:

a) A Paiute legend describes witches (tso-a-vwits) living in the belly of mountain sheep and in snakeskins hidden among rocks, from which they take great delight in repeating in mockery the words of passersby. (Gill & Sullivan 1992, 79).

b) 'The Acoma migration story describes Masewa (son of the sun) leading the people out of the place of emergence, heading for a place called Aako. As they travel they come upon different places they suspect might be Aako. To test each one, Masewa calls out in a loud voice, "Aaaakooooooo!" If the echo resounds, the people stay to test the place further. If the echo is not good, they simply pass it by. At a place just east of Acoma, the echo is perfect, and Masewa announces that this is Acoma.' (Gill & Sullivan 1992, 4–5). (Interestingly, Petroglyph National Park is located at the eastern border of the Acoma aboriginal land claims, and was found by the author to produce excellent echoes.)

c) A site called 'Wikwip' in California contains rock art for which there ethnographic information records that the paintings were made by men preparing for ceremonial dances. The site name means Echo Rock, and is derived from the sound-focusing acoustical characteristics of the cave (Hedges 1993).

d) The Navajo Night Chant (Yeibichai) includes offering of prayers to the divinity Echoing Stone on the first day of purification (Highwater 1984).

e) The Twin Palongawhoya (Echo) features prominently in Hopi creation myths (Williamson 1984).

f) Cherokee: 'Talking Rock creek in upper Georgia . . . is a translation of the Cherokee Nûñyû'-gûñwani'skï, "Rock that talks", and refers, according to one informant, to an echo rock somewhere upon the stream ...' (Mooney 1900). There are many diverse Native American traditions that describe talking rocks or hold that the 'rocks will speak'; this phrase should perhaps be taken literally, since at many rock-art sites one can experience words bouncing off the rock surface where the art occurs, which does indeed give the impression that the rock is speaking.

g(i) Zuñi: 'Átahsaia, the cannibal demon . . . howled his war-cry, "Ho-o-o-thlai-a!" till Teshaminkia, the Echo-god, shouted it to the maidens.' (Cushing 1901) See also the Zuñi Corn Maidens story, and the echo of women's laughter in water-vases (Judson 1912).

g(ii) Zuñi: 'Next day the hunter returns to Grandmother Spider unharmed. She sends the hunter to fetch home to her the previous day's kill of antelope. Then she constructs a rack (hewn) consisting of a long cedar pole (which the hunter supplies) with cross bars of cedar attached by means of yucca fiber. On this the hunter carries the copious jerked meat from his last kill of antelope home to his native place at Matsaka. On the way he obtains a baton (hewn) from Grandfather Echo, and this he uses after his return home to transform his old rival the witch boy permanently into a kachina (spirit being), Echo Man.' (Judson 1912)

h) Tsimshian: '. . . inside the large house with carved front he heard many people singing. . . So he went in, but he saw nobody. Still he heard the voices . . . This was the house of Chief Echo. Then Txä'msem heard the chief speak to his slaves and tell them to roast a dried salmon; and he saw a carved box open itself and dried salmon come out of it. Then he saw a nice dish walk toward the fire all by itself.' (Thompson 1929).

i) Vancouver Island: 'The Kwakiutl myths of ancestry are different for all its members, but certain supernatural beings are present throughout all the tribes . . . These creatures include, sky beings, sky elements, forest and mountain beings, sea beings, and others. The Thunderbird and his younger brother Kolus are members of the sky beings. . . The sky elements are the Sun, Moon, and Echo. The echo is associated with speech and ventriloquism.' (Thompson 1929)

Central America:
The Aztec earth and cave god Tepeyollotl 'Heart of the Mountain' or Tepeolotlec 'Lord of Beasts' was thought to cause echoes: 'Tepeolotlec was the same as the echo of the voice when it re-echoes in a valley from one mountain to another. This name "jaguar" is given to the earth because the jaguar is the boldest animal, and the echo which the voice awakens in the mountains is a survival of the flood . . .' (Spence 1913).

South America:
In Chile, rock art is found in locations associated with a mythological being known as 'sereno', who lives where the water sounds; a rock-art painting called Diablo is located at a site that makes a noise that frightens the villagers when the wind of a dust devil strikes the rock (Claudio Mercado pers. comm. 1998).

Asia:
a) echoes have religious significance to members of an indigenous tribe of India called the Korku. This tribe continues to produce rock art today, using echoes as a selection criteria for choosing which caves to paint (Somnath Chakraverty pers. comm. 1996).
b) Malaysia: 'There are echo-spirits of the mountains, like men and women in shape. If one of them visits a mortal woman, she bears an albino child. A former Dato of Kinta lived with a female echo-spirit in a cave in the face of a limestone bluff, a beautiful woman called the Princess of the Rice-fields by the Hot Spring. One of his followers took another echo-spirit to wife. In three weeks she bore him a son, whom no mortal woman could suckle . . . In Kelantan there are several milder forms of exorcism, practised by traffickers with special spirits, such as the nature spirits of yellow sunsets and the echo spirits.' (Winstedt 1925)

Africa
Bantu: 'Sudika-Mbambi the Invincible was the son of . . . the daughter of the Sun and Moon. . . . Scarcely had he made his appearance when another voice was heard, and his twin brother Kabundungulu was born. . . . Sudika-Mbambi is the thunder in the eastern sky and Kabundungulu the echo which answers it from the west.' (Werner 1933).

Chapter 5

The Sound Paradox: How to Assess the Acoustic Significance of Archaeological Evidence?

Francesco d'Errico & Graeme Lawson

Like archaeoastronomy the archaeology of acoustic environments reveals a paradox: the phenomena which it seeks to interpret are often susceptible of the most detailed scientific scrutiny yet their purposive nature remains largely unverified and their meanings inscrutable. The paper takes an epistemological approach to ancient acoustics, with special reference to portable objects as well as to large-scale structures and spaces. It proposes a set of criteria which may be applied to help evaluate the degree of intentionality represented in such objects and places. Medieval musical finds from recent excavations are reviewed in relation to two more ancient and contrasting interpretive case-studies: the celebrated Middle Palaeolithic perforated cave-bear bone from Divje babe II, Slovenia and the 22 fragments of bone pipes with finger-holes from Upper Palaeolithic levels of the Grotte d'Isturitz, France. These are of such antiquity (c. 45 thousand and up to c. 35 thousand years ago respectively) that their apparent similarity to modern analogies cannot be relied upon to justify claims of intention and purpose. We review the evidence for their manufacture, use and contexts. From this emerge some principles, some of which, we suggest, may be applicable to architectural problems.

Inherent in the acoustimetry of archaeological sites is an interpretive problem which, in our view,[1] weakens many of its conclusions. In spite of the pioneering exploration that has undoubtedly been done, and the wealth of data that it has so far generated, there remains a difficulty in establishing scientifically to what extent — if at all — the recorded phenomena represent actual behaviours, reflecting conscious cultural choices on the part of the builders or users of sites and monuments. In this respect the research seems to us, from an epistemological point of view, to operate in the much same mode as archaeoastronomy.

In archaeoastronomy there is a striking paradox between, on the one hand, the sophisticated techniques by which researchers can measure the orientation of a building and verify that it was aligned on a particular star, say 4000 years ago, and on the other, the difficulty they face in demonstrating that this alignment was deliberate and had some real meaning for the prehistoric users of that building. The archaeology of sound exhibits a similar paradox. In many cases investigators can measure very precisely the acoustic properties of culturally-created or used environments, but then encounter a problem in demonstrating *through the evidence* (as distinct from commonsense reasoning) either that notable acoustic features must be interpreted as the consequence of a will to produce and/or use them or that (where they may be accidents of design or nature) they subsequently influenced behaviour in any discernable way. The question arises then as to what informed criteria we might usefully employ to support the hypothesis of a deliberate use of an 'acoustic' space or the acoustic use of an 'acoustic' object.

In order to identify viable criteria we must first remember that culturally created sound is common to all known human societies and is reflected in a myriad of acoustic outcomes. Convergences may exist, for example amongst the 5-, 6- and 7-note modal structures evidenced in the musics of ancient China, or ancient Greece, or the European Middle Ages (for summaries of which see Yung 1980; Winnington-Ingram 1980; Powers 1980). However, unlike most animal species whose production of sound is determined by their physiological and parental status, or group affiliation, and which produce sets of sounds almost automatically (at some seasons but not at others, or at particular times of day or in particular places) humans' social production of sound is almost entirely culturally determined. This means that, although convergences may sometimes result, each society may choose to produce its own characteristic palette of sounds, selected and articulated in its own distinctive manner: exhibiting preferences for very different natural or artificially-created settings, at different times and in different social contexts, expressed by different people (for example belonging to different age or gender groups) and using different types of instrumental or vocal devices. Different societies may attach quite different meanings to the same sounds. What makes humans unique in this respect is also that non-verbal sounds are produced and used at multiple levels, and that innovations may be easily introduced and passed from one group to another. The virtual absence of universals means that the character of behaviours associated with sound-related archaeological evidence must always be considered as a matter of inquiry and may not be assumed. The remoteness in time of many archaeo-acoustical subjects (whether places or things) means that neither can they be assumed to be homologous with our own experience or the experiences of any other living cultures.

Identifying such criteria and applying them to archaeological items that possibly reflect the oldest instances of culturally-created sounds may help test scenarios of the evolutionary significance of music. A number of studies have suggested that the human brain possesses neural specialization for producing and processing music (for example Peretz & Morais 1993; Perry et al. 1999; Johnsrude et al. 2000). This implies that musical habilities may have arisen in human evolution as a response to selective pressures, in order to fulfil specific roles. Music may have evolved as courtship display (Darwin 1871; Miller 2000), as a way to promote social cohesion (Brown 2000; Freeman 2000), as a form of coalition signalling system (Hagen & Bryant 2003), or as a somehow unforeseen, advantageous by-product of human adaptations such as motor control, habitat selection, emotional expression (Mithen 2005), and language (Pinker 1997). Most of the proponents of these various scenarios find support in studies concerned with the production of sound in the animal world and in cross-cultural analyses of the function music plays in ethnographically known societies. Evolutionary scenarios based on the mere observation of the present world, however, have a serious epistemological weakness if they do not attempt to test their predictions empirically against processes which reach back in time. In archaeoacoustics, happily, empiricism is a watch-word: we characterize past behaviour through archaeological research, and thus may approach early human sound-expression through identification of objects and of natural or artificial spaces which may have been used to produce sounds, through the recognition of traditions and the evaluation of their impact on past societies.

What criteria can we devise that could help us to identify which archaeological traces betray the existence of acoustical behaviours, and of what kind they are? To arrive at our proposals we will make reference to our experience in seeking to interpret three distinct groups of finds of 'musical' interest: an assemblage of undoubtedly acoustic finds from Upper Palaeolithic levels of the Grotte d'Isturitz, in the Atlantic Pyrenees of France; some musical finds from various medieval sites in western Europe; and a controversial find of perforated animal bone from the Middle Palaeolithic site of Divje babe II, Slovenia. We will show how the bone pipes from Isturitz seem to us to compare in many ways closely with medieval musical bone pipes, and how they contrast significantly with the so-called 'flute' from Divje babe. We will show how the formal sophistication and consistency of the Upper Palaeolithic finds establish 'beyond reasonable doubt' their operation as sound-producers, and thus enable us to move on to consider the detail of that sound-production. We will show, conversely, how the failure of Divje babe to satisfy any but the most general criteria for considering it to be 'musical' is confirmed by the contextual taphonomic analysis of this find. Finally we will discuss the implications of these case studies for ancient architectural acoustics, and whether the approach we have followed may provide criteria to assess the acoustic nature of 'macro-acoustic' (i.e. topographical and architectural) features.

Case studies

Upper Palaeolithic bone pipes

Two seasons of excavations conducted in the Grotte d'Isturitz during the early part of the last century, by E. Passemard in 1914 (Passemard 1944) and by R. and S. de Saint-Périer in 1939 (Saint-Périer & Saint-Périer 1952), yielded more than twenty separate specimens of deliberately-worked and perforated bird bone, ranging widely in date from the Magdalenian back into the Aurignacian; in other words, from about 10,000 to 35,000 years BP (Buisson 1990; 1994; Lawson & d'Errico 2002; d'Errico et al. 2003). Amongst the best-preserved

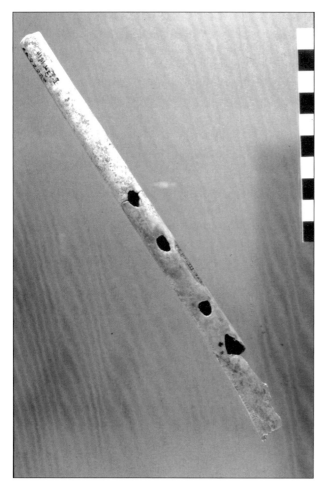

Figure 5.1. *Complete pipe made from a vulture ulna; from the Gravettian layers of the Grotte d'Isturitz, Pyrenées Atlantiques, France. Musée des Antiquités Nationales, Saint Germain-en-Laye. (Photo: F. d'Errico. Scale: 1 cm.)*

Figure 5.2. *Near-complete pipe made from a vulture ulna, from the Gravettian layers of the Grotte d'Isturitz, Pyrenées Atlantiques, France. Musée des Antiquités Nationales, Saint Germain-en-Laye. (Photo: F. d'Errico. Scale: 1 cm.)*

and oldest pieces are two four-hole pipes — one complete (Fig. 5.1) and the second almost so — both attributed to the Gravettian (around 21,000 to 27,000 years BP). Of a third, Aurignacian piece, the earliest, the substantial surviving portion includes one finished end and no fewer than 3 finger-holes (Fig. 5.2).

There is no doubt that these objects were produced by human hands, using a variety of flint tools. In addition to marks made in trimming and shaping them each bone has been given organized series of engraved markings, set out across its surfaces. A connexion with sound-production and pitch-manipulation seems also to be beyond doubt. The perforations not only *look* like finger-holes of musical pipes but have been carefully positioned and cut, and their elaboration has included tell-tale marginal platforms. The objects, in short, seem both 'designed' and properly finished; and they have a functional musical, or quasi-

musical, capability. In addition, following completion, each has undergone extensive manual manipulation — of a kind consistent specifically with use in antiquity as finger-hole pipes.

Besides establishing apparently purposeful manufacture and acoustic feasibility our analysis[2] revealed surprisingly long-lived morphological consistencies, which seem to indicate not only purpose but continuities in that purpose. These can be seen not only within the Gravettian pipes (competently-worked finger-holes, equal in size, four in number, arranged in two off-centre pairs; obliquely-aligned marginal platforms; similar scratched markings; same choice of material) but also extending into the Aurignacian (competent manufacture, choice of material; at least three, probably more, well-formed finger-holes with obliquely angled platforms; differentially spaced; the same plain, polished terminal). This measure of agree-

Figure 5.3. *Bone pipe of deer metatarsal from West Cotton, Raunds, Northamptonshire, England. (Photo: G. Lawson, courtesy of Northamptonshire Archaeology.)*

ment is significant in pipes that could be separated in time by thousands of years, and its importance is highlighted by a discontinuity, revealed during the same process of analysis, with the forms of the later, Magdalenian pieces. Those appear, almost paradoxically, to be much more crudely made. Amongst newer Aurignacian finds, meanwhile, are three fragmentary pieces from a cave at Geissenklösterle, near Ulm in Germany, dated at *c.* 33,000 BP (Hahn & Münzel 1995; Hein 1998; Conard & Bolus 2003; Zilhão & d'Errico 2004; Conard *et al.* 2004). These again exhibit competent workmanship and complexity of form. In two cases the instruments show a similar preference for wing-bones of large birds (albeit of swan radius rather than vulture ulna as at Isturitz). The more recent specimen is made of mammoth ivory and was apparently carved in two separate halves that were subsequently bound and glued together along a perfectly prepared, airtight seam. All three specimens bear similar linear series of incisions; and, most remarkably, they again possess at least three well-formed finger-holes. The holes again have platformed margins; and they are spaced unequally in such a way that the larger gap clearly falls — as it did repeatedly at Isturitz — between holes 2 and 3. In the gaps are also 'three-scratch' divisional markers of the kind seen at Isturitz. Considering the possible diversity of design evidenced by archaeological bone pipes of different periods, this is a *very* close match.

Medieval bone pipes and find-contexts
Functional continuities of this kind are familiar in the designs of instruments of later periods. One comparative sample, the excavated bone pipes of medieval Europe, is worth considering as context to some of these and other points of principle. In its own right it has been the focus of intensive research by one of us (GL) over many years, involving both microscopic study (Lawson 1982) and practical experiment (on-going, of which an outline can be found in Lawson 1999).

The strength of indications of purpose and use which characterize the Upper Palaeolithic pipes is again evident, indeed exceeded here. Comparison

with instruments documented by ethnography, in its widest sense, is admissible — with caution — because of their chronological and cultural proximity. Not only do some finds occupy the same geographical distributions as related folk-instruments, but they also persist to such late dates that typological homology — evolutionary continuum — can be shown between them, or at least proposed and justified. One such medieval type, consisting of flutes of large-bird ulna with three finger-holes towards the distal end, corresponds closely in form and capability to post-medieval and modern wooden three-hole flutes (often called 'tabor-pipes' because traditionally played left-handed while the right hand beats a drum or 'tabor'). Here correspondence between particular function and archaeological form is very close, and exhibits refinement through time.

In much the same way another medieval type, flutes of sheep or goat tibia with four or more finger-holes, relates closely, in both mode-of-operation and tone, to later pipes of 'penny-whistle' and 'recorder' kind. So also are Roman and medieval wooden Pan-pipes almost identical in form and manufacture with modern survivals; medieval Jews' harps are obviously made, and intended to be played, in much the same way as their modern equivalents; and so on. But — and this must be stressed — even if we lacked evidence of such ethnographical continuities, the finds themselves preserve sufficient evidence to enable us to make connexions between form and intended function, and to trace both geographical and temporal continuities in such purposes and functions.

Even among bone pipes (and these make up only a small part of the music-archaeological record) there are now numerous instances. One is to be found in pipes of deer metapodial which have recently begun to be identified in Eastern England (Fig. 5.3). These reed-voiced pipes are on several counts distinct from flutes made from other bones, and seem to represent a discrete cultural tradition, albeit occupying the same temporal and geographical space (Lawson forthcoming). We have already set out elsewhere[3] a description of other instances, from Roman Pan-pipes to early medieval six-string lyres (Lawson 2004). In all these cases it is not so much continuity with modern instruments that establishes connexions between object and behaviour as it is the analysis of forms (design), the correlation of functional capability to use-wear traces, and of course the integration of contextual data.

Small marks next to the finger-holes of bone pipes found in Middle Saxon Ipswich, Suffolk, and medieval

Castle Acre, Norfolk (Lawson 1982), show that behind their placement lay *prediction*, probably connected to tuning (i.e. the achieving of a desired series of pitched sounds). At Schleswig in North Germany (Reimers 1979; Reimers & Vogel 1989), what appear to be unfinished bone flutes of medieval date, found associated with other evidence of manufacture, reveal the same planning process, stage-by-stage (Fig. 5.4). Existence of use-wear in a complete but (to our ears) strangely tuned swan ulna from Norwich, Norfolk, of *c.* AD 1200, not only showed *how* the object had been used but established the very fact that it had. In demonstrating the successful musical employment of that tuning over a significant period, it increases the probability that it was in fact intended (Lawson & Margeson 1993). Examination of context, including associated finds, of bone pipes at Redcastle Furze, Thetford, Norfolk, in the Late Saxon period, show a suggestive association with other leisure pursuits at a location (a cellared building at a street-corner) which might have been a meeting-place (Lawson 1995; 2004). At Alvastra Kloster, the principal Cistercian house in medieval Sweden, musical identification of a series of bone objects as tuning-pegs for stringed instruments (Fig. 5.5) is supported by their association with numerous finds of other more certainly musical types, and in addition by a quantity of spooled Cu-alloy wire of a type and length consistent with instrument-stringing (indeed of the very instruments to which the putative pegs were thought to belong). In short, here in the Middle Ages, but also in other periods of Old World history and protohistory, we are looking at sound-related behaviours and purposes whose indications of association with tool-use are of a very high order indeed.

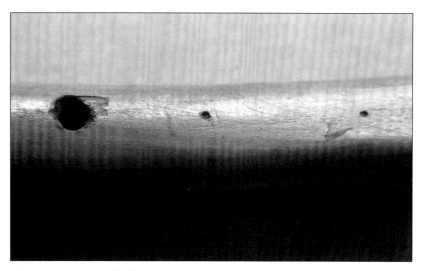

Figure 5.4. *Unfinished bone flute of sheep/goat tibia from Plessenstraße, Schleswig, Germany, showing knife-point markers made prior to drilling the finger-holes. Medieval. (Photo: G. Lawson, courtesy of Archäologisches Landesmuseum, Schleswig.)*

Figure 5.5. *Bone tuning-pegs from Alvastra Kloster, Sweden. Medieval. (Photo: G. Lawson, courtesy of Statens Historiska Museum, Stockholm.)*

Middle Palaeolithic questions

When we come to look at objects from the Middle Palaeolithic for which broadly similar functions have been proposed, the contrast could hardly be greater.

Indeed in no case has it yet been possible, in our view, to demonstrate a convincing association with any sound-related human behaviour. We can reason and argue that such tool-use should be *expected* in the Middle Palaeolithic. Indeed for all of us interested in ancient acoustics and for a number of scholars working on the emergence of modern cognition (McBrearty & Brooks 2000; d'Errico *et al.* 2003; Zilhão & d'Errico

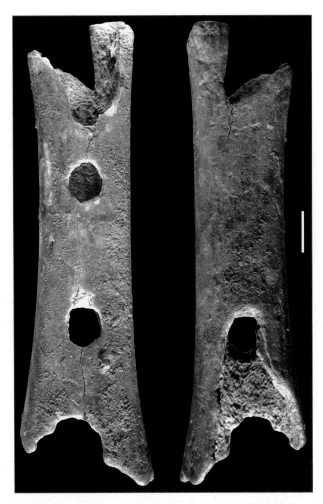

Figure 5.6. *Perforated cave-bear femur from Divje babe II Cave, Slovenia, interpreted by a number of authors as a Mousterian flute. (Scale: 1 cm. Photo: F. d'Errico.)*

We will take as an example the so-called 'Neanderthal flute' from Divje babe II cave, Slovenia, possibly the most controversial music-archaeological find of recent years (Fig. 5.6).

It consists of a juvenile cave-bear femur from a site containing a palympsest of Mousterian and cave bear occupations. Musical identification, as initially proposed, was based on the presence of two round holes in the diaphysis and the purported remains of two others, one at each broken end. To the finders these suggested the finger-holes of flutes, on which basis it was published as 'the oldest musical instrument in the world' (Turk *et al.* 1995; 1997; Turk 1997). There is indeed a superficial resemblance. However, there are essentially two serious obstacles to the interpretation: one taphonomic and another 'palaeo-organological'.

Taphonomy is the science which studies the modifications affecting living organisms when they die. It has become in the last few decades a major area of research in Prehistoric archaeology; involving dozens of laboratories, and hundreds of scientists, in investigating how bone was modified, during prehistoric times, by humans and by a range of natural causes. We know that a number of natural agencies produce modifications which may be erroneously interpreted as manufacture or use, and that these modifications may affect musical interpretations just as any other. Bone taphonomy and music-archaeology are therefore complementary scientific disciplines.

A number of natural processes can produce perfectly rounded holes in bone. Holes are frequently encountered in bones swallowed and regurgitated by hyaenas (d'Errico & Villa 1997). Perforations can also be produced in bone by insects and their larvae, by chemical erosion and mechanical abrasion in the soil, by rodents and, in particular, by carnivores.

Perforated animal phalanges, often interpreted as whistles, have been reported from Middle Palaeolithic sites (e.g. La Quina, Combe Grenal, Bocksteinschmiede, Prolom II; for a discussion see Scothern 1986; 1991; d'Errico & Villa 1997). Chase has used modern reference data to show that these perforations should be interpreted instead as carnivore punctures (Chase 1990), a hypothesis previously put forward by Martin (1907–10) for the majority of perforated phalanges at La Quina. A long-bone shaft with a single perforation, found in the Middle Palaeolithic levels of Haua Fteah, Libya, was published as a broken whistle by McBurney (1969). One of the shaft's broken edges bears a concavity and has been interpreted as the remnant of a second hole, aligned with the first. The complete hole, however, is interpreted as a carnivore puncture by Davidson (1991), who points out the absence of stone-tool marks and the morphology of the hole

2003) it seems both an attractive and a perfectly plausible proposition. Yet the material evidence remains unsupportive. Compared with the relative ease with which later pipes can be interpreted, even in the Aurignacian, such difficulties seem to us to offer a useful analogy for challenges presented in several areas of prehistoric site-acoustics.

The task we face in interpreting Middle Palaeolithic finds can be separated into two broad challenges. The first challenge is to determine whether the find is human-made or whether its form or its condition is the outcome of other agencies — such as the actions of animals or other taphonomic processes. The second is to decide whether the find embodies in its form or condition, or in its context, any evidence associated with the acoustical behaviours proposed for it: for example, showing that it has acoustical potential and has been used in ways that are consistent with exploitation of that potential.

walls, which exhibit depressed margins — a common feature of carnivore punctures. In a similar way, the parallel grooves on a mammoth long-bone fragment from a Belgian Middle Palaeolithic site, interpreted as evidence of its use as a 'skiffle' (Huyge 1990), have been re-interpreted as the result of carnivore damage (d'Errico 1991).

Should we consider the perforated cave bear femur from Divje babe as a carved object, possibly used as a flute by Neanderthals, or just a bone punctured by carnivores? Two studies published after the much-trumpetted discovery have challenged its musical interpretation. The first has shown that that holes of the same size, shape and number as those present on the Divje babe femur occur on cave bear bones from Spanish caves where there are no traces of human occupation, suggesting that the perforations on the 'flute' were probably natural and produced by carnivores (d'Errico *et al.* 1998). The second has shown how traces on the object are fully compatible with their interpretation as carnivore gnawing (Chase & Nowell 1998; Nowell & Chase 2002).

In a further study, whose results are reported here for the first time, one of us (FD) has analyzed 77 perforated bones from different levels of Divje babe and from 4 other Slovenian cave-bear sites (Mokriska jama, Potocka zijalka, Koprivska luknja, Krizna jama). Of these, Krizna jama is an entirely natural cave-bear bone assemblage with no recorded human presence. The other sites show, like Divje babe, sporadic traces of human presence associated with massive accumulations of cave-bear bones. In documenting the Slovenian material variables recorded included the body part, the age of the animal, two different measurements of the hole diameter, and the type of bone tissue in which the holes occur. Perforations and other carnivore damage observed were replicated with dental elastomer and submitted to microscopic analysis. The same procedure was applied to 6 perforations produced experimentally by the finds' original discoverers using limb bones of brown bear subjected to indirect percussion with a soft hammer (Turk & Bastiani 2000; Turk *et al.* 2001; 2003).

In the Slovenian comparative sample there are many indications that perforations are the result of carnivore damage, providing points of comparison which are valuable in assessing the Divje babe object's

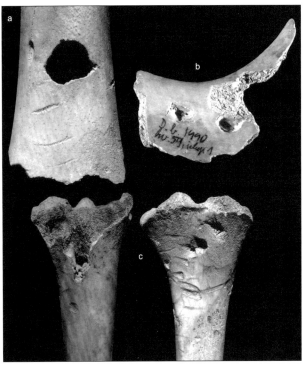

Figure 5.7. *Cave-bear bones from (a–b) Divje babe and (c) Mokriska jama, bearing perforations and punctures associated with typical carnivore damage. (Photo: F. d'Errico.)*

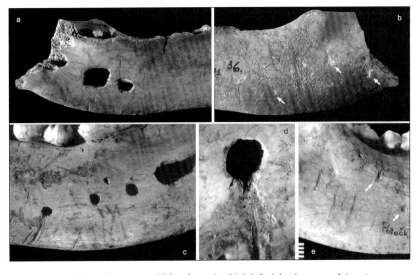

Figure 5.8. *Cave-bear mandibles from (a–b) Mokriska jama and (c–e) Potocka zijalka bearing alignments of rounded perforations associated with typical carnivore damage (scoring and pitting); (d): close-up view of (c) showing a deep scoring originating in a hole produced by a carnivore. White arrows indicate pitting resulting from counter-bites. (Photo: F. d'Errico.)*

claim to be a bone flute. In more than 70 per cent of cases other traces are also recorded which are typical of carnivore damage; in 40 per cent we find different types of damage, such as pitting and scoring, associa-

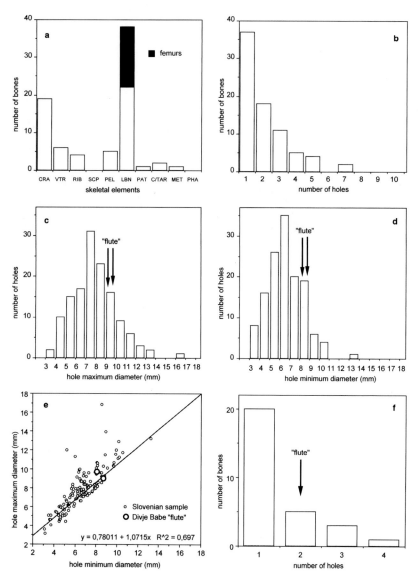

Figure 5.9. *Occurrence and size of holes on cave-bear bones from four Slovenian sites (cf. text for details): a) occurrence of holes on skeletal elements; b) number of holes found per bone; c–d) frequency distribution of hole diameters; e) correlation between minimum and maximum diameters ; f) number of holes recorded on compact bone.*

The ages of the animals corroborate the hypothesis of a natural origin for the perforations on the 'flute'. Just as the 'flute' comprises a juvenile femur, 73 per cent of the perforated bones also belong to young bears. Furthermore, whilst holes are present in almost all bones they are particularly abundant on limb bones, and, amongst these, femurs (Fig. 5.9a). The presence of two, or possibly three, perforations on the 'flute' cannot be considered as a possible proof of a human origin, as this is a common feature in the studied sample (Fig. 5.9b). The relatively large size of the holes does not indicate an anthropic carving either, since the maximum and minimum diameters of the holes on the putative flute are close to the mean value of those of the comparative sample (Fig. 5.9c–d). Moreover, the correlation between maximum and minimum diameters indicates a clear tendency towards slightly elongated holes; the same pattern that we observe when measuring the two complete holes of the suggested flute (Fig. 5.9e). The fact that the holes of the 'flute' occur in the centre of the diaphysis is not a proof of their anthropic origin. In the Slovenian sample, 28 per cent of the holes occur in compact bone. It is true that the majority of bones with holes in the compact bone have just one hole, but bones with two or more holes are also present (Fig. 5.9f), and many of these holes occur in the diaphyses of limb bones. Many show a striking similarity to those on the 'flute'. A femur of a young cave bear from Mokriska jama is a case in point (Fig. 5.10b). It bears two sub-circular holes on the same face, almost in the same anatomical position as the two holes on the 'flute', while the opposite face shows traces of scoring and pitting. This specimen represents perhaps the best demonstration of the natural origin of the holes on the 'flute' as it carries exactly all the features present on the purported instrument — with the exception of the openings at the ends. Such openings are features that would certainly have been produced by further carnivore damage.

Advocates of the musical interpretation (Turk *et al.* 2001) have conducted experiments in order to show that the distance between the two holes does not

ted on the same bone (Fig. 5.7). The perforations often show features distinctive of punctures produced by carnivores, having irregular edges, depressed margins and flaking of the outer wall of the bone where it is pushed into the depression. 20 per cent of the bones show counter-bites in the form of opposing perforations, or perforations opposed to impressions produced by tooth pressure (Fig. 5.8). In 10 per cent of the sample there are grooves emerging from the perforations, suggesting displacement of the tooth across the bone surface after puncture.

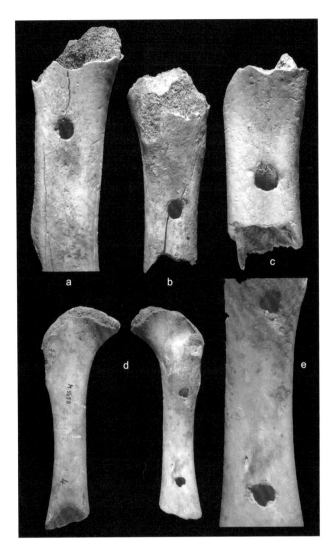

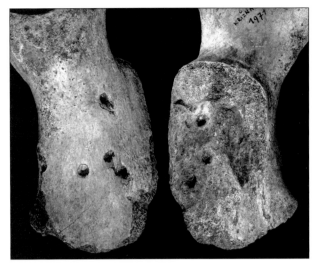

Figure 5.11. *Cave-bear coxal bone from Krizna jama bearing multiple carnivore punctures on both aspects. (Photo: F. d'Errico.)*

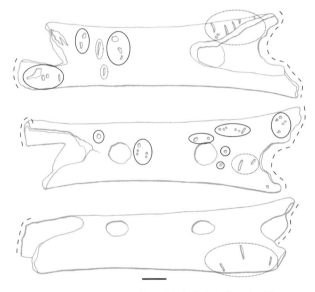

Figure 5.10. *Cave-bear limb bones from Mokriska jama bearing perforations on the diaphysis similar in size and shape to those on the purported flute from Divje babe: a–d) cave-bear limb bones; e) close-up view of (d). (Photo: F. d'Errico.)*

Figure 5.12. *Drawing of the Divje babe 'flute' with tracings indicating the locations and types of carnivore damage. Plain circles represent pitting; dotted circles scoring; interrupted line indicates crenulated morphology and smoothing typical of carnivore gnawing. (Scale: 1 cm. Drawing: M. Vanhaeren.)*

correspond to that separating the apexes of carnivore teeth. This distance, however, offers no real help in differentiating human-made from natural holes since there is proof that the same bone could be punctured repeatedly (Fig. 5.11). If a carnivore makes repeated bites a new hole may occur at any distance from the first. Therefore the distance between the holes cannot be a diagnostic criterion.

In sum, these results demonstrate that holes of the same size, shape, number and location as those on the 'flute' are common on cave-bear bones from Slovenian Pleistocene cave-bear assemblages and are produced by carnivores.

Our direct analysis of the object confirms that a large carnivore is the most likely source of the per-

forations. The two ends of the bone show the typical rounded and crenulated morphology of bones modified by carnivores. In addition the semi-circular notch on the anterior face of the bone can be interpreted as the result of the counter-bite opposite to the distal hole (Fig. 5.6).

Microscopic analysis of the bone surface identifies several other traces of carnivore action (Fig. 5.12). The posterior face of the bone reveals, near its distal

Figure 5.13. *Macrophotos of the posterior aspect of the Divje babe 'flute' indicating punctures and scoring partially covered by concretions. (Scale: 1 cm. Photo: F. d'Errico.)*

Figure 5.14. *Macrophotos of the anterior aspect of the Divje babe 'flute' showing typical carnivore punctures. (Scale: 1 cm. Photo: F. d'Errico.)*

end, traces of scoring and pitting close to the distal hole (Fig. 5.13). Pitting was also detected around the proximal hole. Of all the carnivore traces the most remarkable can be seen on the opposite face where clear tooth impressions, associated with scoring, are recorded near the proximal end (Fig. 5.14).

Not only was this bone seriously damaged by carnivores but the distribution of different types of carnivore damage across the bone surface is consistent with interpretation of the two holes as resulting from

carnivore action. The large, deep impressions found on the anterior face near the proximal end, indicating a strong pressure exerted by carnivore teeth, can reasonably be interpreted as the counter-bite of the proximal hole. The presence of pitting near the two holes suggests that carnivore teeth touched this area repeatedly. In sum, *all* the traces observed on the bone point to a natural origin for the holes. Not one anthropogenic trace was detected. Experiments conducted by the advocates of the 'flute' hypothesis (Turk *et al.* 2001) seem to show that indirect percussion with a soft hammer can produce holes which are macroscopically similar to those on the bone. This thay have taken as evidence that the perforations could have been produced by humans. However, our microscopic analysis of 6 of their experimental holes identified in three cases clear traces of the use of stone tools, in the form of V- shaped incisions perpendicular to the hole's edge. Similar incisions were found nowhere on the putative 'flute' or on any of the other examined perforated cave-bear bones.

Even if we were to accept that the soft hammer technique can produce holes that are perfectly identical to those produced by carnivores, can we use this as evidence that the perforations on the 'flute' might have been produced by humans? The question we face being one of natural science, we need to apply the principle of uniformitarianism, i.e. that natural processes current today have occurred in a similar manner in the past. This means that we can attribute little heuristic relevance to experiments that try simply to mimic a natural process in order to argue that human agency cannot be excluded, when many converging contextual reasons indicate that a natural agent is by far the most likely.

In conclusion, all the taphonomic and contextual evidence we have been able to adduce suggests that the perforations on the so-called Divje babe flute were produced by a large carnivore, probably a cave bear. This outcome, to be sure, will come as no surprise to any student of the history and practice of 'music-archaeology', to whom the problem is, by now, a thoroughly familiar one: that holes, even near-circular ones in bone tubes, are by no means unique to musical instruments. Indeed the archaeological record of later periods is full of bone-objects-with-perforations, many of which have attracted enthusiastic musical attributions only to be proven, on subsequent inspection, to have had quite different origins and purposes. All manner of objects can appear musical, especially when broken: from casket hinges, so-called bone 'toggles' and 'needle-cases' to the strangely perforated residues of button-making, bead-making and other craft activities. Others prove quite accidental. Such negative diagnoses have tended to go unreported in the archaeological literature because the objects are so quickly reclassified under other heads; nevertheless they have long cautioned music-archaeologists against accepting musical attribution solely because of the presence of perforations. Such caution is especially necessary where, as in the case of Divje babe, a find is being proposed for which there are, as yet, no supportive contemporary parallels. Caution becomes *essential* when what is at stake is of such importance as the very existence — or absence — of musical behaviour before the Upper Palaeolithic.

The difficulty is compounded at Divje babe, as so often, by the incomplete state of the putative object. From faunal comparison we can reconstruct with ease the bone's original morphology and dimensions; but even with these data, the breakage of both ends and the absence of any more complete parallels mean that we simply cannot determine what overall form the putative artefact would have taken when whole — and especially how it may have been voiced. So from the start we are asked to make some quite significant leaps of faith. For example, the stocky character of the original femur and the distribution of the holes along almost its full length already appear to cast into question the aptness of the object to any musical use, at any rate of the melodic sort with which we are familiar today. This impression has encouraged some commentators to attempt to compensate by 'completing' it in various ingenious ways, to enable it not only to work better as a multi-pitched pipe but even to generate

tunings resembling modern diatonic scales (Fink 2002, 86). Such tunings cannot possibly be achieved by this layout of holes within the total possible length of the bone, so some kind of extension then becomes necessary. Although extension is not *per se* impossible, that such additional complexity has to be invoked to make it fit the theory introduces a further epistemological weakness into the argument. So a question mark hangs over the second organological problem too: the object's aptness to its proposed acoustic purpose.

This does not demonstrate that Neanderthals were unable to manufacture and play musical instruments. It only means that we cannot use this object to support such a hypothesis.

Emerging 'Music-archaeological' criteria

Emerging from these studies we can identify a number of criteria which might be useful in the investigation of enigmatic phenomena of other sound-related kinds. They are generally — even conventionally — applied in music-archaeology today.[5] In ascending order, weakest first, they are:

A1. Feasibility.
Does the object have acoustical feasibility — i.e. does it 'work' or can it (or more properly, a replica or reconstruction) be made to function in an acoustical way — today?

A2. Ethnographical parallels.
Is there any modern ethnographical parallel whose general form or detail supports the proposed acoustical purpose?

A3. Ancient documentary support.
Does any contemporaneous document (text or image) support the proposed acoustical purpose?

A4. Contemporary archaeological support.
Is there any better-preserved, contemporaneous archaeological evidence consistent with the proposed acoustical purpose? Failing that, does the material culture more generally support any kind of acoustical awareness?

A5. Efficiency.
How efficiently does the design of the object perform today as an acoustic system — i.e. how far is it adapted to its putative acoustical purpose?

These are surely all valid criteria, as far as they go. But we argue that further refinements are necessary to achieve a reasonable degree of certainty: contextual, 'internal' and comparative. We may think of them as a set of observational challenges which invite an evaluation or 'points score':

B1. Non-contemporary parallels.
Are there any close archaeological parallels from other periods whose acoustical significance is better understood?

Medieval pipes achieve top score here. The Isturitz finds score very well; and so — superficially — does Divje babe.

B2. Context and associations.
Is there anything in the immediate archaeological circumstances of the find which may support associated acoustical behaviours or preferences?

Medieval finds achieve top scores again. Isturitz scores well too: its space is highly resonant and there is much evidence of human activity, including traces of painting. By contrast Divje babe scores only on the bare fact of environmental enclosure.

B3. Manufacture and exploitation.
Does the subject exhibit any detail of manufacture or use which supports the proposed acoustical operation: any indication (e.g. wear or damage) that the object was exploited in some acoustically-related way?

The medieval finds achieve top scores again. Isturitz scores well on both. But Divje babe rates no score at all.

B4. Internal consistency of form.
Does the subject combine more than one such feature in a way that supports acoustical purpose? And if so, how many? Examples in pipes might include position and alignment and shape of holes, and adaptations to their margins.

Medieval finds and Isturitz score extremely well. At Divje babe the presence of the holes and their shape and linear alignment achieve scores (naturally, since these are the elements which first struck the discoverers as musical) but their positioning and marginal adaptation do not.

B5. Relationship to earlier and/or later objects of broadly similar kind.
Are there any patterns of connexion, especially of onward development through time? And do these connexions exhibit consistency with acoustical purpose?

Amongst medieval finds such relationships are clear,

and consistently musical. Onward development in later examples includes such practical refinements as thumb-holes and increasingly sophisticated voicing ducts. Isturitz pipes too seem to exhibit long-term continuity, even Tradition. At Divje babe only the straight alignment of its holes compares with the Upper Palaeolithic instruments; and it is — so far — isolated, without any earlier comparisons.

B6. Appropriateness of design choices.
Is there any evidence of choices in materials and structures which seem especially appropriate? Useful examples might include consistent choice of bones subsequently widely favoured by other cultures for musical purposes.

Isturitz scores well with large-bird ulna, which subsequently finds favour throughout ancient world music. The proposed choice of bear-bone at Divje babe is at present unique; femur of any kind is rarely utilized.

B7. Practical contra-indications.
Is the subject free of practical contra-indications? Examples might include such impractical features as: bones which have not had their epiphyses removed; holes whose placement makes them awkward or impossible to finger; holes whose shaping is unsuited to an airtight finger-tip seal.

Isturitz is entirely consistent with modern models of 'practicality' in musical pipes. At Divje babe the holes (and proposed holes) are practical to finger but in no way developed. Without artificial extension beyond the original length of the bone their wide spread is inconsistent with scalar exploitation of the kind identified in the Upper Palaeolithic and later (although such differences in organisation might be allowable in some cultures). But overall, the test is difficult to apply because the bone is so incomplete.

B8: Essential omissions.
Are any predictable acoustics-related details absent? Examples might include absence of smooth finish to internal bores or to finger-hole margins, absence of sharp edges to voicing-lips (in flutes). (Absence of signs of wear is already itemised under (3) above.)

The early Isturitz pipes lack a proximal sharp edge or sound-hole (otherwise known as the 'window', a normally D-shaped terminal feature) characteristic of later air-jet voiced flutes and whistles. They therefore attract no score as 'flutes'. However their terminals are consistent instead with another principle widely exploited in prehistoric times, the lip-reed (trumpetembouchure) method of voicing, so they still score highly under that classification. The manufacture of the later (Magdalenian) Isturitz pipes seems strangely crude compared with earlier ones, and like Divje babe they suffer from incompleteness; but in other respects they show no acoustic inconsistencies, and have been used. Divje babe lacks almost all predictable indications except the size and alignment of its holes.

B9. Evaluation of practical inconsistency.
In consequience of B7 above, how many present properties are we having to ignore or excuse to make an acoustic interpretation work?

In the principal classes of medieval pipes there are no inconsistencies; at Isturitz very few, none in the complete pipes. At Divje babe we must somehow explain away the evidence of natural agency.

B10. Evaluation of absences
In consequence of B8 above, how many absent elements are we having to invent — in order to make the subject function in an acoustic way?

Often in the Middle Ages, in individual flutes, we lack softer organic elements such as the block or 'fipple', or in reed-pipes the reed. In Roman and medieval times we often lack the mouthpiece of an individual horn or trumpet. However, even where physically absent such elements are often indicated by traces or implied by design adaptations; and their forms are known from other finds. The absence of blocks at Isturitz is not significant because the pipes are clearly of a kind that is capable of functioning without them. At Divje babe, on the other hand, because only the metaphysis and two complete holes remain we must invent the forms of both ends, and maybe more besides.

Proposed 'Archaeoacoustic' applications

Now we can see from all this that, under such a regime, finds from sites such as Thetford, in late Anglo-Saxon England, and Schleswig's Plessenstrasse, in 11th- and 12th-century Germany, rate very highly at most levels as relics of acoustic behaviours; and we can also see that Isturitz (and indeed Geissenklösterle and other Upper Palaeolithic sites) achieve scores which are closely comparable. Moreover, if we turn to some of those other types which form the normal currency of music-archaeologists — such as the lyres and harps of Sumerian civilization some 5000 years ago, or the cast bronze bells of Iron Age China, or indeed Peter Holmes's bronze horns and trumpets (for which see Chapter 6) — we can observe that behavioural as-

sociation is extraordinarily well established. These are self-evidently acoustical devices. Consequently inquiry has long since moved on to address their detailed workings and relationships, leading students to start asking questions like: 'was the ancient Egyptian long-necked lute strummed or plucked?' or 'to what system of tonality were medieval Pan-pipes tuned?' or 'what was the nature of the contacts between lyre-players in 6th-century England and their counterparts in Sweden and Germany?' They rarely need to question the acoustic essence of their subjects. When they do so they expect them to achieve high scores, and naturally tend to treat with scepticism any that do not. So how — in hard-nosed music-archaeological terms — do 'acoustic monuments' compare with such finds when they are subjected to the same process and the same or broadly similar criteria?

A1. Feasibility.
Does the monument or space have acoustical feasibility — i.e. does it 'work' or can it be made to work in an acoustical way — today?

A2. Ethnographical parallels.
Is there any ethnographical parallel whose general form or detail supports the proposed acoustical purpose?

A3. Ancient documentary support
Does any contemporary document (text or image) support the proposed acoustical purpose?

A4. Contemporary archaeological support.
Is there any better-preserved, contemporaneous archaeological evidence consistent with the proposed acoustical purpose? Failing that: does the material culture more generally support any kind of acoustical awareness?

A5. Efficiency.
How efficiently does the design of the monument or space perform today as an acoustic system: how far is it adapted to its putative acoustical purpose?

These all seem perfectly applicable, and a survey of the case histories presented elsewhere in this volume will show under how many different heads they achieve scores. But then come the more detailed questions:

B1. Non-contemporary parallels.
Are there any close archaeological parallels from other periods whose acoustical significance is better understood?

B2a. External context and associations.
Is there anything in the site's external archaeological

context — in its surrounding landscape and its relationship to other sites — which may support associated acoustical behaviours or preferences? In this case we might consider any associated musical finds in the vicinity, or distances to other features within earshot, or any other natural or man-made features which seem to have acoustic significance.

B2b. Internal context and associations.
Is there anything in the site's internal archaeological context — for example, in archaeological deposits enclosed within its space — which may support associated acoustical behaviours or preferences? In this case we might consider any associated musical finds and any other acoustic-seeming features.

B3. Manufacture and exploitation.
Is there any feature in or on the site's structural fabric (whether in its construction or treatment or resulting from its use) which suggests that the building or space was built for some acoustic purpose, or exploited in some acoustically related way? Under this head we might evaluate the integrity or efficiency of proposed acoustic structures (for example, of reflectors or baffles, or of air-column or Helmholz structures).

B4. Internal consistency of form.
Is there more than one such indication on the site, and is there therefore any internal acoustic consistency: any combination or coincidence of such features within the monument or space itself which supports acoustical purpose?

B5. Relationship to earlier and/or later examples of similar kind.
Are there any patterns of connexion, especially of onward (or 'backward') development through time? And do these connexions exhibit consistency throughout with acoustical purpose?

B6. Appropriateness of design choices.
Is there any evidence of specially appropriate choices in materials and structures (e.g. choices of timber or masonry constructions, subsequently widely favoured by other cultures)?

B7. Practical contra-indications.
Is the subject free of practical inconsistencies (e.g. impractical features and other contraindications)?

B8. Essential omissions.
Are there any embarassing absences of predictable acoustics-related details? (e.g. absence of smooth rendering of surfaces, or of paved floors, or smooth dressing of vertical surfaces, etc.)

B9. Evaluation of practical inconsistency.
How many such inconsistencies are we having to ignore or explain laboriously to make the interpretation work?

B10. Evaluation of absences.
How many absent elements are we having to draw in — or invent — in order to make it work?

All of these too seem reasonable questions to ask; but now we begin to see rather greater variation in the scores achieved. Many rate poorly or not at all.

Conclusions

Should failure of a site or site-type to satisfy any more than a few of the most general of these tests worry us? The present writers think that maybe it should, a little, and that at least a note of caution should be sounded here.

Some monuments, to be sure, especially those of historical periods, seem to score sufficiently well to confirm us in the view that acoustical perceptions and behaviours would have accompanied them and may even have contributed to their development. The documented acoustical character and purposes of medieval church choirs and Greek and Roman theatres (discussed elsewhere in this volume by Iegor Reznikoff, Graeme Lawson and Eleonora Rocconi) seems beyond doubt, particularly those exploiting the resonant use of concealed jars and similar devices. In Prehistory the selective marking of Upper Palaeolithic resonant spaces and the recurrence of echo associations at some native American rock-art sites (proposed respectively by Iegor Reznikoff and Steve Waller) seem *archaeologically* even more convincing. But what of European megaliths and their related earthworks? There are undoubtedly phenomena to be observed in and around such sites today, and the same or similar phenomena would very probably have been experienced there in the past. It is fascinating, and perfectly fair, to speculate as to what purpose such properties might have served or what effects they might have had on the perceptions and behaviours of ancient people who visited their spaces. Yet so far we have seen few suggestive convergences in the primary evidence (that is, in the physical structures of individual sites). It is rare to find an acoustic property which appears to coincide with any architectural feature of which it is not itself the direct consequence (in chambered tombs a possible exception might be the small secondary apertures of Newgrange, reported in this connexion by

Frances Lynch, 1973, 148–9). Moreover, there are few helpful parallels, and some unhelpful ones, outside the Neolithic and Bronze Age. Perhaps the closest European match for Bronze Age stone circles is to be found in the late Iron Age and early medieval ship-shaped stone settings of Scandinavia, where similar acoustic properties may readily be experienced. Among these are many which cannot possibly have served any such purpose because they are simply too small: it is difficult not to conclude therefore that their builders' prime consideration was simply to symbolize in a structural way the shapes of ships and boats which we know were important to those cultures, and that sound can only have been an accidental component. In short, megalithic acoustics seem to us — so far — to have achieved a level of scientific credibility equivalent only to that of the Divje babe find; which is to say, sadly: not a very high one.

* * *

In conclusion, whether we are talking about the mobiliary or the monumental, it seems to us that simply having acoustic potential is not enough, in itself, to confirm claims of acoustical behaviour. Equally unhelpful is the commonsense argument that ancient people's acoustic awarenesses and responses should 'stand to reason', when this requires the acceptance that their perception of their world must be like ours. They had ears, of course, like ours; but also like our cousins the other great apes. We simply cannot make assumptions about their hearing, or the meanings they attached to what they heard, when these are precisely what we are trying to understand. Consequently such arguments, although of philosophical interest, do not offer an adequate basis on which to proceed to further levels of scientific interpretation. The megalithic question still remains: how can we show that an alignment of prehistoric stones possesses any more acoustic significance than, say, the rows of grave-stones in a modern municipal cemetery, or the trees in a forest?

Perhaps it would be unfair to expect *too* unambiguous a signal so soon in the investigative process. Even medieval church architectures, which we know from independent sources had a profound effect in shaping aspects of the evolution of Western liturgical music, have so far given up few tell-tale clues of the kind which we would look for in a musical instrument. And even among instruments of the same period there are whole classes of simpler kind which score badly or not at all. Friction-drums, to take just one example, the ceramic 'rommel pots' pictured in the hands of medieval and later musicians, are notoriously difficult to identify at any time, because without their skin membranes or associated sticks they possess in themselves almost *no* unique, diagnostic elements; but they surely existed. Such elusiveness in an epoch which we know to have been rich in sound shows how foolish it would be to *dismiss* notions of acoustical awareness simply because such signs are not readily forthcoming. But the task of identifying those signs is clearly going to continue to test our ingenuity.

Notes

1. Of the two writers, d'Errico is a prehistorian investigating the emergence of modern behaviour; Lawson is an archaeologist interested in the origins and development of music and related sound-based behaviours. Both are concerned primarily with material culture and its significance in modelling the emergence of modern cognition. D'Errico's work was supported by funds from the CNRS in the framework of the ESF Programme Origin of Man, Language and Languages (EC Sixth Framework Programme under Contract no. ERAS-CT-2003-980409). The French Ministry of Foreign Affairs and the Slovenian Academy of Science were instrumental in making the Divje babe project possible. Lawson's work on the Isturitz material was funded in part by a grant from the McDonald Institute for Archaeological Research. We are very much indebted to Marian Vanhaeren, Bordeaux, for her tireless help with the figures and for her critical reading of the manuscript.

2. Both writers have benefited greatly from the courtesy and hospitality of the staff of the Musée des Antiquités Nationales, Saint-Germain-en-Laye, and especially from the kind co-operation of Mme Marie-Hélène Thiault.

3. In a paper read to the International Study Group for Music Archaeology, at Kloster Michaelstein, Germany, in September 2002.

4. The writers wish to express their appreciation to Ivan Turk for giving Francesco d'Errico access to the the Divje babe material and the cave bear bone assemblages from the other Slovenian caves, and for helpful discussions on the archeological and taphonomic context of the find. The results we present in this paper could have never been achieved without his generosity.

5. Such a process of validation was first articulated by Sweden's Cajsa Lund as long ago as the 1970s (see especially Lund 1984).

References

Brown, S., 2000. The 'musilanguage' model of music evolution, in *The Origins of Music*, eds. N.L. Wallin, B. Merker & S. Brown. Cambridge (MA): MIT Press, 271–300.

Buisson, D., 1990. Les flûtes paléolithiques d'Isturitz (Pyrénées Atlantiques). *Bullétin de la Société Préhistorique Française* 87, 10–12, 420–33.

Buisson, D., 1994. Les flûtes paléolithiques d'Isturitz, in *La pluridisciplinarité en Archéologie musicale*, vol. I:

VIème rencontres internationals d'archéologie musicale de l'ICTM, Saint-Germain-en-Laye, ed. C. Homo-Lechner. Paris: Maison des Sciences de l'Homme, 259–75.

Chase, P.G., 1990. Sifflets du Paléolithique moyen (?). Les implications d'un coprolithe de coyote actuel. *Bulletin de la Societé Préhistorique Française* 87, 165–7.

Chase, P.G. & A. Nowell, 1998. Taphonomy of a suggested Middle Paleolithic bone flute from Slovenia. *Current Anthropology* 39, 549–53

Conard, N.J. & M. Bolus, 2003. Radiocarbon dating the appearance of modern humans and timing of cultural innovations in Europe: new results and new challenges. *Journal of Human Evolution* 44, 331–71.

Conard, N.J., M. Malina, S. Münzel & F. Seeberg, 2004. Eine Mammutelfenbeinflöte aus dem Aurignacien des Geissenklösterle. *Archäologisches Korrespondenzblatt* 34, 447–62.

Darwin, C., 1871. *The Descent of Man and Selection in Relation to Sex.* London: John Murray.

Davidson, I., 1991. The archaeology of language origins — a review. *Antiquity* 65, 39–48.

d'Errico, F., 1991. Carnivore traces or mousterian skiffle? *Rock Art Research* 8, 61–3.

d'Errico, F. & P. Villa, 1997. Holes and grooves: the contribution of microscopy and taphonomy to the problem of art origins. *Journal of Human Evolution* 33, 1–31.

d'Errico, F., P. Villa, A.C. Pinto Llona & R. Ruiz Idarraga, 1998. A Middle Paleolithic origin of music? Using cave bear bone accumulations to assess the Divje Babe I bone «flute». *Antiquity* 72, 65–79.

d'Errico, F., C. Henshilwood, G. Lawson, M. Vanhaeren, A.-M. Tillier, M. Soressi, F. Bresson, B. Maureille, A. Nowell, J.A. Lakarra, L. Backwell & M. Julien, 2003. The emergence of language, symbolism and music — an alternative multidisciplinary perspective. *Journal of World Prehistory* 17:2, 1–70.

Fink, R.,2002. The Neanderthal flute and origins of the scale: fang or flint? A response, in *Studien zur Musikarchäologie III. Archäologie früher Klangerzeugung und Tonordnung,* eds. E. Hickmann, A.D. Kilmer & R. Eichmann. (Orient-Archäologie Band 10.) Rahden, Westf.: Verlag Marie Leidorf, 84–7.

Freeman, W., 2000. A neurobiological role of music in social bonding, in *The Origins of Music,* eds. N.L. Wallin, B. Merker & S. Brown. Cambridge (MA): MIT Press, 411–24.

Hagen, E.H. & G.A. Bryant, 2003. Music and dance as a coalition signaling system. *Human Nature* 14:1, 21–51.

Hahn, J. & S. Münzel, 1995. Knochenflöten aus dem Aurignacien des Geissenklösterle bei Blaubeuren, Alb-Donau-Kreis. *Fundberichte aus Baden-Württemberg* 20 (Aufsätze), 1–12.

Hein, W., 1998. Zur 'Rekonstruktion und Funktion jungpaläolithischer Knochenflöten'. *Musica Instrumentalis* 1, 120–28.

Huyge, D., 1990. Mousterian skiffle? Note on a middle palaeolithic engraved bone from Schulen, Belgium. *Rock Art Research* 7:2, 125–32.

Johnsrude, I.J., V.B. Penhune & R.J. Zatorre, 2000. Functional specificity in right human auditory cortex for perceiving pitch direction. *Brain* 123, 155–63.

Lawson, G., 1982. Bone flutes, in Excavations at Castle Acre Castle, Norfolk, 1972–77: country house and castle of the Norman Earls of Surrey, by J. Coad & A. Streeten. *The Archaeological Journal* 139, 252.

Lawson, G., 1995. Bone flutes, in *Excavations at Redcastle Furze, Thetford, 1988–9,* by P. Andrews. (East Anglian Archaeology 72.) Gressenhall: Field Archaeology Division, Norfolk Museums Service, 116 & (118) fig. 87.

Lawson, G., 1999. Getting to grips with music's prehistory: experimental approaches to function, design and operational wear in excavated musical instruments, in *Experiment and Design: Archaeological Studies in Honour of John Coles,* ed. A. Harding. Oxford: Oxbow Books, 133–8.

Lawson, G., 2004. Music, intentionality and tradition: identifying purpose, and continuity of purpose, in the music-archaeological record, in *Studien zur Musikarchäologie IV,* eds. E. Hickmann, A.D. Kilmer & R. Eichmann. (Orient-Archäologie series.) Rahden, Westf.: Verlag Marie Leidorf, 61–97.

Lawson, G., forthcoming. Tuning and tradition: the earliest Northumbrian bagpipes and their relationship to finds from archaeological excavation. *Archaeologia Aeliana* 5th Series, 34 (2005).

Lawson, G. & F. d'Errico, 2002. Microscopic, experimental and theoretical re-assessment of Upper Palaeolithic bird-bone pipes from Isturitz, France: ergonomics of design, systems of notation and the origins of musical traditions, in *Studien zur Musikarchäologie III. Archäologie früher Klangerzeugung und Tonordnung,* eds. E. Hickmann, A.D. Kilmer & R. Eichmann. (Orient-Archäologie Band 10.) Rahden, Westf.: Verlag Marie Leidorf, 119–42.

Lawson, G. & S. Margeson, 1993. Musical instruments, in *Norwich Households: Medieval and Post-medieval Finds from Norwich Survey Excavations 1971–8,* by S. Margeson. (East Anglian Archaeology Report 58.) Gressenhall: East Anglian Archaeology, 211–15.

Lawson, G., C. Scarre, I. Cross & C. Hills, 1998 (1996). Mounds, megaliths, music and mind: some thoughts on the acoustical properties *and purposes* of archaeological spaces. *Archaeological Review from Cambridge* 15(1) ('Senses & Perception' issue), 111–34.

Lund, C.S., 1984. *Fornnordiska Klanger: the Sounds of Prehistoric Scandinavia.* Musica Sveciae series MS101 (His Master's Voice HMV 1361031). Stockholm: Kungl. Musikaliska Akademien & EMI Svenska. [Subsequently reissued 1991 on CD by Kungl. Musikaliska Akademien, as MSCD101].

Lynch, F., 1973. The use of the passage in certain passage graves as a means of communication rather than access, in *Megalithic Graves and Ritual: 3rd Atlantic Colloquium, Moesgård 1969,* eds. G.E. Daniel & P. Kjaerun. Copenhagen: Jutland Archaeological Society, 147–61.

Martin, H., 1907–10. *Recherches sur l'évolution du Moustérien dans le Gisement de la Quina (Charente), Industrie osseuse 1.* Paris: Schleicher Frères.

McBrearty, S. & A.S. Brooks, 2000. The revolution that wasn't: a new interpretation of the origin of modern human behaviour. *Journal of Human Evolution* 3, 453–563.

McBurney, C.B.M., 1969. *The Haua Fteah (Cyrenaica) and the Stone Age of the Southeast Mediterranean*. Cambridge: Cambridge University Press.

Miller, G., 2000. Evolution of human music through sexual selection, in *The Origins of Music*, eds. N.L. Wallin, B. Merker & S. Brown. Cambridge (MA): MIT Press, 271–300.

Mithen, S., 2005. *The Singing Neanderthals: the Origins of Music, Language, Mind and Body*. London: Weidenfeld & Nicolson.

Nowell, A. & P. Chase, 2002. Is a cave-bear bone from Divje Babe, Slovenia, a Neanderthal flute?, in *Studien zur Musikarchäologie III. Archäologie früher Klangerzeugung und Tonordnung*, eds. E. Hickmann, A.D. Kilmer & R. Eichmann. (Orient Archäologie 10.) Rahden, Westf.: Verlag Marie Leidorf, 69–81.

Passemard, E., 1944. La caverne d'Isturitz en pays basque. *Préhistoire* 9, 1–84.

Peretz, I. & J. Morais, 1993. Specificity for music, in *Handbook of Neuropsychology*, vol. 8, eds. F. Boller & J. Grafman. New York (NY): Elsevier, 373–90.

Perry, D.W., R.J. Zatorre, M. Petrides, B. Alivisatos, E. Meyer & A.C. Evans, 1999. Localization of cerebral activity during simple singing. *NeuroReport* 10, 3979–84.

Pinker, S., 1997. *How the Mind Works*. New York (NY): W.W. Norton.

Powers, H.S., 1980. Mode, in *The New Grove Dictionary of Music and Musicians*, vol. 12: *Meares to Mutis*, ed. S. Sadie. London: Macmillan, 376–450.

Reimers, C., 1979. *Benflöjter från det Medeltida Schleswig*. Stockholm: Kungl. Musikaliska Akademien, Riksinventeringens rapporter series, nr. 22 (typescript, 22 pp.)

Reimers, C. & V. Vogel, 1989. Knochenpfeifen und Knochenflöten aus Schleswig, in *Ausgrabungen in Schleswig. Berichte und Studien*, vol. 7. (Das archäologische Fundmaterial I.). Neumünster: Karl Wachholtz Verlag, 19–42.

de Saint-Périer, R. & S. de Saint-Périer, 1952. *La grotte d'Isturitz III, les Solutréens, les Aurignaciens et les Moustériens*. (Archives de l'Institut de Paléontologie Humaine. Mém. 25.) Paris: Institut de Paléontologie Humaine.

Scothern, P.M.T., 1986. The musical evidences of the Palaeolithic. A Palaeo-organological survey, in *Second Conference of the ICTM Study Group on Music-Archaeology*, vol. I: *General Studies*, ed. C.S. Lund. Stockholm: Kungl. Musikaliska Akademien, 73–80.

Scothern, P.M.T., 1991. The Music-archaeology of the Palaeolithic within its Cultural Setting. Unpublished PhD dissertation (2 volumes), University of Cambridge.

Turk, I. (ed.), 1997. *Mousterian Bone Flute and Other Finds from Divje babe I Cave Site in Slovenia*. Ljubljana: Institut za Arhaeologijo.

Turk, I. & G. Bastiani, 2000. The interpleniglacial record in the Palaeolithic site of Divje Babe I (Slovenia): some of the more important results of the 1980–1999 excavations. *Societa Preistoria Protostoria Friuli-Venezia Giulia, Trieste* 8, 221–44.

Turk, I., J. Dirjec & B. Kavur, 1995. Ali so v sloveniji nasli najstarejse glasbilo v europi? [The oldest musical instrument in Europe discovered in Slovenia?]. *Razprave IV. Razreda SAZU*. 36, 287–93.

Turk, I., J. Dirjec & B. Kavur, 1997. A-t-on trouvé en Slovénie le plus vieil instrument de musique d'Europe? *L'Anthropologie* 101(3), 531–40.

Turk, I., J. Dirjec, G. Bastiani, M. Pflaum, T. Lauko, F. Cimerman, F. Kosel, J. Grum & P. Cevc, 2001. New analyses of the 'flute' from Divje Babe I (Slovenia). *Arheoloski vestnik* 52, 25–79.

Turk, I., G. Bastiani, B.A.B. Blackwell & Z. Horusitzky, 2003. Putative Mousterian flute from Divje babe I (Slovenia): pseudoartefact or true flute, or who made the holes. *Arheoloski vestnik* 54, 67–72.

Winnington-Ingram, R.P., 1980. Greece. I: Ancient in *The New Grove Dictionary of Music and Musicians*, vol. 7: *Fuchs to Gyuzelev*, ed. S. Sadie. London: Macmillan, 659–72.

Yung, B.N., 1980. China. IV: Scales; Modes in *The New Grove Dictionary of Music and Musicians*, vol. 4: *Castrucci to Courante*, ed. S. Sadie. London: Macmillan, 261–2 & 262.

Zilhão, J. & F. d'Errico, 2003. The chronology of the Aurignacian and Transitional technocomplexes. Where do we stand? in *The Chronology of the Aurignacian and of the Transitional Technocomplexes. Dating, Stratigraphies, Cultural Implications*, eds. J. Zilhão & F. d'Errico. (Trabalhos de Arqueologia 33.) Lisboa: IPA, 313–49.

Zilhão, J. & F. d'Errico, 2004. An Aurignacian 'Garden of Eden' in southern Germany? An alternative interpretation of the Geissenklösterle and a critique of the *Kulturpumpe* model. *Paléo* 15, 69–86.

Chapter 6

The Scandinavian Bronze Lurs: Accident or Intent?

Peter Holmes

During the Bronze Age, large, conical lip-reed (brass) instruments were manufactured in Scandinavia. Most of the instruments which have survived are in parts, offering a unique opportunity to examine the DNA of the these 'twins'. This paper reports on a study of the available extant instruments in which the author carried out detailed measurements of the instruments in an attempt to establish their metrological credentials. Analysis of the measurements taken suggest that some systematic attention was paid to the control of the conicity of their tubes and to their general dimensional stability both during prime manufacture and assembly and that pairs of instruments match each other very closely. Manufacturers showed clear intent in their activities and, it is suggested, understood both the concepts of design and manufacture at a level of abstraction which hints at the use of engineering rather than craft practices. The analysis suggests that the concept of conicity was understood in some way and that a technique or techniques had been developed which allowed the manufacturer to replicate objects to within very close limits. The manufacture of lurs, it is suggested, was a very highly-developed occupation requiring a deep level of understanding of form and manufacture.

This paper discusses the developments that took place on a group of musical instruments, generally referred to as 'lurs' or 'bronze-age lurs', which were found throughout Scandinavia and have been dated to the late Bronze Age. These instruments are generally horn-shaped in cross section and are blown by the player as a brass or lip-reed instrument. They were generally found in pairs with one curving from the mouthpiece around to the left and the other curving to the right, the instruments being referred to as 'left-wound' and 'right-wound lurs'. The instruments are generally identified by their findspot, such as 'Maltbæk' and, to identify individual instruments in a pair, their ID in the author's data base is used — the Maltbæk pair being SD128 and SD129. These numbers correspond with those allocated by Broholm (Broholm *et al.* 1949) but run from 100 onwards where Broholm's ran from zero.

Almost any open-ended but sealed tube may be blown as a brass or lip-reed instrument and will yield a sound. If the tube is irregular in cross section, the tones that it will yield may be difficult to predict, as

will the relationship between the different notes. As the tube tends towards either a cylindrical or a conical form, the harmonic structure of its musical output will become more predictable. In the limit, when an instrument becomes either totally cylindrical or totally conical in its cross section, the harmonic structure of its sound output becomes quite readily predictable from the laws of physics. In this limit, a conical tube which is suitably excited is capable of sounding all the notes of the harmonic sequence while a cylindrical one will sound only the odd-numbered harmonics. If it is known what the intended output of an instrument it is then possible to identify intention in the developmental stages of a series of instruments, assuming that the appropriate knowledge and essential craft skills are passed on from one generation of maker to the next.

Lip-reed instruments have been developed from a variety of sources, a common one being the horns of animals which, because of their essentially conical form, became the prototypes for conical instruments and are given the generic name 'horn'. The conical

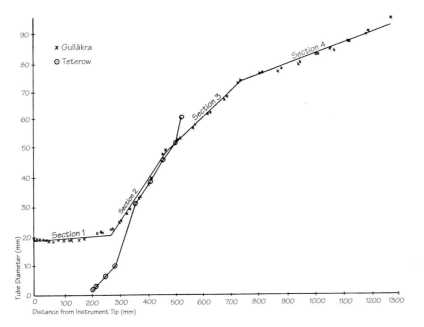

Figure 6.1. *The Gullåkra lur and Teterow horn.*

cross section of the bore of a horn is the feature which identifies it as a 'horn' and not a 'trumpet' and the degree of conicity of the bores is considered in this paper, its angle being measured in milleradians (mrad) or thousandths of a radian.

One of the many disadvantages of animal horns is that they come in the size and shape that the animal provides and, even though the animal may provide two horns, there is no guarantee that they will be a matching pair, nor that they will look particularly pretty when the animal has worn them all its life.

Musical-instrument manufacturers have long become adept at 'improving' on the animal's product, initially by providing additional fitments that improve the appearance of the instrument that nature donated, as well as improving its playing characteristics. The earliest evidence of such activities, as far as the lurs are concerned, are those from Bochin, Teterow and Wismar in northern Germany (Schmidt 1915) and the added pieces that adorn the tip, middle and end of the horn and are cast in bronze. The relatively small added elements on these instruments are decorative and mainly aesthetic in effect.

However, before the first extant 'lur' (from Gullåkra) had appeared, these extensions had become significant in musical terms and had extended the performance characteristics of the lur, as well as its appearance. Nevertheless, the Gullåkra lur retained the archaic form of its precursor horn within its own structure.

Figure 6.1 shows the structure of the Gullåkra instrument with the shape of the Teterow instrument superimposed upon this. In this graph it can be seen how the central and end part of the Teterow horn is replicated in the early middle part of the Gullåkra lur. The overall form of the Teterow instrument can be partially described by reference to its overall shape, expressed in terms of its semi-vertical angle of 81 mrad and this compares roughly with that of the second slope of the second section of the Gullåkra lur of 68 mrad.

At the tip (mouthpiece) end of this instrument, the tube extension is nearly cylindrical, with a very-small semi-vertical angle of 7.3 mrad, yielding a tip diameter which is only 2.6 mm smaller than that diameter which meets the centre section. In a similar way, the bell section expands at a much slower rate than the centre section, having an overall semi-vertical angle of 19.2 mrad.

The Gullåkra lur appears to have been developed by adding two sections to its central section, both of which have much smaller slopes than this central portion. If the desire of the maker was to extend the instrument's length from the 300 mm or so of a horn like Teterow, the reduction of slope would have been necessary to avoid an excessively small diameter at the mouthpiece end on the one hand and an excessively large diameter at the bell on the other.

Mathematically-speaking, the shape of the Gullåkra lur can be expressed in terms of the relationship between distances along the tube (y) from the tip, to the diameter of the tube at any point. In the case of the Gullåkra lur, the x/y relationship, taken over the whole instrument is:

$$y = 0.0715x + 0.11524$$

with a regression coefficient — goodness-of-fit factor — of 0.9800 and E(Max) — the maximum deviation from the 'best-fit' straight line through the points of 17.00 mm. However, the second section of this tube, from $y = 273$ mm to $y = 464$ mm, has a slope approximately twice as steep as that of the tube as a whole.

Most of the lurs retain the four-section structure of the Gullåkra lur but tend to have a much more uniform overall slope and the value for E(Max) on these is much less. Putting this in mathematical terms, the later instruments tend towards the development of a more-uniform slope from tip to bell end, such that the relationship:

$$y \text{(distance along tube)} = m \text{ (slope)} \times x \text{(tube dia.)}$$

holds very closely throughout the entire length of the instrument.

On the Maltbæk instruments, for instance (Fig. 6.2), although the correlation coefficient (r) of 0.9534 is less than that of Gullåkra ($r = 0.9800$), the value of E(Max) is much lower at E(Max) = 8.6 mm. This points to the maker's intention to produce a more-conical lur and to his ability actually to do so.

In addition, the Maltbæk lurs were made as a pair, one being left-wound and one right-wound, clearly another intentional feature. As a pair, these two instruments are physically very similar, the maximum dimensional difference between the diameters of the two instruments at any point along the tube being only 2 mm, this difference occuring at the junction of the tube and bell sections. In the diagram, the author's reference ID is used to distinguish between the two instruments, these being SD128/9.

Another group of instruments, from Brudevælte, consists of three pairs of instruments SD101/2, SD103/4 and SD105/6, five of these being available for study (SD106 currently being in Russia). On these instruments, the structure of the slopes has been virtually reduced to a three-slope structure, the three slopes on these instruments varying very little from the best-fit straight line which is generated by analyzing the data from their x/y points as a whole (Fig. 6.3).

The regression coefficient $r = 0.9951$ for the data from these instruments and the maximum 'error' from this line is about 2.5 mm, values very close to this existing at both intersections of slopes and at the bell exit diameter The data suggests strongly that these instruments are built to a defined design which incorporates a set slope of the order of this best line slope. The remarkable similarity in dimensions of these two instruments can be seen in their x/y plots, the largest difference between individual instruments at any point being of the order of 1 mm, while the average difference is almost zero! The five Brudevælte instruments are, thus, dimensionally very similar.

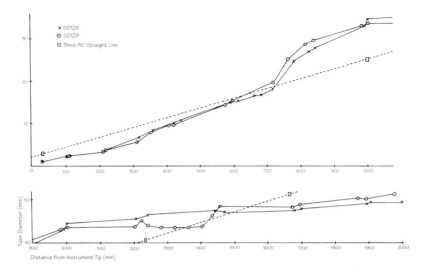

Figure 6.2. *The Maltbæk lurs.*

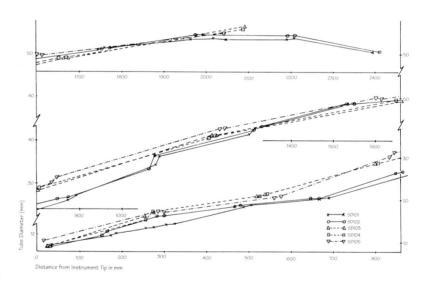

Figure 6.3. *The Brudevælte lurs.*

One pair of instruments, from Folrisdam, have a particularly conical tube, the relationship between their x/y measurement being expressed in the equations:

$$y = 0.0275x + 6.964$$
correlation coefficient (r) = 0.9930 Instrument SD124

$$y = 0.0277x + 6.653$$
correlation coefficient (r) = 0.9943 Instrument SD125

The standard errors for this data are: $Syx(1) = 1.327$ and $Syx(2) = 1.411$ (Fig. 6.4).

Taken on their own, this data suggests that the instruments are intended to be constructed from a tube which is quite conical. However, this tube itself

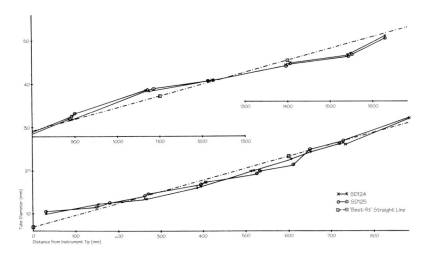

Figure 6.4. *The Folrisdam lurs.*

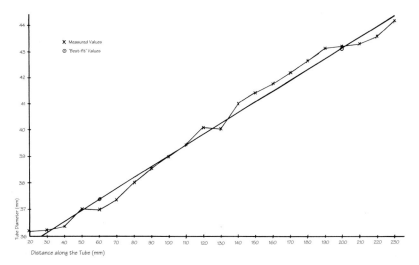

Figure 6.5. *The Rossum lur tube.*

is made up from three sections which are individually even more conical and have even smaller standard errors. The three slopes of individual section of the two instruments are:

Slopes (SD124) = 0.277, 0.332, 0.245
Slopes (SD125) = 0.270, 0.332, 0.200

These instruments differ in another significant way from the other instruments in that they lack the steeper central section seen on the majority of lurs, suggesting that the maker had a concept of the overall instrument and had set out to create a single slope along the entire tube.

The apparent precision in the overall slope of the two lurs is mirrored in the individual sections which demonstrate an equally-significant relationship. In the section from the tip of the Folrisdam instruments to a point 610 mm downstream, the x/y relationship is one of a straight line with standard errors (Syx) of 0.20/0.60. As the tubes are curved in two planes, the precise conicity of the instrument is not apparent but, were the curvature to be removed to yield a straight conical instrument, it would open out uniformly, with a slope of 0.27 in such a way that the diameters at all points are within 0.3/0.9 mm (actual values) of the best-fit straight line values.

Most instruments have an overall form which is less uniform than the Folrisdam ones but, even on these, individual segments are manufactured in such a way that their conical cross section is uniform and the plot of their x/y points yields a straight-line relationship. Even on the Gullåkra lur, although E (max.) is high at 17 , its third unit of slope has a straight-line correlation coefficient of $r = 0.9947$. (13 values) On Maltbæk, slope 2 has a value of $r = 0.9976$ with a mean tube diameter variation from the best fit line of 0.26 mm.

One lur tube, that from Rossum (SD133) was fragmentary and it was possible on this to measure the tube diameter at 10 mm intervals down the tube, the figures obtained being shown on Figure 6.5. the data was analysed in the same way as for the other lur data and the resulting straight line derived from this had a correlation coefficient of 0.9958. The maximum deviation of any point from this straight line was about 0.35 mm, again demonstrating the ability to manaufacture to a predetermined design.

The roundness of tubes

All the lurs are 'round' in the sense that they have a round appearance but the early presumed 'pre-lurs' are round to an extent that can be gauged by eye and manufactured by hand. This contrasts with other lurs which have a much higher degree of roundness. The roundness of instruments was assessed for this study by measuring tube diameters at a number of points around their periphery. It must be said that the numbers of stations measured were wholly inadequate for

Table 6.1. *Tube roundness.*

Instrument	Roundness (mm)	No. of stations
Rørlykke SD 120	2.30	4
Rørlykke SD	1.90	4
Gullåkra SD135	1.32	4
Brudevælte SD	0.74	4
Maltbæk SD128	0.65	8
Brudevælte SD	0.62	24
Brudevælte SD	0.61	11
Revheim SD	0.59	13
Revheim SD	0.54	15
Rossum SD	0.47	7
Brudevælte SD103	0.38	6
Maltbæk SD	0.36	7
Folrisdam SD	0.28	5
Garlstedt SD	0.24	10
Folrisdam SD124	0.10	4

definitive statements to be made about the roundness of instruments but they yielded a set of indicative figures which, at least, present a rough picture of the level of roundness achieved by the makers.

Among the simplest of the lurs, the Gullåkra instrument is considerably more round than the Wismar group but its out-of roundness can still be detected both by eye and by feel. Running along the axis of this instrument can be felt decidedly flatter areas suggesting that the cross-section is a form of polygonally-deformed circle. From the five stations measured, a mean roundness of 1.32 mm was found. Two stations of the five were round, to within 0.90 mm although, even here the out-of-roundness was visibly detectable.

It was clearly the intention of the makers to produce round lur tubes and the roundness of the tubes measured does roughly correlate with the closeness of fit of the tubes to a conical model. However, at some level of roundness, it becomes impossible to detect any further improvement so any increase in roundness above this figure must be a product of improved manufacturing technique. Table 6.1 gives roundness values of the instruments which were measured, the figures being presented in order of increasing roundness.

Between the two limits in the above table, there is a considerable gap with the least round tubes most probably being capable of being made by eye and the most round almost

certainly being produced by some generating process. Perhaps the gap between the 1.32 and 0.74 figures represents a change on manufacturing process. Whatever the story is, it seems clear that the maker had the intention of making a round object and, of applying to this task, the most suitable manufacturing technology that was available.

The design of the lurs

As the lurs are made in matched pairs, they provide clear visual evidence that they were either made to be similar to each other or they were made to a common standard. Two sets of lurs, those found at Brudevælte and the pair from Rørlykke may provide some further guide as to the true story.

The Rørlykke pair are not a 'pair' in the lur sense as they are both right-wound. However, their overall form is very similar, the shape and type of the decoration bands is identical and the level of technology displayed in the casting of each instrument is clearly similar. One of the instruments was fragmentary when found and has been reconstructed for display purposes but when the data collected from this reconstruction was analyzed, the two plots of the lur pair did not coincide. It was found that, when the plot of the reconstructed lur was adjusted by adding in 29.60 mm of mouthpipe, a close coincidence of plots was obtained. It was concluded, therefore that a portion of tube had been lost and, hence, the instrument had been incorrectly reconstructed. Once this adjustment had been made to the data, the diameters of the tubes are within a millimetre or so of the same diameter with the maximum tube divergence being about 4 mm. The tubes are strikingly similar over most of their

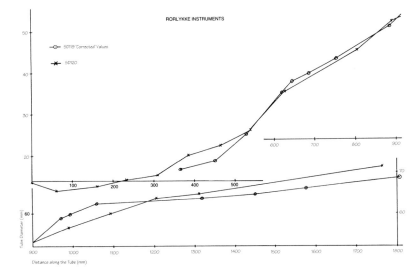

Figure 6.6. *The Rørlykke lurs.*

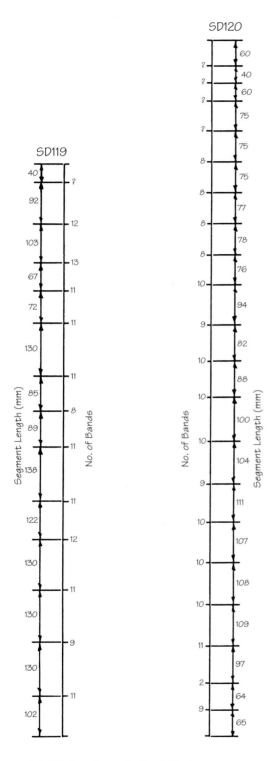

Figure 6.7. *The bands on the Rørlykke lurs.*

length and, over the section between $y = 525$ mm and $y = 880$ mm the tubes are virtually identical. Although the tube's morphology does diverge over certain sections it still seems to be produced to an overall design, such that the divergence is 'corrected' and the tube dimensions again coincide downstream.

Both instrument tubes are decorated by sets of circumferential parallel bands but at no point on the tubes does the number of bands match up, either in position on the tube or in the number of bands in a given set. Instrument SD119 has an average of 11 bands per group while SD120 has an average of 9. The sections demarcated by the bands do not coincide with the actual portions of tube which were made and then joined together by cast-on sections with meandering edges — these being generally referred to as meander joints. However, these meander joints are in different positions on the two lurs indicating that the process of making the two pieces did not simply consist of making one and then copying it or making the two together.

This pair of instruments was made to the same design (as indicated by their dimensional similarity), although the two individual instruments were probably made at different times. To do this, the maker must have stored the information needed to create individual instruments and this was clearly seen as paramount with details like where the joints should be and what decoration should be applied being subsidiary to the instrument's overall morphology.

The largest group of instruments found together is the Brudevælte group and at the time of the find, three pairs (SD 101/2, SD 103/4, SD 105/6) or six instruments were recovered. One (SD106) was subsequently given away and is now in a Russian museum so five remain available for study.

These instruments are all similar in form, have roughly similar bell discs, are pretty well as round as each other and appear to be from the same school of manufacture. However, one pair, SD 101/2, is sufficiently different from the two other pairs to suggest that it was either manufactured earlier than the other instruments or was made by a less accomplished craftsman. The features which illustrate this difference are:

i) Segment length: the mean lengths for instruments SD 101/2 are 180.2/190.8 mm while those for the other instruments are:

> SD103/104 332.7/331.9 mm
> SD 105 326.5 mm

ii) The x/y data for instruments SD 103/4 and SD 105 follows a straight line relationship with

> E (max.) = 3.0 mm (103/4)
> E (max.) = 4.5 mm (105)

while that for instrument, SD 101/102, although following a very similar relationship shows a much greater variation from this,

E (max.) = 6.6 mm

iii) The mouthpipes on SD 101/102 are roughly semi-circular as on the majority of other lurs while those on SD 103/104 and. SD 105 have a straight portion immediately downstream of the mouthpiece.

iv) The bell discs of SD 103/104 and 105 are larger and contain a greater number of decorative elements than SD 101/102, while these latter instruments are decorated with six bosses and six equally-spaced sets of concentric circles the other instruments have both a completely circular set of these circles and other patterns made up from them.

v) The bell tubes of SD 103/4 are cast with only a thin band, possibly as on Rossum while SD 10l/2 have much thicker feature here.

These differences suggest that these instruments were probably made at different times but their overall tube morphology is very similar. Their overall slopes are 0.022/0.021, 0.024/0.025 and. 0.026 and at a point 1.67 m from their tips, all 5 (6?) are within one millimetre of the same diameter. Thus, if these instruments were made at different times but to a similar design, the information that defines this design must have been stored in some way which allowed the instruments to be replicated.

The design and manufacturing philosophy of the lurs

Of all the lurs, The Folrisdam instruments, SD 124/125, are the ones whose design appears to be most deliberate as the tube of the instrument can be represented by a straight-line equation such that all diameters along the 1.7 m instrument are within 3 mm of that calculated mathematically. Structurally, it is made up of three sections which were joined together following manufacture.

We will never know just how the maker set out to manufacture these instruments but whichever way he chose, his intention was clear, to make a precisely-conical instrument. This he could have done by making two sets of three sections and then joining these together or by starting at one end and progressively constructing the instrument. Either way, it would have been necessary to monitor progress by checking the diameter of the tube and making any adjustments that might be necessary at each stage.

Intentionality in the operation can be seen in the way differences from the presumed model of slope build up and are then corrected. Assuming that the instrument/yard manufacture was started at the mouthpiece end of the mouthpipe yard, the maker produced a tube of increasing diameter from about 10 mm to about 22 mm. (Figures from SD 125.) Then, 610 mm from the instrument tip, having manufactured a length of tube that opened out with a slope of 0.0208 to within about 0.4 mm below the best-fit straight line value, he increased the slope on yard 2 to 0.0350. Again this yard was manufactured closely to this slope the mean variation from it being 0.2 mm. Thus, at this point 610 mm from the instrument tip, he was clearly aware of the change in slope i.e. he had made it deliberately. It seems likely therefore that he was clearing the cumulative error that had built up at that point, where, presumably it had reached a detectable value (2 mm?). His change of slope produced a second section that crossed back over the 'best-fit' line, correcting this 'error'.

Section 2 was then manufactured with a consistent slope up to 1.075 from the tip where the slope was changed from 0.0350 to 0.0181. On section 3, this slope was again closely followed, the mean error here being 0.17 mm. In section 2, as with section 1, a variation from the overall best-fit line appears to have accumulated during its manufacture being at its greatest value of 2 mm at the intersection of yards 1 and 2. However, these yards do run smoothly into each other suggesting that the variation from the overall best fit line that now exists was designed into the specification and was not a measuring error.

Were the manufacturer to have made the instrument in individual sections, he would need to have ensured that the end diameter of section 1 would fit the entry diameter of section 2 and if he were to make all the sections at the same time he would need to have had some technique for storing the dimensional information that allowed the tubes to mate accurately enough.

Whatever route was taken to manufacture the parts of these instruments, it was clearly a deliberate one which had been developed over a period of time and was planned each time a new manufacturing project was attempted.

The assembly of complete instruments

Once the component parts of the instruments had been created they were assembled into finished instruments with just the same care and precision. Table 6.2 and Figures 6.8 and 6.9 show measurements taken on two pairs of the Brudevælte instruments in order to illustrate the dimensional repeatability of the assembly process. Some of these measurements record the distance between points on the instruments which are created from several components which have been

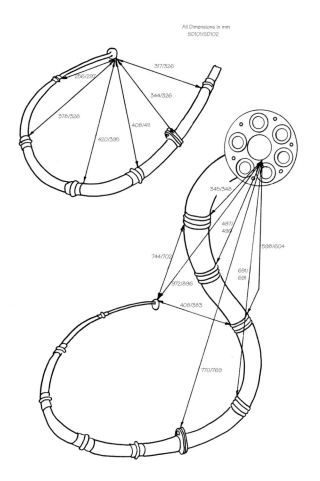

Figure 6.8. *The Brudevælte lurs SD101/2.*

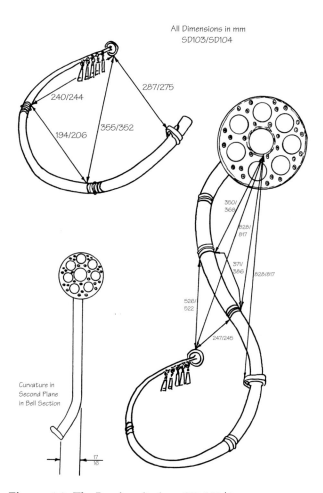

Figure 6.9. *The Brudevælte lurs SD 103/4.*

assembled together. An example of this is the measurement of 355/352 mm which spans two tube sections and results from the assembly of two components. This is clearly closer than can be set by eye alone and points to a deliberate act of selective assembly which was designed to achieve two virtually dimensionally identical objects.

This effect is even more noticeable on the bell yard of SD 101/2 (Fig. 6.8). On this, the dimensions from the tip of the bell mouth to the segment bands are shown in Table 6.2.

These figures for the repeatability between items and the uniformity of this repeatability over the four

Table 6.2. *Assembled dimensions on Brudevælte 101/2.*

SD 101	SD 102	Difference	
		Per cent	**Absolute (mm)**
345	348	3	0.86
487	490	3	0.61
598	604	6	0.99
770	769	1	0.13

readings leave no doubt as to the deliberateness of the dimensions. Their achievement can only derive from careful assembly of the segments when casting these together. Undoubtedly the chords measured here were used as check measures on assembly, presumably to achieve identical forms on instrument pairs.

The conceptual grasp of the process of manufacture

Getting into the mind of the lur maker is probably the biggest challenge of all! There were undoubtedly many different craftsmen involved in the manufacture of these instruments and they all show — admittedly to different degrees — the intention to produce conical instruments. The most difficult question of all hinges on the question of the level of abstraction applied to the process of designing/creating these instruments. It is possible that an instrument was kept as a template for the storage of the data about a lur and that the necessary dimensional information was extracted from this when making new instruments. In view of the precision with which instruments were reproduced, this method would call for some technique to extract the dimensional information very accurately and to transfer it to the new instrument. The data seems to suggest that the level of reproduceabilty is greater than could be achieved by eye alone. At the next level of abstraction, the storage of data in an abstract

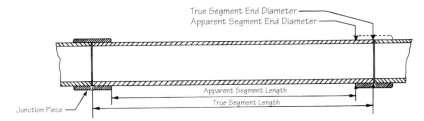

Figure 6.10. *Calculation of significant segment size.*

form, say as gauges or length standards, would call for no further refinement in the technique but for a more abstract model of the lur, i.e. as a set of dimensions. Whether the intent was to store these for purposes other than making lurs is not known but that would represent a significant step in the path to developing the concept of mensuration.

The maker could, thus have used the following physical devices to store the dimensional information needed to recreate a lur (listed in increasingly-abstract order):

a) An actual instrument (or a pair) kept as a copy;
b) The sections of a dismembered instrument (i.e. following prime manufacture);
c) The cores of an instrument for use as generators of form;
d) The cores of an instrument in the form of a straight cone;
e) Station markers or gauges storing dimensional information specific to set locations on the tube;
f) Dimensional data stored in the form of units by some means.

The six possibilities above all point to the deliberate intent of the manufacturer to create lurs but, as we know not which was used, tell us nothing about the level of conceptualization that was applied to the instruments. Perhaps, in a step-by-step process, the idea of the increase in diameter of a tube with the distance along its length led to a generalized understanding of taper but not in the way that we understand it today — in a mathematical or quasi-mathematical way.

Were the makers to have progressed to stage of storing dimensional information as units of length, this would free them from restrictions imposed by physical models and their imperfections. It could. also lead the maker towards a geometrical analysis of his product, significantly different from that of earlier instrument makers who simply copied a shape.

The use of standard units of measure

Although this cultural region provides no evidence of the use of units of length, much evidence exists from other areas for the use of units from much earlier periods In Egypt and Mesopotamia for example, as early as 3000 BC, standard. lengths were used, being kept in temples and. royal palaces (Hodges 1970, 110; Wilder 1973, 94.) However, such units as are known have the finger width as the major sub-division and, being defined on a very variable anthropometric feature, such a unit would. appear to be far too coarse for use in defining the tube morphology of a lur.

Butler & Sarfartij, reporting in 1970, identified a possible unit of measurement on a ceremonial bronze sword which had been deposited as a votive offering in Jutphaas in the province of Utrecht. The find appears to date from the middle Bronze Age — based upon stratigraphy — which in this area dates to 1200–1000 BC. Their view was that a unit of 26.5 mm was used to construct this sword — a unit that they entitled the Jutphaas inch or J-inch.

A search was made for a similar unit in the lurs, the major problem lying in the identification of the elements to which the craftsman would have applied units. It was only possible to measure over the surfaces which are now exposed but these may not have been the ones the maker chose as he had access to surfaces which are now covered. An attempt was made, therefore to extrapolate the data collected in order to recreate the actual dimensions that might have been used to gauge the progress of the manufacturing process by utilizing the estimated dimensions at the ends of segments rather than at the points where bands or cast-on bosses end, as illustrated in Figure 6.10.

All the lurs were analyzed in this way, the discussion below referring to the data for Brudevælte 102. A set of diameters was calculated for the presumed ends of sections. In doing this, the assumption was made that the slope of the tube between the two ends of the junction piece was uniform. This appears to be a valid assumption when considering the data from the Rosum instrument, on which a section of tube was analyzed in detail and found to be of a uniform slope.

A unit of 4.5 mm was found to give a series of multiples values for diameters which coincided quite accurately with the calculated segment end diameters. For purposes of shorthand notation this unit

Table 6.3. *The Brudevælte inch (brin).*

Corrected value of tube dia. (mm)	No. of brins to obtain corrected value	Nearest integer no. of brins	Value of integer number (mm)	Difference columns 2 and 3 (mm)
9.1	2.02	2	9	–0.1
14.2	3.16	3	13.5	–0.7
18.7	4.16	4	18	–0.7
20.4	4.53	5	22.5	2.1
26.5	5.89	6	27	0.5
48.5	10.78	11	49.5	1.00
51.5	11.44	11	49.5	–2
54.3	12.07	12	54	–0.3
54.1	12.02	12	54	–0.1
50.6	11.24	11	49.5	–1.1

is referred to as a (bronze-age inch) or 'brin', in the case of Brudevælte (102) the value of 4.5 mm being a Brudevælte brin. Table 6.3 expresses the nearness of the measured lengths to multiples of brins in two ways: Column 1 shows the number of brins needed to generate the measured. value while Column 4 shows the value obtained from an integer number of brins and Column 5 the difference between the integer number and the actual measured. value.

Column 5 on Table 6.3, seems to substantiate the view that 4.5 mm is a relevant unit of measure as most of the difference values are very low. In addition each of the 2nd to 5th segments seems to be one brin longer than the preceding one while the diameters of segments 7, 8 and 9 increase at only half that rate. This may account for the large variation from an integral number of brins seen on line 7 of Table 6.3 as this may result from the desire to increase the tube diameter more slowly. Were the application of a unit of measure to these figures false, then a range of error values from 0 to ±2.25 mm would be expected, with a numerical mean of 1.125. The mean error of the figures in Table 6.3 is 0.85, counting the two large figures and 0.55 omitting these.

For the brin to be proved conclusively as a standard unit of measure, it would need to be recognized generally on this instrument as well as on others related to it. However, the other dimension which concerned the craftsman, the length of segments is considerably larger in scale than the diameters of tubes and the brin is a rather small unit to be searching for in this context. In fact, the segment lengths of Brudevaelte 101/2 do show some tendency to be integer multiples of 4.5 mm but not an overwhelming one. When using a compound multiple of 4.5 mm, i.e. one of 10 times 4.5 mm, a mean error of 7.75 mm is obtained, as opposed to the error of 11.25 mm that

would be expected were the dimensions to be unrelated to this unit. Similar situations are found on other lurs where tantalizing glimpses of units are obtained but no hard evidence found.

With such a small unit and relatively poor means of measuring and replicating, one would expect considerable dimensional drift to occur as as standards are copied to be handed on. This would make it unlikely for identical standard units to be detected on instruments which might have been made generations apart.

Earlier comparative analyses of the lurs

The metrological data from the lurs appears to show some sort of systematic development but the analysis leaves open the question of how the trends found in this study correlate with other systematic studies of the lurs. Several writers have set out to establish typological/chronological classifications for the lurs, notably Oldeberg in 1947 and Broholm in 1965. Table 6.4, which is derived from Lund (1986, 48, table II) superimposes the metrological data on the analysis by Broholm.

The metrological data, patchy as it is, shows pretty well the same sequence as that proposed by Broholm, suggesting that the technological sequence could also be mapped over to a chronological one. The lur pair that does not map as accurately as the main body of instruments is that from Revheim in Norway. However, this pair is markedly different from the other lurs, is very much smaller in size and was found at the most northwestern edge of the lurs' distribution.

Conclusion

The lurs represent a unique resource for investigating intent. Not only are they made in pairs but they are also lip-reed instruments whose desired morphology may be predicted given a desired performance characteristic.

In this paper, the morphology of the instruments has been analyzed under the assumption that their manufacturers were actually attempting to create 'musical' instruments in the modern western sense, i.e. ones with which a player could sound a series of notes which accurately conform to the theoretical harmonic series of notes. If this was their aim, they succeeded admirably and ensured that generation after generation, they managed to refine the instruments' form to conform ever more closely to an ideal conical musical instrument, as well as creating instrument pairs that were extremely close mirror images of each other..

It is only possible to guess what techniques needed to be developed in order to make pairs of thin-sectioned cast and per-fectly-conical musical instruments and the intimate detail of the craftsman's endeavour escapes us. However, what it entailed in general terms is another matter. The manufacture could not have been done without a high level of conceptualization of both the design and manufacture of these instruments and the creation of intermediate artefacts — tools — which would aid in the process. Such a level of planning of manufacturing processes we tend today to characterize as 'engineering' and perhaps this is how we should describe the manufacture of the bronze lurs. Their manufacturers planned and executed their manufacturing endeavours with great skill and foresight and, undoubtedly with clear intent.

Table 6.4. *A comparison of typological/chronological and metrological sequencing.*

Period	Broholm 1965	E(Max)	Regression coeff.	Round-ness	Max diff. between insts in pair
Period III *c.* 1300–1100 BC	Froarp				
	Gullåkra	17.00	0.9800	1.32	N/A
	Rørlykke SD119		0.9070	2.30	3.6*
	Rørlykke SD120		0.9730	1.90	
	Skåne				
Period IV *c.* 1100–900 BC	Dauding				
	Hallenslev				
	Lommelev				
	Lübzin				
	Maltbæk SD	8.60	0.9470	0.65	3.5
	Maltbæk SD		0.9534	0.36	
	Nyrup				
	Påarp				
	Rossum				
Period V *c.* 900–600 BC	Blidstrup				
	Borgeby				
	Boslunde				
	Brudevælte SD101		0.9755	0.74	2.5
	Brudevælte SD102		0.9881	0.62	
	Brudevælte SD103		0.9969	0.61	1.6
	Brudevælte SD104		0.9951	0.38	
	Brudevælte SD105		0.9941		N/A
	Daberkow				
	Garlstedt			0.24	
	Länglöt				
	Radbjerg				
Period VI *c.* 600–500 BC	Folrisdam SD	1.33	0.9930	0.28	1.6
	Folrisdam SD	1.41	0.9943	0.10	
	Revheim SD		0.9805	0.59	
	Revheim SD		0.9703	0.54	

References

Broholm, H.C., W.P. Larsen & G. Skjerne, 1949. *The Lurs of the Bronze Age*. Copenhagen.

Butler, J.J. & H. Sarfatij, 1970. *Another Bronze Ceremonial Sword by the Plougescant – Ommerschans Smith.* (Berichten van de Rijksdienst voor het onheidkundig Bodemonderzoek, vol. 20–21.) Amersfoort.

Hodges, H.W.M., 1970, *Technology in the Ancient World*. London: Pelican.

Holmes, P., 1976. The Evolution of Player-Voiced Aerophones Prior to 500 AD. Unpublished PhD thesis, London.

Holmes, P., 1986. The Scandinavian bronze lurs, in *The Bronze Lurs: Second Conference of the ICTM Study Group on Music Archaeology, Stockholm*, vol. 2, ed. C.S. Lund. (Royal Swedish Academy of Music 53.) Stockholm: Royal Swedish Academy of Music, 51–125.

Lund, C.S. (ed.), 1986. *The Bronze Lurs: Second Conference of the ICTM Study group on Music Archaeology, Stockholm*, vol. 1. (Royal Swedish Academy of Music 53.) Stockholm: Royal Swedish Academy of Music.

Oldeberg, A., 1947. A contribution to the history of the Scandinavian bronze lur in the Bronze and Iron Ages. *Acta Archeaologica* XVIII, 1.

Schmidt, H., 1915. *Die Luren von Daberkow, Kr. Demmin.* (Praehistorische Zeitschrift VII.) Berlin.

Wilder, R.L., 1973. *The Evolution of Mathematical Concepts.* New York (NY): John Wiley & Sons.

Chapter 7

Theatres and Theatre Design in the Graeco-Roman World: Theoretical and Empirical Approaches[*]

Eleonora Rocconi

In the Classical world the two main actorial qualities, loudness and clearness of voice, were strengthened by some simple acoustical devices typical of Greek theatre design since its beginnings: the almost complete absence of reverberation (due to the absence of a roof), which made the speech more intelligible, and the profusion of early reflected sounds (the most important of which come from the orchestral reflection) which enhanced the audience's perception of the actor's voice and chorus' song. But empirical enquiry into archaeological ruins carried out in recent years by scholars need to be supported also by a careful investigation of theoretical sources, which show a consciousness of these phenomena by the ancients since the fourth century BC, and by thorough examination of the different performing arts which took place there through a historical perspective. On a broader level, it seems quite evident that there was indeed amongst ancient Greeks and Romans an acoustical intentionality underlying their building of theatres, which was mindful of acoustical laws, even if their ancient scientific approach was mainly an empirical-deductive one.

In the Classical world the development of dramatic performances in which music had the leading role is well known: since the institution, at the end of the sixth century BC, of the Athenian festivals in honour of Dionysus (the Greek god of wine and religious frenzy), there were dramatic competitions in Greece between what we nowadays regard as the most important performing arts of the ancient world: tragedies and comedies. Both these forms of drama have still not well known beginnings[1] but, in their standard shape, they show a combination of speech and music assigned respectively to actors (from one to three) and to a chorus which sang and danced at the same time, most probably in unison. The instrument most commonly accompanying the musical sections was the *aulos*, a double-reed wind instrument particularly associated with the Dionysian deity.

We know that, until the beginning of the fifth century, performances took place in the Agora, the main square of Athens located at the foot of the Acropolis. This is indicated both by references in literary sources[2] to a dancing ground there and by the archaeological

presence of large post-holes indicating supports for wooden grandstands (known as *ikria*). After the collapse of this wooden scaffolding between 499 and 496 BC,[3] dramatic contests were moved out of the Agora and an auditorium was built on the south slope of the Acropolis, inside the precinct of Dionysus. Although this auditorium became a stone building only in the seventh decade of the fourth century, from its beginning it probably had the same design we can admire in later archeological ruins: a circular platform of packed earth for the chorus' dancing, called the *orchestra* (< *orcheomai*, literally 'space in which the chorus dance'), and a semicircular seating scheme properly called the *theatron* (< *theaomai*, literally 'place for seeing')[4] surrounding the orchestra, made of timber and located against the hillside (to give it a steep seating rake, typically of 20 to 34°). The approaches to the orchestra were called *parodoi* or *eisodoi*, literally 'entrances'.

The main reasons for this building choice were surely on the one hand the safeness (the vaulting techniques, without which theatres could not be constructed as independent structures on level sites, were only later on developed by the Romans); on the other hand there was the matter of visual perspective, unquestionably very good in an outdoor theatre design of this type, the best viewing having been obtained by gradually increasing the slope of the *cavea* from front to rear. However, as we know that at least since the sixth century BC great attention was given in Greece to acoustical phenomena (the Pythagorean tradition comes to mind), it seems more than probable that acoustical reasons were involved too, and in recent years many scholars, including archaeologists, engineers and experts in architectural acoustics, have carefully observed and measured the acoustical properties of the ancient theatres.

As a matter of fact, sight and hearing constituted a unified sensory field for the Greeks, and quite often literary sources remark on the vocal talents an actor must have: *euphōnia* ('goodness of voice'), *megalophōnia* ('loudness of voice') and *lamprotēs* ('clearness, distinctness').[5] If we focus our attention on the last two qualities, it is easy to understand the reason for their importance: loudness is necessary in an open-air theatre that could attract and contain an audience from 14,000 to 17,000 people (we know, for instance, that Sophocles chose not to perform in his own plays, as had been traditional among Greek playwrights, because of his *mikrophōnia*, 'weakness of voice'); clearness is indispensable too for speech intelligibility, to enable the audience to follow the exhibition properly.

These two actorial qualities were strengthened by some simple acoustical devices typical of Greek theatre design: the almost complete absence of reverberation (due to the absence of a roof), which made speech more intelligible, and the profusion of early reflected sounds — that is to say, sounds reaching the listener within 40–50 milliseconds of receiving the sound directly — which enhanced the audience's perception of the sources: the actor's voice and chorus' song.

The most important effect was without doubt the orchestral reflection, which increased the range of satisfactory listening from 42 metres — the distance limit for speech transmission in quiet conditions — to 60 metres.[6] Amongst theoretical pieces of evidence the pseudo-Aristotelian *Problems* (fourth century BC) and the *Natural History* of the Roman writer Pliny the Elder show a consciousness of this phenomenon by the ancients:

> Why are choruses less distinct when the orchestra is covered with straw? Is it due to the roughness that the voice, falling on a surface which is not smooth, is less united, so that it is less? For it is not continuous. Just in the same way light shines more on a smooth

surface because it is not interrupted by any obstruction (Pseudo-Aristotle *Problems* XI 25).

> There are other factors besides about the voice that deserve mention. It is absorbed by the sawdust or sand that is thrown down on the floor in the theatre orchestras, and similarly in a place surrounded by rough walls; and it is also deadened by empty casks (Pliny *Natural History* XI 270).

The steeper the slope of the *cavea*, the more the sound waves coming from the orchestra were pushed uphill: each succeeding row was so high above the preceding one that the sound could reach all ears without interruption. For the ancients 'the travelling air causes the sound' (*Problems* XI 6), and its refraction (*anaklasis*) depends on the quality of the surface on which the sound falls. The smoother and thicker the surface is, the stronger the reflections of a sound will be:

> Why do newly plastered houses echo more? Is it because there is more refraction of sound (*anaklasis*) owing to the smoothness of the surface? The surface is smoother because it is unbroken and continuous. But we must try it not when it is quite wet, but when it is already dry; for there is no refraction of sound from wet clay. This is why stucco produces more echo. Possibly the immobility of the air also contributes to the result; for when the air is massed together it throws back what falls on it with more violence (Pseudo-Aristotle *Problems* XI 7).

> Why is it that if one buries a large jar or empty pot with a lid on, the building echoes more, and also if there is a well or cistern in the house? Is it because, since echo is refraction (*anaklasis*) the air must be compactly enclosed, and have something from which it can be refracted, when it strikes on what is thick and smooth? For in these conditions the echo is most noticeable. So the well and the cistern combine the qualities of narrowness and compactness, but jars and pots have thickness in their sides, so that the same results occurs in both cases. For hollow bodies produce more echo; and for this reason bronze produces more echo than other metals. It is not strange that this happens when they are dug in; for the voice carries downwards no less than in any other direction. Generally speaking, it seems to be carried in all directions and in a circle (Pseudo-Aristotle *Problems* XI 8).

The Greeks seem also to have had clear ideas on the geometry of reflection, according to which the angle-of-incidence of a sound is exactly the same as the angle-of-reflection:

> Why is it that, since the voice is air which has taken shape and is travelling, the shape is so often dissolved, but echo, which occurs when air in this condition strikes something hard, is not dissolved, but we hear it clearly? Is it because it is refracted and not scattered? Consequently the whole persists, and two

similar shapes arise from it; for refraction occurs at a similar angle (*pros homoian gōnian*). Hence the sound of the echo is similar to the original sound (Pseudo-Aristotle *Problems* XI 23).

Despite all this theoretical knowledge of the acoustical phenomena attested by Peripatetic sources, the first document which connects it explicitly to architecture appears only in the first century BC, in the treatise *On Architecture* of the Roman writer Vitruvius. According to the author, who probably based his account on the theoretical work of the fourth-century BC musicologist Aristoxenos of Tarentum (a pupil of Aristotle), a theatre needs to be built on 'a site in which the voice may fall smoothly and reach the ear with a definite utterance and without the interference of echoes' (*On Architecture* V 8). Places are distinguished by him in *katēchountes* (as if to say places which 'push back the sounds'), those in which the voice, when first it rises upwards, meets solid bodies above so it is driven back and, settling down, overwhelms the following utterance as it rises; *periēchountes* (literally 'pushing sounds all around'), those in which the voice moves round, is collected and dissipated in the centre, so that the terminations of the words are lost and the voice is swallowed up in a confused utterance; *antēchountes* (literally 'resonant'), those in which the words, striking against a solid body, give rise to echoes and make the termination of the words double to the ear; and finally *synēchountes* (literally 'strengthening the sounds'), those in which the voice reinforced from the ground rises with greater fullness and reaches the ear with clear and eloquent accents.

According to some modern opinions, in the ancient theatres additional sound reflections were obtained through two other devices: the tragic and comic masks, which served to make the actor's voice more resonant, and the vertical surface of the stage-house (called *skēnē*), on which the sound was in its turn reflected.

The face mask suggestion is based on a passage of Aulus Gellius (second century AD), where we read an incorrect interpretation of the Latin term *persōna*, which means 'mask':

> The head and the face are shut in on all sides by covering of the *persōna*, or mask, and only one passage is left for the issue of the voice; and since this opening is neither free nor broad, but sends forth the voice after it has been concentrated and forced into one single means of egress, it makes the sound clearer and more resonant (*claros canorosque sonitus facit*). Since then that covering of the face gives clearness and resonance to the voice (*clarescere et resŏnare vocem*), it is for that reason called *persōna*, the o being lengthened because of the formation of the word (Aulus Gellius *Attic Nights* V 7).[7]

Actually, etymological evidence shows that the word *persōna* does not come from *per* + *sŏnare*, because the vowel *o* is short in the verb; moreover we know that until the end of the fourth century BC these masks were made of linen or leather, materials which could hardly have enhanced the voice level in the way a megaphone might (as still many scholars state in their books).

With regard to the *skēnē*, we should remember that originally it was simply a curtain, only later transformed in a painted wooden panel (*skēnographia*).[8] Moreover, we have no certain evidence for the presence of a raised rectilinear stage (called *logeion*, literally 'speaking-place', by the Greeks) in the fifth century BC: according to some scholars' opinions, in Classical times the actors acted in the orchestra, not on a stage,[9] so the sound-reflecting properties of the stage-house's vertical surfaces at that time were practically insignificant.

This archaic theatre design was successively remodelled: in the fourth-century BC theatres were fabricated in stone (a much more reflecting — but intrinsically less resonant — material in terms of sounds) and a stage of the height of approximately one metre surely appeared. This stage was increased to at least three metres in Hellenistic times (thanks to the growing importance of actors in drama), an unfavourable circumstance for the reflected wave since its angle to the audience plane was thereby remarkably reduced.[10] Such a deficiency was probably corrected by the presence of wooden panels (called *pinakes*) incorporated in the *skēnē* as sound reflectors, and by the shape of the *proskenion*, the vertical front wall of the stage, facing the orchestra, which certainly had the effect of spreading laterally the reflected sounds onto the lower steps of the auditorium. The proscenium niches often show rectangular and semicircular elements in succession, as some archaeological ruins still show (for example, the Theatre of Ostia, for which see Canac 1967, ch. 2 fig. 7): we should not forget that, as the ancient Greeks knew, 'hollow bodies produce more echo' (*Problems* XI 8, quoted above).

In the Roman period theatre design changed further: the building was no longer placed against a natural slope and it was equipped with a high *skēnē* structurally linked to the semi-circular auditorium. Such a stage-house was different from earlier ones in its constituent parts, perhaps also in their acoustical role: the lower part did not have reliefs, it was smoother, enabling a better reflection sound; the higher part showed statues, columns and reliefs. The orchestra became semicircular (Fig. 7.1) and consequently the much deeper stage appears closer to the *cavea*[11]: it was therefore required to be low, allowing the voice to reach the lateral steps of the auditorium and to

Figure 7.1. *Theatre of Segesta (Sicily), an example of a semi-circular Roman orchestra.*

ing by its contact the hollows of the several vases, will arouse an increased clearness of sound, and by the concord a consonance harmonizing with itself ... (Vitruvius *On Architecture* V 5).

Archaeological evidence shows that this system really existed, despite the scepticism of some scholars,[12] and its main purpose seems to have been to create the possibility of obtaining harmonies and *sostenuto* effects for singers and musicians.[13]

This leads us directly to another important question, that is to say the variety of performances which could take place, since the Greek age, in Classical theatres. As a matter of fact, the ancient world basically knew two different types of competitions: the *skenikoi agones*, in other words dramatic competitions involving music (of the type we have already mentioned), and the *thymelikoi agones*, music and dance contests which took place near the *thymelē*, the altar of Dionysos which stood in the orchestra.[14] It has been commonly observed that the acoustics of ancient theatres are particularly suitable for speech, solo or unison singing and chanting and solo musical instruments (typical of the ancient drama), but less satisfactory for orchestral music because of the almost total absence of reverberation. Now, we know that in the second half of the fifth century a roofed theatre for musical performances — the *Odeum* — was built in Athens (and, later on, almost everywhere in the Greek and Roman world); however, according to the distinction between *skenikoi* and *thymelikoi* competitions, it seems reasonable to think that open-air theatres were both used for dramatic and musical performances before the construction of the *Odeum*, and perhaps continued to do so even later.

In this connection, a particularly interesting hypothesis was set out by an Italian archaeologist, Luigi Polacco, about a discovery in the theatre of Syracuse, in Sicily (Fig. 7.2). In the middle of the orchestra was excavated a rectangular cell of 2.70 × 2.45 metres (2.80/2.90 metres in depth), surely not useful for scenic reasons.[15] Polacco thinks that its utility lay in being a hollow which could function as a sound-box for a platform placed over it he calls *thymelē* (the word more generally means 'wooden table'). Iconographical evidence shows the practical use to which such a platform was put by singers and musicians (even if it wasn't necessary there always was a cell beneath it) and a 'much resonant

maintain good visual conditions for those seated in the orchestra (as a matter of fact, in the Roman world the orchestra was normally occupied by senators — because of the disappearance of the chorus — and therefore it could no longer perform a useful role as a reflector).

So additional acoustical devices were required, as for instance the presence of a colonnade (*porticum*) surrounding the upper levels of the *cavea*, which could have served as a sound reflector. A most interesting feature is the use of *ēcheia*, bronze vases of different dimensions placed on different spots in the *cavea* with the intention of making certain notes sound louder than others, described to us by Vitruvius but actually already known by Peripatetic sources (see *Problems* XI 8, quoted above):

> ... bronze vases are to be made in mathematical ratios corresponding with the size of the theatre. They are to be so made that, when they are touched, they can make a sound from one to another of a fourth, a fifth and so on to the second octave. Then compartments are made among the seats of the theatre, and the vases are to be so placed there that they do not touch the wall, and have an empty space around them and above. They are to be placed upside down. On the side looking towards the stage, they are to have wedges put under them not less then half a foot high. Against these cavities openings are to be left in the faces of the lower steps two feet long and half a foot high ... Thus by this calculation the voice, spreading from the stage as from a centre and strik-

thymelē' is quoted in a literary fragment of the early fifth century BC:

> What is this hubbub? What are these dances? What arrogance has come upon the loud-chattering Dionysian altar / *polypataga thymelan*? (Pratinas fr. 1 Snell *apud* Athenaeus *The Deipnosophists* 17b–c).

As far as roofed music-halls are concerned (*ōideia*, literally 'public buildings for musical performances' < *ōidē* = 'song'), the archaeological evidence has been less generous, because none of these roofed theatres survived in full. A literary account[16] describes the *Odeum* in Athens as a building with multiple columns and beams to hold up the roof (the lack of technology made this the only possible structure with which to support large surfaces in the fifth century BC).[17] The acoustics of such an indoor theatre would have been very complex compared with the acoustics of an outdoor theatre: many reflected and reverberant sounds would interact with the direct sounds, causing such inconvenient acoustical effects as annoying echoes in the auditorium and an over-reverberance inherent to the monumental volume of the building. However, I do not regard this as proof of an absolute lack of scientific understanding of room acoustics by the ancients, as some scholars have resolutely stated.[18] We have plenty of evidence about ancient knowledge of acoustical phenomena, and we can be reasonably sure that the construction of a roofed theatre with the explicit intention to play music inside resulted from the demand of having a more reverberant auditorium, even if the *ōideia* were later on employed also for other activities apart from musical performance.

To sum up, empirical enquiry into ancient theatres carried out in recent years by scholars may be weakened if it is not supported by a careful investigation of theoretical sources and by thorough examination of the different performing arts which took place there through a historical perspective. On a broader level, it seems quite evident that there was indeed amongst the ancient Greeks and Romans an acoustical intentionality underlying their building of theatres, which was mindful of acoustical laws,[19] even if their scientific approach was mainly an empirical-deductive one.

For the Greeks the creation of a work of art was a quest for a purely abstract geometry which, through mathematical proportions, could express that symme-

Figure 7.2. *Theatre of Siracusa (Sicily), panoramic view.*

try and proportion the ancients regarded as synonymous with 'the beautiful' in visible things:

> Being beautiful is being well-proportioned and measured (Plotinus *Enneads* I 6.1).

Notes

*   Translations of the ancient Greek and Latin texts comes from the Loeb Classical Library's editions, quoted in the bibliography under the name of the translator.

1. On this topic our main source is Aristotle's *Poetics*, which relates the origins of the drama to extemporary beginnings: according to him (*Poetics* 1449a), the tragedy finds its roots in the choral lyric devoted to Dionysus, called 'dithyramb'; the comedy in the phallic songs performed at the village festivals by a processional chorus. As a matter of fact, in its earliest forms the drama was essentially choral, with only one actor (most probably the chorus' leader) dialoguing with it.

2. Pollux VII 125; Photius s.v. *ikria*; Suidas s.v. *ikria*.

3. Suidas s.v. *Aischylos*; Suidas s.v. *Pratinas*.

4. The meaning of the word *theatron*, which corresponds to the Latin *cavea*, was later on extended to signify the all building.

5. Cf. Plato *Laws* 817c; Diodorus of Sicily *Library of History* XV 7 and XVI 92; Aristotle *The Art of Rhetoric* 1403b.

6. Barron 1993, 228.

7. This passage is based on an older writing, Gavius Bassus' *On the Origin of Words* (first century BC).

8. Aristotle ascribes the introduction of the scene-painting to Sophocles (see *Poetics* 1449a).

9. For a discussion of this problem (furnished with a rich bibliography), see Di Benedetto & Medda 1997, 28f.

10. Canac 1967, 107ff.

11. Vitruvius *On Architecture* V 6: 'thus the stage will be made wider than that of the Greeks because all the actors play their parts on the stage'.
12. See the comment at this chapter of Vitruvius' treatise in Gros 1997, 687ff.
13. For this interpretation, see Landels 1967.
14. Musical contests occured since the archaic age at religious festivities in different time of the year (e.g. the Panathenaic festival in Athens). It seems more than probable that, after its building, the Dionysian theatre became the favourite place for this kind of exhibitions. For a detailed collection of ancient sources on this topic, see Frei 1900 and Bethe 1901.
15. The cell does not show any undergound connection with other galleries, so that it could have hardly had the function of a Charonian staircase (a scenic passage for the ghosts' apparitions from the underworld).
16. Plutarch *Pericles* 13.9.
17. See some modern restoration drawings of the Odeum, based on the archeological remains, in Izenour 1992, fig. 1.2 b–e.
18. Izenour 1992.
19. Vitruvius *On Architecture* V 3: 'Therefore the ancient architects following nature's footsteps, traced the voice as it rose, and carried out the ascent if the theatre seats. By the rules of mathematics and the method of music, they sought to make the voices from the stage rise more clearly and sweetly to the spectators' ears'.

References

Anti, C., 1951/1952. L'acustica fattore determinante della storia dei teatri greci e romani. *Atti e memorie dell'Accademia Patavina di scienze, lettere ed arti. Classe di scienze morali, lettere ed arti* 64, 25–49.

Barron, M., 1993. *Auditorium Acoustics and Architectural Design*. London: E & FN Spon.

Bethe, E., 1901. Thymeliker und Skeniker. *Hermes* 36, 597–601.

Canac, F., 1967. *L'acoustique des théâtres antiques: ses enseignements*. Paris: Édition du Centre National de la Récherche Scientifique.

Di Benedetto, V. & E. Medda, 1997. *La tragedia sulla scena*. Torino: Einaudi.

Frei, J., 1900. *De certaminibus thymelicis*. Basel: ex officina E. Birkhaeuser.

Granger, F., 1969. *Vitruvius, On Architecture*, vol. I: *Books 1–5*. London: Heinemann.

Gros, P., 1997. *Vitruvio. De architectura*. Torino: Einaudi.

Gulik, Ch.B., 1969. *Athenaeus: the Deipnosophists*, vol. VI: *Books 13–14.653b*. London: Heinemann.

Hett, W.S., 1969. *Aristotle*, vol. XV: *Problems. Books 1–21*. London: Heinemann.

Hunninger, B., 1956. Acoustics and acting in the Theatre of Dionysus Eleuthereus. *Mededelingen der Kon. Nederl. Akademie van Wetenschappen*, 19/9, 303–39.

Izenour, G. I., 1992. *Roofed Theatres of Classical Antiquity*. New Haven (CT) & London: Yale University Press.

Landels, J.G., 1967. Assisted resonance in ancient theatres. *Greece and Rome* 14, 80–94.

Leacroft, R. & H. Leacroft, 1984. *Theatre and Playhouse: an Illustrated Survey of Theatre Building from Ancient Greece to the Present Day*. London & New York (NY): Methuen Drama.

Pickard-Cambridge, A., 1968. *The Dramatic Festivals of Athens*. Oxford: Oxford University Press.

Polacco, L., 1990. *Il teatro antico di Siracusa (pars altera)*. Padova: Editoriale Programma.

Poulle, B., 2000. Les vases acoustiques du théâtre de Mummius Achaicus. *Revue archéologique* n.s. 1, 37–50.

Rackham, H., 1969. Pliny. *Natural History*, vol. III: *Books 8–11*. London: Heinemann.

Rolfe, J.C., 1969. *Gellius. Attic Nights*, vol. I: *Books 1–5*. London: Heinemann.

Shankland, R.S., 1972. The development of architectural acoustics. *American Scientist* 60, 201–9.

Shankland, R.S., 1973. Acoustics of Greek theatres. *Physics Today* 26, 30–35.

Chapter 8

The Evidence of the Use of Sound Resonance from Palaeolithic to Medieval Times

Iegor Reznikoff

Many studies have shown that various monuments, from Palaeolithic to medieval times, have resonant qualities. However, almost none of these studies gives any evidence of the awareness or genuine use of these sound qualities by those who constructed the monuments or worshipped in them. What real evidence do we have of the conscious use of resonance in ancient times? Here are given four kinds of evidence which we have studied: two from Palaeolithic caves and two from Antiquity and the Middle Ages.

In recent years many studies have tried to show the resonant qualities of caves, rock formations, temples or megalithic constructions, which are known to have been visited, decorated or constructed by ancient civilizations. Instances include Palaeolithic decorated caves (for a general study see Reznikoff 2002), rock-art sites (see Waller 1993; Chapter 4 this volume),[1] exteriors and interiors of ancient temples in Mexico (Lubman 1998) or in France,[2] and famous megalithic sites (see Watson & Keating 1999; Chapter 2 this volume). But in most cases the question remains unanswered whether the resonant or sound quality of the studied location was appreciated and used as such in ancient times by contemporary people who constructed, painted or marked it and, hence, certainly celebrated in some way within that location or monument. Nowadays orchestras and musicians dislike strong resonance, because it too easily leads to congestion of sounds, and also because it is incompatible with the modern tempered (non-natural) tuning of musical instruments.[3] But what about ancient civilizations?

Even when the quality of the resonance in a place seems obvious to us and must surely have been known to ancient people also, it does not mean that they used this resonance or even appreciated it, since we do not even know, for certain, whether they sang or celebrated with sounds there. And if we believe that indeed they did so, it is only on the basis of the general argument that in oral traditions people sang for whole days and often all night long, especially when marking important events of life. But this, of course, doesn't

prove anything for a given monument: after all, either outside or inside this resonant monument or location contemporary people could have remained silent!

A typical example concerns the resonance of the main chambers of the great Pyramid in Egypt; some experiments — rather *New-Age* in style — were done there, and I have often been asked whether, as a specialist of resonance, I have ever tried to sing there myself. But apart from the delight of simply being there, even if the chambers resonated marvellously, it would not mean that they were constructed for the purpose of sounds, or that such a sound quality was exploited there in some performance or celebration. The same can be said of many of the other studied sites or monuments. For instance, of the various examples given in the well-documented book by P. Devereux (2001), very few studies seem to offer effective evidence of the genuine use of resonance in ancient times.

When a musical *instrument* has been identified as such, it is *de facto* clear that it was used as a musical instrument. However such an identification may sometimes be quite problematic, as was recently demonstrated for prehistoric bone pipes by F. d'Errico (2002), or may remain an open question; for example, it is unclear whether some rhombus-shaped objects in the Upper Palaeolithic should be interpreted as sound producers or as pendants (neck ornaments). Of course the fact that an object produces seemingly worthwhile sounds does not mean that it has been conceived and used as a musical (or simply sound-making) instrument; but in general the identification of a musical instrument is often straightforward. The problem is harder with natural lithophones, in the Upper Palaeolithic, since they were not built on purpose and it is therefore questionable whether they have been used, even if there are some marks on them, whether man-made marks or 'natural' ones. Moreover, even where such marks really do prove to have a human origin, can we be sure that they relate specifically to sounds? Some marks clearly are man-made (for example in the case of red marks or small pictures on sounding stalactites). This, however, still does not prove musical use: there are such marks elsewhere on non-sounding stones and walls. The evidence does not usually lead to firm conclusions. However, it is perhaps convincing enough (see e.g. Dams 1985; Reznikoff 2002, 46; Ablova 2003).

Completely different is the problem of establishing the use of resonance in natural caves, open spaces with echo effects, or even man-made spaces (temples, churches). Given such a space, how is it possible to show that it was used also for its sound quality, and — to come to the main question — *what real evidence do we have of the conscious use of resonance in ancient times?*

The evidence can be supplied by:

a) written records of the time;
b) marked signs or ornaments that can be proved to relate directly to the resonance of the space considered or at least to some parts of it;
c) (for man-made spaces) special architectural features that are obviously acoustical.

The easiest of these to address are of course (a) and (c). Selected below are four sets of evidence that we have studied; two in Palaeolithic caves (related to point (b)) and two belonging to Classical Antiquity and medieval times (related to point (c)). Let us first, however, consider point (a).

Ancient literature

Support from ancient literature is unfortunately almost non-existent. For the most ancient times — the Stone Age — there are of course no written sources at all. For later periods, when some rare texts mention what can be understood as resonance or, more explicitly, echo effects, the sources never, as far as I know, relate to a specific extant monument which is known to us, the only exception being the theatre of Epidaurus. For instance, in the ancient tradition of Finland (known from oral traditions transcribed in the nineteenth century as *Vanhat Runot*, Old Verses, or from the famous novel *The Seven Brothers* by A. Kivi) we learn that echoes were often used in open spaces; but where precisely, and how, we are not told.[4]

The most beautiful, dramatic and complete account of the use and awareness of echo can be found in the life of St Germanus of Auxerre (died AD 448) as told in his life, *Vita S. Germani* (III, 17–18) written around 480 by Constantius of Lyon (Constance de Lyon 480 (1965), 155–9) and later recounted by Bede the Venerable in his famous *Historia Ecclesiastica Gentis Anglorum* completed in 731. Germanus was called to Britain to help to evangelize the invaders, actually the pagan Saxons. The British, who are Christians, had to fight hard against them. A battle was prepared, the troops were facing one another. Because the Picts joined the Saxons, the Christians forces were weaker and the outcome appeared likely to be tragic. But they were not weak in spirit and Germanus — known already for a saint — is with them. He gives voice to the triple Easter Alleluia, for indeed it was Eastertide. As Bede writes, 'the whole army joined in this shout, until the surrounding hills echoed with the sound' (Bede, *Hist. Eccles.*, I, 20). At once, the enemy was convinced that there were British troops hidden in the hills all around them. 'The enemy column panicked, thinking that the very rocks and sky were falling on them' (Bede, *Hist. Eccles.*, I, 20). Terrified they fled the battlefield, put to flight by the Easter Alleluia and its echo.

This battle (*c*. AD 429) took place either at Verulam (St Albans, Hertfordshire) or at Mold (Flintshire, Wales).[5] It is very remarkable that the *incipit* of the Easter Alleluia (on the word *alleluia*, before the melisma) sounds very like trumpets of Victory and can indeed be easily shouted out; it sheds light also on how this Alleluia has to be performed: as the song of our Lord's Victory over Death.[6]

Of course there are many other accounts of the use of echo in the ancient literature (e.g. in Ovid's *Metamorphoses* VIII, 10–20), but the one above is, no doubt, the most impressive.

Concerning resonance, probably the oldest text that mentions it clearly, is found in the Life of St Vincent of Saragossa (Spain, end of the third century AD) as related in the *Acta Sanctorum* (on the 22nd of January, i.e. on St Vincent's day) and retold in verse by the poet Prudentius in the fourth century in Spain.[7] During his martyrdom Vincent, after having been tortured, was left alone in a cave; there, after a while, he started to sing, praising the Lord for the marvels of Creation. Prudentius writes: 'to the sweet song of the martyr, as an emulating voice, answered the echo of the concave space'. The guards, listening, heard many voices singing with Vincent; impressed by the beauty of the sounds but wondering who could be singing with the martyr they came and looked but, of course, they found him alone. This happened several times, and in the end they came to the obvious conclusion:

Vincent must be being accompanied by a choir of angels.[8]

This explanation 'by angels' is often referred to in early medieval texts when describing the sound of a voice singing in a church and what appears to be the choir of harmonics heard in the resonance. It occurs, for example, in Bede's *Historia Ecclesiastica Gentis Anglorum* (IV, 3). Although, as indicated above, we do not know what churches (or cave) were referred to. But it proves, at least, that in those times people were aware of and did marvel at the quality of resonance of their churches. This, as shown below, is confirmed by a much more direct and obvious form of evidence: their architecture (point (c) above). So, to conclude, there is not much precise information available from the literature before the Renaissance. Let us now turn to point (b) which brings us back to prehistoric times.

Statistics

A meaningful connection between man-made signs and the resonance of a cave (or of an open space in connection with rock art), can, in my view, be established only on a statistical basis. Only such a systematic study is reliable: if among signs and pictures some are found to correspond to resonant locations, then we can assert this relationship as shown, if the positive connections are statistically significant. Otherwise doubt remains: perhaps the connection appears just by coincidence.

For a statistical study to be effective, it must be based first for a given cave (or space) and then, by collecting several such studies, one might begin a general comparative study of a range of decorated caves (or open spaces). There have been, until now, very little such statistical studies. Some of them, however, have produced very clear results; at Le Portel (Ariège, France), I obtained an estimate of the correlation of 80 per cent and at Niaux (Ariège) of up to 90 per cent, of pictures found in *well-resonating* locations; it has to be said, however, that at Niaux almost all the pictures are located in the *Salon Noir*, which has very rich acoustics, like a Romanesque chapel, and therefore, of course, almost all the pictures there are in correspondence with this beautiful resonance (Reznikoff 1987, 155). At Arcy-sur-Cure (Burgundy) the correlation is also very high and can be estimated at more than 80 per cent; in other words, most of the pictures are concentrated in the most resonant parts of the cave (Reznikoff 2002, 48).[9] The values we attach to such estimation depend, of course, on the criteria we choose to define what we mean by a *well-resonating* or *good-sounding* location; so a serious discussion is needed.[10] In some caves, such as Oxocelhaya (Pays Basque), the problem, and therefore the criteria, can be complex; in others the result

may depend very much on the criteria chosen — and yet the precise criteria to choose may not be obvious. But even when in a cave there seems to be a high correspondence value some doubt may remain for a particular picture or sign. Given such an individual case, can we be sure that it really was intended to relate to the resonance we hear? It is remarkable that in some cases the answer is in the affirmative. It gives us our first strong evidence.

Red dots in Palaeolithic caves

Among the clearly non-figurative signs often found in prehistoric painted caves are red dots or marks, made of ochre or sometimes of haematite. These dots have a more-or-less round shape, about 2 cm in diameter. Because of this small size they can be found in various locations, including those where, for some reason, a picture could not be painted: perhaps, for example, because the surface is not smooth enough. Since we can exclude pictorial reasons for marking such dots in particular places the question arises as to why they might have been painted where they are. For example, in a long narrow tunnel where one has to crawl, one may find an isolated red dot appearing suddenly on the roof or side wall, whereas there was neither one before that point nor after it, and no other paintings appear to be present at all. What rationale can be given to explain such a situation? An answer is given by the remarkable relationship between such dots and the sound qualities of their locations. As a general rule, *the red dots or marks are related closely to the resonance of the part of the cave where they are located.*

This result, which we reported in 1983 (Reznikoff 1987, 309; Reznikoff & Dauvois 1988, 241 & 244),[11] has received clear verification in some narrow recesses or tunnels (*boyau* in French). In two of these tunnels, one of approximately 6-metre length at Oxocelhaya and one of some 10 metres at Le Portel, a red dot appears at the very location of maximum resonance. Such dots can be found by blind trial in which the investigator, progressing through the tunnel in darkness, puts on the light when maximum resonance is reached and inspects the walls: the red dot is there. Since (1) there is apparently no other reason for painting the dot where it is and (2) the correspondence with the point of maximum resonance is precise, the conclusion, as astonishing as it may seem, is straightforward: the red dots have a sound-resonant meaning. As to probability: if one admits a possible margin of inaccuracy of, say, 10 cm for the location of maximum resonance, the likelihood of locating the dot accidentally at the right location would be 100 to 1 for a tunnel 10 m long and 60 to 1 for one 6 m long. This yields odds for both tunnels combined of 6000 to 1. But at Le Portel, at Oxocelhaya and in other caves, there are other red dots too: one of them in a part of a 10-metre gallery and many others in smaller locations, which still correspond to maxima of resonance, although not in such a spectacular way as I have described above. Considering several locations together, the odds of all these correspondences having come about purely by chance would reduce to something of the order of a million to one. These are very long odds. When we add to them the apparent absence of any other rational explanation, the acoustic meaning of such signs begins to appear very convincing indeed.

Of course, prehistoric people were not studying the acoustics of their tunnels, as such. Our explanation is that since they progressed almost in darkness, they had to make sounds, or in a narrow tunnel just to hum with closed mouth (on a sound like *mm* or *hm*), using the sound as a kind of sonar: the response of the cave or of the tunnel to this signal might tell whether there is space ahead and where to to progress. Reaching the location of maximum resonance (the acoustical main antinode) is very impressive: the whole tunnel resonates to a simple *hm* and the sound can be heard outside the tunnel, in the main cave (there are often pictures in front of the entrance of the tunnel). Progressing further inside the tunnel, one naturally finds oneself pausing at this remarkable sound location. And the dot shows precisely where this living sound point lies, possibly identifying it for use later on. This is our first prehistoric evidence.

Small decorated niches and recesses in Palaeolithic caves

But if the evidence of the red dots proves Palaeolithic people's awareness of resonance, one should expect there to be some more evidence of this. And indeed such dots or marks are also found inside or in the immediate neighbourhood of niches or small recesses. These recesses are too small to have a distinct point of maximal resonance; actually, the whole recess may resonate. As a general rule, *niches or recesses that are painted (with red dots, some marks or pictures) resonate strongly*. This rule applies also to niches, in the immediate vicinity or just in front of which such decorations are found.

Of course one should not expect all sounding niches to be decorated: there are usually too many niches in the cave. But it is interesting to observe that some of the decorated niches sound so easily and so strongly, even just with a single breath or a tiny sound, that it is inconceivable that the person who decorated the niche could have remained unaware of

this phenomenon. It is what we call a *Camarin* effect (Reznikoff 2002, 44).

Decorating them entails making them resonate. There are such niches or recesses in several caves; moreover some possess exceptional decoration.

Probability is unnecessary here to establish awareness of resonance. Clearly those who marked them necessarily experienced a strongly resonance. To summarize our two first arguments, we may say that since Palaeolithic times the sounding quality of tunnels, recesses or niches was known and often used as such. And the same goes for the cave as a whole or for parts of it.

In fact, niches, recesses or alcoves were used as natural *resonators*. They prefigure and introduce our next piece of evidence: the deliberate introduction of small artificial niches, namely vases, into architectural constructions, in order to improve their sound quality.

Acoustic vases in theatres and churches

The principal reference to the use of acoustic vases, or *echea*, in Classical times is to be found in the *De Architectura* of Vitruvius. The vessels used were made of bronze or *terracotta,* earthenware, and according to Vitruvius *De Architectura* (I, 1, 9 and V, 4), were set out in niches around the seating-tiers of some theatres. They were tuned in unison or at the fifth and/or fourth of a main tone, within a range of one or two octaves, in order to amplify the sound of the voice (i.e. the singing voice as in the prosody or poetry of Antiquity). As far as I know, no such pots have been found in what are now the ruins of ancient theatres (see however Bruel 1951), but there is no reason to disbelieve Vitruvius; he is very precise and clear in his account. On the other hand acoustic earthenware pots are found and very well known in later churches. In some extant churches there are still more than a hundred pots *in situ* and there were more in some churches which no longer survive (for example 150 in the ancient church of Orval, in Belgium). Such pots are found throughout Christian antiquity. They are recorded, for example in the fourth-century church of St Victor in Marseille; they are very frequent in Romanesque and Gothic architecture and were still used in Baroque churches. They are found throughout the whole of Europe, including churches of the Russian and Byzantine tradition. Curiously, there are even two acoustic vases situated in the upper corners opposite to the stage of the Rachmaninov hall in the Conservatoire of Moscow, this hall being originally a church (end of the nineteenth century).

The fact that the pots appear in Christian contexts both West and East indicates that their origin goes back to Classical Antiquity; and this should not be surprising since we know that the works of Vitruvius were known and taught in the learned spiritual tradition transmitted by monasteries and monastic schools since Antiquity. There is no known use of pots in Roman temples, and it may be that there was no special interest in sound and resonance in temples in Antiquity (although for the use of the *absida*, see below). In the fourth century Christian tradition adopted, under the Emperor Constantine the Great, the Pantheon of Rome with its famous dome, built in the second century AD, as its prototype for the design of churches: firstly in Jerusalem's Holy Sepulchre and then at St Sophia of Constantinople, in the fourth century (reconstructed in the sixth). With the advent at the Pantheon of the semi-spherical dome, curves were now introduced into religious architecture: not just domes, but also vaults. Just as in the curved spaces of theatres, and because of the priority given to the voice in singing the Holy Scriptures, good acoustics were looked for; and sounding devices, such as pots, were used from time to time.

There is no mention in Christian literature, as far as I know, of acoustic pots in churches until the late Middle Ages, around the fifteenth century.[12] But of course we need to remember that there is virtually no literature about architecture or the construction of churches during the same period; so if we were to go simply by the evidence of literature we might have to conclude that there were no churches built at all! However, whenever pots are mentioned in later sources, it is always in relation to acoustics and *singing*. As Mersenne comments, in the seventeenth century, the pots are set 'in the arches or vaults of churches to help the voices of those who sing'. He explains that the pots are intended to *keep* and *reinforce* the sound (Mersenne 1636, 35).

Strangely, some modern studies of these vases have denied their usefulness from the acoustic point of view, but it must first be understood that their subjects were isolated vases examined in laboratory conditions and not sets of vases analysed *in situ*, in the resonant milieu of the church; moreover, they explored separated frequencies, for example of a speaking voice, and not of continuous singing tones. When one has such a voice and a trained ear, although one or two isolated vases in a church may not change the sound very much at all, the result with a full set of pots is very significant. The sound quality is greatly improved, through a process of reinforcement and *smoothing*, especially around the main frequencies of the vases — usually within the pitch-range of the male voice (100–400 Hz). Indeed in some resonances there are discontinuities in the resonant response: some tones

(pitches) sound well, offering a good response, and yet suddenly some tones almost disappear: the resonance, in other words, is heterogeneous. To take an actual example, in the exceptional resonance of the church of the abbey of Thoronet (Provence) all the sounds — across a wide range of the human voice — elicit an equally good and indeed remarkable response, including lower tones. While in the church of the abbey of Sylvacane (also in Provence), as in many other churches, responses to some tones are weaker than others, especially at lower frequencies. There are, as far as I know, no pots in Sylvacane. Perhaps the resonance there proved good enough without them. These properties of sets of pots, reinforcing and equalizing or smoothing the resonance, have been confirmed by acoustical studies (Floriot 1978; Fontaine 1981).

In most cases pots are distributed in the vaults; but they are also sometimes found in the walls of the choir, at different heights. In the church of Thoronet there are some small cavities at the top of the vault. No pots are contained in them. Nevertheless they appear to have no other architectural rationale: perhaps they were put there to receive pots in the event that the church did not sound as expected; but it does, as we have seen, extremely well.

That there is some acoustic intention behind these devices has never been questioned; for trained musicians, they do have a distinct acoustic effect, and are therefore clear evidence of conscious use and appreciation of sound resonance in churches. In summary, such interest in resonance and its various musical qualities has evidently persisted since ancient times, from Vitruvius to Mersenne and beyond, and is attested both in the ancient literature and from archaeological observation, corresponding to points (a) and (c) above.

The round shapes of these pots and their frequent association with vaults, introduces us to the employment of cylindrical and spherical surfaces in overall architectural construction as further ways of improving sound qualities of buildings.

The apse

One of the main characteristics of churches in Christian antiquity is the vaulted apse (from the Greek *absis*: circle, vault; *absida* in Latin). This can be related to the general use of curved surfaces in architecture. In the fourth century AD, when Christian culture and art emerge and become open to the learned and spiritual knowledge of Antiquity, the masters of architecture and the arts are of course the Romans. From Gaul to North Africa and the Near East they built palaces, theatres, arenas, bridges, aqueducts, bath-complexes (*thermae*) and temples. They mastered the technique of vaulting, particularly for thermae. But the first *religious* monument where the technique was exploited was, as we have seen, the Pantheon of Rome with its famous dome. Built in the second century BC and then rebuilt in the second century AD, it has for more than 1800 years remained structurally perfect, not a stone has moved. Probably because of its name, but also certainly for the beauty and ideal of a dome representing the sky's vault, Constantine the Great (died AD 337) adopted the Pantheon as his architectural model for the further development of the Christian church. Since then, domes and vaults have been used in Western, Byzantine and Russian traditions, and, transmitted by Byzantine architects, were adopted for the Muslim mosque. Subsequently their use spread all over the world. The same techniques of vaulting necessary for domes and half-domes were used for apses and vaulted naves.

One of the advantages of a vaulted ceiling, properly constructed, is that, since it does not use wood, it can last for ever, as we can see from the dome of the Pantheon or the much larger dome of St Sophia of Constantinople (sixth century AD). The vault of the abbey church at Thoronet, completed in AD 1200, also remains perfect to this day, as do the vaults of so many other churches and cathedrals. The second advantage of vaults derives from the quality of the resonance they induce. Resonance is reinforced and improved by curved surfaces. According to the elementary laws of propagation and reflection of sound, cylindrical and spherical surfaces not only concentrate and focus sound but also enhance and prolong the harmonics (overtones) of the original sound.

So, despite the great technical difficulties involved in erecting a vault, its advantages are obvious; however, because there are other architectural advantages as well it is not possible to argue that acoustics were the only consideration in erecting vaults.

The apse is quite a different matter. The apse has the shape of a half-dome (or semi-cupola); sometimes even of two separate half-domes, one placed above the other. There is absolutely no architectural reason for such a complicated construction, when a simple flat wall would be perfectly adequate, exactly as it is at the entrance of the church, at its west end. The reason for the complex curved shape of the apse is obviously acoustic: it focuses the sound of the singing voice facing the apse where the altar is located (from the earliest times, the celebration was sung by the priest). From there the voice can be heard very distinctly up to 100 m away. Because of the apse's shape and of the vaults above, the whole church may resound quite extraordinarily, even with a single voice singing, particularly

in natural intervals; the resonance and the richness of the harmonics often give the impression of a singing choir, the choir of angels mentioned above, following the ancient Christian tradition.[13]

This is the most remarkable evidence of the practical knowledge and use of sound resonance. It certainly represents the highest acoustic achievement in architecture, especially in the Romanesque churches of the eleventh and twelfth centuries. As a work of acoustical engineering, the church of the abbey of Thoronet is a wonder of the world.[14]

Curiously enough, the acoustical rationale behind the complex shapes of apses is never explained in architectural studies or descriptions of churches. In our modern cloth-eared age it is rather suggested that the acoustical properties we hear 'decorate' the architecture, its vaults and arches, whereas it is of course quite the other way around: the architecture was conceived to serve the praise of the Divine World and therefore of the sound. The singing voice of the celebrant must be heard and the beauty of the chant must be enhanced by an appropriate treatment of the building: by an apse and a vaulted nave.

Historically speaking, the origin of the medieval apse is to be found (1) in the absida of the Roman temple, where it is semi-circular but with a flat ceiling; and (2) in the niches constructed in walls to house statuary. Such niches, with the statue removed, became what were called *martyria*: niches with hemispherical ceilings, erected for family worship of the dead and ancestors (Grabar 1943–46). Here again the curved shape focuses the sound and reinforces some higher overtones. This quality was to be mastered with the erection of apses in churches from the fourth century onwards.

Sometimes an adverse acoustic consequence of a dome is that it can concentrate sound under its own volume; a well-proportioned apse, on the other hand, may correct or at least offset this flaw, when the celebration of the Divine Offices is performed at the altar and the celebrant is facing the apse.

In the Western tradition, perhaps for this very reason, large domes are used much less frequently than in Byzantine and Russian traditions. It seems that it is clearness of sound and a relative openness which characterize Western church architecture, contrary to the late Orthodox tradition, where an iconostasis separates the apse and the altar from the transept and the nave, destroying the resonance.

It is very interesting that St Bernard (died AD 1153) decided, for the sake of the simplicity he wanted for the Cistercian order, that the wall at the altar side should be flat, without any apse. This of course was simpler to achieve, from the architectural point of view, but not necessarily beneficial from the acoustic one. There was opposition from within the Order; and when he died, apses began to reappear, despite the difficulty involved in erecting them. The abbey church of Thoronet, which belonged to the Cistercians, however, has a magnificent, deeply-curved apse and no fewer than four apsidal chapels. The many churches that adopted the flat end-wall, for example the abbey churches of Sylvacane (Provence) and Fontenay (Burgundy), do not sound the same as those with apses; when one sings from the choir there is an obvious scattering of the sound, quite contrary to the focusing which an apse achieves. The sound is less clear, less powerful, although it may still be very beautiful because of the vaulted ceiling of the choir and the nave.[15]

Conclusion

We can see, through the ages, continuity in the discovery and use of resonance and of its marvels: naturally vaulted galleries, curved recesses and round niches, or artificially-made pots and apses or vaulted choirs and naves. From the Palaeolithic caves to antique theatres and churches with the same curved lines and forms, resonance was appreciated for celebrations, chanting and singing, with the human voice praising the Invisible and its resonating mysterious sounds. In fact these curved lines are also those of our skull, palate and throat which have in a very real sense an apsidal structure, serving a similar projectory function.

It is remarkable that alongside these architectural and acoustical adaptations, which are common to caves, temples and churches, there is one other common element: pillars, whether made from the junction of stalactites and stalagmites, forming fluted columns,[16] or man-made pillars of ancient Greek and Roman palaces, theatres and temples, and of course medieval churches. It is as if the same cave, the same sanctuary, the same cathedral was rediscovered or reconstructed ever since our first and deepest sanctuary: in the womb of our Mother — woman, earth or God (Reznikoff 2005). Nowadays this understanding and practice of architectural sound is lost; or rather, as I pointed out in the introduction, it is concerned with quite different needs: because, of course, resonance must be avoided for modern orchestras, ensembles and their music. Opera and concert halls today are thus built according to a completely different acoustic premise. The magic practice singing with echoes is forgotten.

Moreover, even when performances take place in a temple or sanctuary, it doesn't mean that the performers always use and appreciate its ancient resonance. Today, almost all of the concerts performed in Romanesque churches ignore or even, by means of stages, curtains and other devices, try to avoid the often remarkable acoustics of these churches. But here we meet a genuine difficulty: to really sing *in a resonance*, that is, fully using its acoustic character, we need to sing in *just intonation* i.e. in the natural pure intervals of resonance, and not those of the modern equally-tempered scale. Just intonation was, of course, precisely one of those natural tonalities which characterized ancient singing. These intervals are still, although decreasingly, practised in the musical traditions which have preserved the spirit of Antiquity by oral transmission of their learned spiritual chant and music. For many of us, a rigorous practice of natural intervals in strong resonances has been a wonderful school for just intonation and an entry-point into ancient modal chants. This opens onto a wide world that extends, as we have seen, from the depths of caves and the rituals of ancient temples and churches to choirs of angels sounding in everlasting divine harmony.

Notes

1. See also Reznikoff 2002, and for a study around lakes, in Finland, Reznikoff 1995. See also Goldhahn 2002.

2. See the author's studies on the resonance of Romanesque and Romanesque-Gothic churches in the booklets of the CDs quoted in the footnotes below.

3. In the marvellous resonance of the church of Vézelay (Burgundy, France), I used, for early Christian chant performed in natural intervals, the most resonant (Romanesque) part of the basilica, while M. Rostropovitch, for his recording of the Bach's Suites for cello solo, used the less resonant (Gothic) part of it. Listen to the two CDs *Le Chant de Vézelay* (Le Vase de Parfum), Studio SM, (1221.16), Paris, 1992, and *Le Chant de Vézelay* (Marie-Madeleine au Tombeau), Studio SM, (1221.62), Paris, 1993, and to M. Rostropovitch, *J.S. Bach, Suites pour violoncelle*, 2 CD, Emi classics (5554922), 1995 (recorded 1991); also in DVD (5991599).

4. My record-breaking performance, with, by chance, ideal conditions on the lake of Valamo in Finland, scores at twelve echoes. It was real magic.

5. For Verulam, see Lot 1939, 97; and for Mold, see Usher 1639, ch. XI. At Mold there is still a Maes-Germen Valley. These two references are taken from R. Borius, see Constance de Lyon 480 (1965), 86–7.

6. Cf. *Le Chant du Thoronet* (CD), Studio SM, Paris 1980, where this Alleluia is performed.

7. A. Prudentius, *Peristephanon*, Hymnus V (St Vincent's Passion), v.313–16.

8. St Vincent is therefore the patron saint of those who sing in a resonance and particularly the patron saint of the musical archaeologists working on the resonance of monuments and, of course, of caves.

9. At Arcy the correlation is straightforward: the more the

echoes in the cave (up to seven) the more the pictures.

10. See Reznikoff 2002, 42 & 46 (for caves), 50 (for rocks in open spaces where the criterion is based on the number and quality of echoes). The criterion of echoes given by clapping hands as suggested by S. Waller is, in many cases, certainly too poor or too loose a criterion for reliable results. A voice, making sounds in natural intervals is usually the most relevant; it is, of course, anthropologically the richest and most valid tool to study and understand a possible human awareness and use of resonance in caves for rock sites (see below in the text).

11. As we discovered it in Le Portel.

12. See Viollet-Le-Duc 1895, 471–2; Viollet-Le-Duc was probably the first to study acoustic vases, he quotes a text of the year 1432. The pots are mentioned later by Italian Renaissance architects e.g. Francesco di Giorgio Martini (1490). An early modern study is Hills (1881–82, 65–81). This reference is quoted from Tallon (1992); A. Tallon was my former student at the University of Paris. The recent studies are Floriot (1978), his important *Contribution à l'étude des vases acoustiques du Moyen-Age* (1964), and Fontaine (1979; 1981).

13. Cf. *Le Chant de Vézelay* (see note 3).

14. Cf. *Le Chant du Thoronet* (see note 6).

15. Cf. *Le Chant de Fontenay* (CD), Studio SM, (1216.40) Paris, 1989.

16. As in Oxocelhaya (Pays-Basque).

References

Ablova, A., 2003. Ringing stones: the interpretation of archaeological musical monuments, in *Musical Semiotics Revisited*, ed. E. Tarasti. (Acta Semiotica Fennica XV, Approaches to Musical Semiotics 4, Studia Musicologica Universitatis Helsingiensis IX.) Helsinki: Studia Musicologica Universitatis Helsingiensis, 585–90.

Bruel, P., 1951. *Sound Insulation and Room Acoustics*. London.

Constance de Lyon, 480 (1965). *Vita Germani*, ed. & trans. R. Borius. Paris: Sources Chrétiennes.

Dams, L., 1985. Paleolithic lithophones: description and comparisons. *Oxford Journal of Archeology* 4/1, 31–46.

d'Errico, F., 2002. Just a bone or a flute?, in *Studien zur Musikarchäologie* III: *Papers from the 2nd Symposium of the International Study Group on Music Archaeology, Monastery Michaelstein (Germany), September 2000*, ed. E. Hickmann. (Orient-Archäologie 107.) Berlin: Rahden, 89–90.

Devereux, P., 2001. *Stone Age, Soundtracks: the Acoustic Archaeology of Ancient Sites*. London: Vega.

di Giorgio Martini, F., 1490 (1967). *Trattati di Architettura Impequaria et Arti Militare*, trans. L.J. Baldasso. Milan.

Floriot, R., 1964. Contribution à l'étude des vases acoustiques du Moyen-Age. Unpublished thesis, Faculté des Sciences de l'Université d'Aix-Marseille.

Floriot, R., 1978. Les vases acoustiques du Moyen-Age. *Bulletin du Groupe d'Acoustique Musicale* (GAM), 98.

Fontaine, J.M., 1979. *Contribution à l'étude des vases acoustiques disposés dans les églises (XIe–XVIIIe s.)*. Paris: Mémoire Ingénieur CNAM.

Fontaine, J.M., 1981. Un système historique de correction sonore: les vases acoustiques, in *Colloque Qualité acoustique des lieux d'écoute*. Paris: Université de Paris VI, 93–117.

Goldhahn, J., 2002. Roaring rocks: an audio-visual perspective on hunter-gatherer engravings in northern Sweden and Scandinavia. *Norwegian Archaeological Review* 35, 29–60.

Grabar, A., 1943–46. *Martyrium. Recherches sur le culte des reliques et l'Art chrétien antique*. 2 vols. Paris.

Hills, G.M., 1881–82. Earthenware pots (built into churches) which have been called acoustic vases. *Transactions of the Royal Institute of British Architects* 1881–82, 65–81.

Lot, F., 1939. *Les Invasions Germaniques*. Paris.

Lubman, D., 1998. An Archeological Study of Chirped Echo from the Mayan Pyramid at Chichen Itza, Conference at the Acoustical Society of America, October 1998, Norfolk, VA; see www.ocasa.org/memberlinks.htm, also www.eden.com/~tomzap/sounds.html.

Mersenne, M., 1636 (1975). *Harmonie Universelle*, vol. 3: *Livre de l'Utilité de l'Harmonie*. Facsimile edition. Paris.

Reznikoff, I., 1987. Sur la dimension sonore des grottes à peintures du Paléolithique, in *Comptes Rendus Academie Sciences Paris* 305, série II. Paris.

Reznikoff, I., 1995. On the sound dimension of prehistoric painted caves and rocks, in *Musical Signification: Essays on the Semiotic Theory and Analysis of Music*, ed. E. Tarasti. (Approaches to Semiotics 121.) New York (NY): Mouton de Gruyter, 541–57.

Reznikoff, I., 2002. Prehistoric paintings, sound and rocks, in *Studien zur Musikarchäologie* III: *Papers from the 2nd Symposium of the International Study Group on Music Archaeology, Monastery Michaelstein (Germany), September 2000*, ed. E. Hickmann. (Orient-Archäologie 107.) Berlin: Rahden, 39–56.

Reznikoff, I., 2005. On primitive elements of musical meaning, see www.musicandmeaning.net, *Journal of Music and Meaning* 3 (Invited papers).

Reznikoff, I. & M. Dauvois, 1988. La dimension sonore des grottes ornées. *Bulletin de la Société Préhistorique Française* 85/8.

Tallon, A., 1992. Acoustique de l'architecture médiévale. Unpublished mémoire de maîtrise, Département d'Art et d'Archéologie, Université de Paris IV, Paris.

Usher, J., 1639. *History of the Antiquity of the Briton Church*. Dublin.

Viollet-Le-Duc, E., 1895. Pot, in *Dictionnaire Raisonné de l'Architecture Française du IXe au XVIe s.*, vol. VII. Paris, 471–2.

Waller, S., 1993. Sound reflection as an explanation for the content and context of rock art. *Rock Art Research* 10, 2.

Watson, A. & D. Keating, 1999. Architecture and sound: an acoustic analysis of megalithic monuments in prehistoric Britain. *Antiquity* 73(280), 325–36.

Chapter 9

Large Scale–Small Scale: Medieval Stone Buildings, Early Medieval Timber Halls and the Problem of the Lyre

Graeme Lawson

This paper identifies medieval and post-medieval archaeology as a profitable, indeed essential, background to the study of acoustics in prehistoric built environments, being at a point in time where ethnography and archaeology converge, and where ethnographical models may thus be compared with and tested against closely-related archaeological material. It further identifies the design and manufacture of ancient musical instruments and sound tools as useful analogues for ancient architectural design and engineering, and asks whether we might expect there to have been actual connections between their respective acoustic traditions. Two examples illustrate some of the issues at stake. In the first place is a problem which parallels that of Bronze Age megalithic acoustics: ship-shaped stone-settings and timber buildings of the early medieval period in northwest Europe. Records from the early Middle Ages confirm 'Dark Age' timber halls, whose ground-plans survive, to have been places where speech and music, specifically of lyres, played an important part. Lyres are now well-known from excavated finds of the sixth and seventh centuries. Their forms show what appear to be acoustical sophistications, yet these do not seem to result in expansive output characteristics when replicated. Could the forms of the buildings themselves have served to compensate? In the second place is the architectural adoption of instrument-like 'inserts' for acoustical effect, including resonating jars beneath the choirs of medieval churches. The medieval West Front of Wells Cathedral, in the southwest of England, possesses two sophisticated acoustical adaptations, conceived and built into the masonry structure from the outset: these can been shown to have been intended specifically for — and used in — the performance of processional music for Palm Sunday.

One of the very practical problems afflicting acoustical approaches to prehistoric monuments has been the reluctance of archaeology, one of its two parent disciplines, to accept sound as a worthwhile — and sometimes even a valid — subject for archaeological enquiry. Scepticism is right and proper, of course; and archaeoacoustics, if it is to survive and prosper in that scientific environment, must address such doubts. But to investigators it sometimes feels a frustrating up-hill struggle. Despite all the thought and energy devoted to the work, often it seems that the novelty of archaeoacoustics counts against it, especially in relation to funding. Marginalization is the perceived consequence. If ever a subject's development was held back by institutional indifference it is surely this.

However, the acoustician's situation is by no means unique. Students of the archaeology of *musical* sound have had a rather similar experience, which it may be instructive to review briefly. The historical development of their subject, so-called music-archaeology, has already to a large extent rehearsed many of the problems of archaeoacoustics today: it has been characterized largely by individual pioneers, working more-or-less in isolation, struggling to maintain a footing in the archaeological mainstream, sometimes abandoning it altogether. With relatively few exceptions, support — and employment — has tended to come rather from the sphere of ethnomusicological, music-historical and performance studies. Familiar cries from archaeology have been 'surely finds are rare: there can't be enough material', or 'surely this is more to do with music than archaeology'. (As if prehistoric agriculture was more to do with farmers!) Although there have been several research dissertations, up to and including doctoral level, barely a handful of these have been archaeologically based and supported. The same researchers may have given countless student seminars and public lectures, yet still no regular provision has been made (to my knowledge) in *any* university archaeology teaching curriculum. There is still no specialist centre for undergraduate or postgraduate students to go to in order to join a programme of music-archaeological study.

All this has impacted negatively across the whole field, even to the excavation and conservation of our music-related source-material. The special needs of music-archaeological finds in conservation continue to be dealt with haphazardly, on a shoe-string: often fudged, too often ignored. Outstanding, newsworthy finds continue to be viewed as art-relics, of interest to special interest groups, rather than contextualized artefacts of material culture, of importance to us all. The parallels with archaeoacoustics are all too obvious!

Yet such slow progress seems strange when we consider how long music-archaeological research has been active and how far it has now advanced. It has already been in development for more than forty years. In Great Britain its modern beginnings can be traced back to the first pioneering publications of Vincent Megaw and John Coles in the 1960s. Two of the great strengths of Megaw's and Coles's early contributions were the way they each combined their musical and archaeological interests and competences in a seamless, truly interdisciplinary way. In Megaw's work a particular strength has been the way in which, from the outset, he has seen the subject as a multi-period challenge, in which problems of music's early prehistory could and should be addressed in tandem with comparable problems in the Roman period, the Middle Ages and even later times (see especially Megaw 1968). This vision, happily, has slowly infected music-archaeological thinking as a whole, and has been lent further encouragement by the disproportionate quantities in which later finds have since come to light. The Middle Ages in particular have yielded a rich seam, affording valuable opportunities for comparative study within the context of human populations which, although pre-Industrial, we can still be confident were 'culturally modern'. I commend them warmly to the attention of prehistoric acousticians too.

If, developmentally, there is already much common ground between archaeoacoustics and music-archaeology, further correspondence and convergence between them would seem highly desirable — indeed it was one of the principal aims of this meeting. The thought also occurs to me that there are aspects of their respective methodologies which could benefit from such interaction. I therefore want to take this opportunity to set out some examples in which it seems to me that the archaeology of monuments and the archaeology of music do already coincide materially. In making my selection I have chosen three medieval cases in which additional measures of support can be elicited from historical tradition. I should stress that I have done this not in order to 'cheat' — I think we can reasonably infer acoustic intention in at least two of them from their material record alone. I refer to such documents primarily to demonstrate that these ideas are *not* just products of our fevered imaginations but — in keeping with our theme of 'intentionality' — represent real phenomena linked to real acoustic behaviours.

Example 1. Adaptations in ceramics: resonant pots

My first example, which is now quite well known, seems to illustrate this quite neatly. In restoration work on medieval buildings pottery vessels (or their remains) are from time to time encountered, built horizontally into the original masonry and left open at the neck in such a way as to suggest that they may have performed some acoustic function. Generally such pots are indistinguishable from types used in ordinary domestic settings, so their acoustic properties are unlikely to have been purposed by their manufacturers: it is their subsequent treatment — their placement and orientation — that is suggestive. The proposition that they are associated with sound is further corroborated by the nature and purpose of their contexts. Some are located in chapels, or buildings which once served that function (such as the Old Library of Pembroke College, Cambridge).[1] Their employment there would make sense because such small buildings would have had a correspondingly 'small' acoustic; and that may have been regretted in a culture in which prestige in architecture often was associated with a 'large' acoustic. They make still further sense when we note that their employment in buildings of slightly larger dimensions, such as parish churches, is not random but always associated with one very particular part: a small enclosure close to or within the chancel. Two examples from medieval Norwich are illustrated by

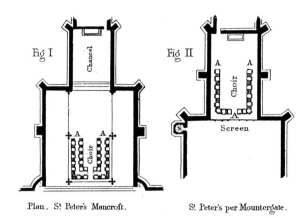

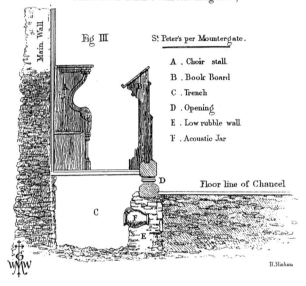

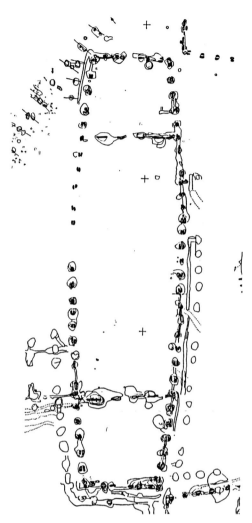

Figure 9.1. *Norwich, St Peter Mancroft and St Peter Mountergate: ground plans and vertical section of medieval choirs, showing underfloor spaces and the locations of 'acoustic jars'. (From McKenny Hughes 1915.)*

Figure 9.2. *Fyrkat, Denmark: ground plan of one of the large timber halls within the Viking-period fortress (House 2V) showing post-hole layout and characteristic curvature (conventionally described as 'boat-shaped'). (From Olsen & Schmidt 1977, fig. 120.)*

McKenny Hughes and are reproduced here (Fig. 9.1; McKenny Hughes 1915). There is clearly an association with some very particular use of this enclosure. The fact that we know from tradition that they are the choirs, precisely where choristers stood to perform liturgical chant, is simply the icing on the interpretive cake. The nature of our enquiry, it seems to me, has already moved on from whether or not these pot-settings are acoustic in purpose. It can now address what they can tell us about the currency of acoustic experience amongst builders, the value attached to it amongst patrons and clients, and any benefits such devices might have conferred upon medieval singers, their art and their audiences.

Example 2. Adaptations in wood: the mead-hall and the lyre

My second example comprises — in terms of architectural space — stone-settings and large timber buildings of the Roman Iron Age and early medieval period in Scandinavia (Lawson *et al.* 1998). The boat-like ground-plans of many of these structures have long been held to justify labelling them 'boat-' or 'ship-shaped', in cultures in which the ship had vital practical as well as social importance and must therefore frequently have held deep symbolic meaning. This may be so, especially of the stone settings, whose orthostats often increase in height towards stem and

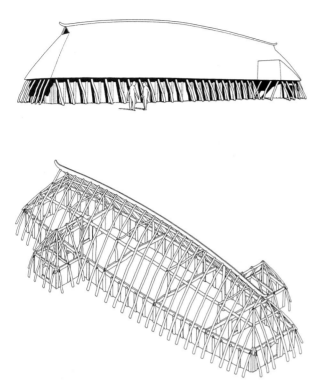

Figure 9.3. *Fyrkat, Denmark: tentative, hypothetical reconstruction of one of the halls, giving an impression of the possible overall shape. (From Olsen & Schmidt 1977, fig. 99.)*

stern. However, the extent to which the timber halls can really have represented ships — except in plan — has never been satisfactorily established. Figure 9.2 shows a late example from the Viking-period fortress of Fyrkat in Denmark. Most investigators are agreed that the bowing-out of the walls must have demanded a corresponding bow in the ridge of the roof (Fig. 9.3). Such ridges are familiar enough, here in Britain, in the shapes of hog-back memorial stones of the same period, which no doubt represent the hall of the dead. But such curvature hardly resembles the straight keel of an upturned boat. Nor is there any boat-like metaphor in the descriptions of such halls in early medieval literature. The name of the most famous of all early medieval mead-halls, *Heorot*, the feasting place of Danish king Hrothgar in the Old English heroic poem *Beowulf*, means 'Hart' (adult male deer, stag). Its gables have 'horns', not prow and stern. But clearly it represents some significant, pressing design choice, for it has introduced considerable complication into the buildings' design and build. There seems little structural advantage in such a shape, unless it is to reduce the height of the gables. Could it have served some acoustical function instead?

As far as I know, no building of this kind has ever been subjected to detailed acoustic modelling;

but even at a glance we can see that the shape is very distinctive and would certainly have responded to sound in a way quite unlike that of a simple rectangular design. Except maybe at the gables, there are *no* parallel walls, an arrangement which would probably have enhanced the audible clarity of speech. It may also have benefitted any persons sitting in the narrower areas furthest from the central hearth trying to hear what was happening there. The idea that these buildings were social spaces where things happened, rather than simply domestic dwellings, is consistent with the archaeological evidence, and enhances the argument. The internal focus of attention, the hearth, seems likely to have been central. The historical evidence advances the case much further. In it we read of the hall-feasts of a warrior elite in which the exchange of heroic speeches and verse occupies a large part of the post-prandial activity. Such lively exchanges — boasting, laments, contemporary heroics and the deeds and genealogies of the ancestors — were central to the culture, so audibility, and especially the intelligibility of speech, would have been extremely important.

If this was indeed the intention behind the boat-like shape it might have a bearing also on the purpose (or subsequent uses) of some of the near-contemporaneous megalithic 'ship' settings. Although these do not seem to have merited explicit mention in the ancient literature, some possess distinctly audible acoustic properties which could also have served such a purpose. If in time we can push this connexion further it could provide a new (albeit still distant) historical perspective on our prehistoric stone alignments. A more immediate prospect, however, may be found in an interesting coincidence of a music-archaeological kind.

Stringed musical instruments of the same period — six-stringed lyres — survive from excavations of graves of kings and warriors of the pre- and early Christian periods (for the most recent finds of which see Lawson 2001). In Old English poetry they are mentioned specifically in the context of the hall, where their principal role seems to have been to accompany the poems themselves. Enough is known of their design and construction to enable us to build accurate replicas and subject them to experimental evaluation. In all cases the materials used, the elegant structures achieved and the ingenuity used to repair subsequent damage reflect considerable investment (anything between 50 and 100 hours of skilled bench-time, for example) and we can only conclude therefore that they must have served some culturally important function. In terms of capability, they certainly generate a sweet, harp-like tone when plucked. Yet even at their loudest, using a strumming technique to which the forms of their bridges seem specially adapted, they hardly output a dramatic volume of sound, considering the milieu in which they are said to have been employed. So here too might be an argument for architectural adaptation. From a purely practical, twenty-first-century point of view, of course, it would have been easier just to build a more responsive instrument. But this might not have been possible in cultural terms. Certainly the designs of these lyres remain static for so long (from their first appearance in the second century to their last in the eleventh) that their forms must have been regulated by some quite powerful tradition (Lawson 2005).

Example 3. Adaptations in stone: acoustic ports in the West Front of Wells Cathedral.

If this second example has seemed to pose more questions than it has answered my final example I hope will redress the balance. In his recent survey of the medieval architecture and embellishment of Wells Cathedral, Somerset, in the southwest of England, and its meaning, Jerry Sampson has drawn attention to some structural developments which appear to be associated with acoustic — indeed musical — behaviours: two rows of external 'port-holes' amongst the statuary set high up on the church's elaborate West Front (Sampson 1998). These are no rough ventilation holes but neat, circular openings in finely-dressed masonry, connecting spaces in the interior of the building with the outside world. Their internal apertures are set at head height above inner platforms, suggesting that they are there expressly to enable anyone standing on the platforms to see, or hear, or project sound through them. Since neither the view nor audible external sound seems sufficient to justify the care that has been taken or the number of holes made, some sound-*making* intention seems a reasonable explanation.

Historical evidence for the uses to which the building and the spaces around it were put, especially in the area immediately outside the West Front, supports this conclusion. Examination of the documentary evidence leads Sampson to propose a connection with the dramatic, almost theatrical, role which such façades came increasingly to serve during the Middle Ages. The earliest Wells *consuetudinary* (or 'customary' — the manuscript manual detailing the yearly round of liturgical and other observances to be made in and around the site) dates from around 1270–1300, and is a direct adaptation of Sarum (Salisbury) use to Wells's particular needs (Sampson 1998, 168). There is much to be read in such manuscripts concerning the musical

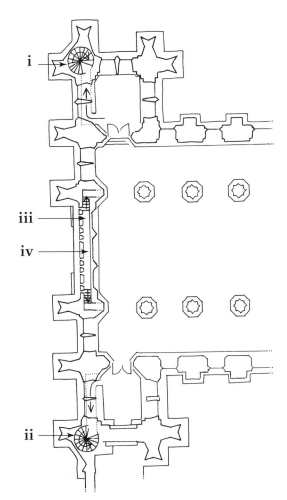

Figure 9.4. *Wells Cathedral, Somerset, England: plan of the West end (i and ii — the NW and SW processional stair-wells; iii — the gallery; iv — masonry screen). (From Sampson 1998: xviii.)*

practices of different churches and their repertoires of chant. But of especial interest to acoustical studies at Wells is a description of the great procession which was to take place annually on Palm Sunday. From it we learn how, on this very important day of the Christian calendar and in front of large crowds gathered in the lay cemetery opposite the West Front (now the open lawn of Cathedral Green), the ceremonial would conclude with a spectacular recreation of Christ's entry into Jerusalem. The whole procession by this time having already made a ritual circuit of the cathedral and its environs, three clerks would sing Matthew's gospel narrative. After each verse, we are told, the leader should sing *En rex venit* and the choristers take it up. At a second station, probably closer in to the great West Door, the procession would halt and choristers would sing the *Gloria laus*, after which the procession would move off-centre towards one of the

Figure 9.5. *Wells Cathedral, West Front, view showing (i) the four quatrefoil niches containing the ?singers' ports and (ii) the row of eight ?trumpet ports high in the gable. (Photograph: Graeme Lawson.)*

aisle doorways where three priests would sing *Unus autem*. The procession would then enter the church through the West Door and progress down the nave to a fourth station in front of the rood screen, to the sound of a solo voice singing the anthem *Ave rex noster*, and on the third repeat the whole choir would join in.

Of all these powerful events (and this is only a brief synopsis of the elaborate detail supplied in the thirteenth-century manuscript) Sampson identifies the *Gloria laus* and the triumphal entry as the key moments affecting the liturgical function of the West Front (1998, 169). In each case the numbers of singers are precisely specified: three priests to sing *En rex venit*, three to sing the *Unus autem*, and in particular seven choristers to sing the *Gloria laus*. Sarum usage specifies they be posi-

tioned not simply on the ground but somewhere high up 'in eminente loco'. At York, where there was no permanent, dedicated provision for this, the erection of some kind of trestle or platform is specified. Here at Wells, however, it seems to have been embodied in the construction of the building itself

Sampson notes the unusual width of the stairwells in the northwestern and southwestern corners of the West Front, which suggests to him a processional function (Fig. 9.4:i–ii). From the way in which such provision has imposed structural difficulties within the rest of the design he infers that this function must have been an important one. Perhaps it was to accommodate a sub-procession of the Palm Sunday procession, and maybe those of other feasts too. One of the routes which opens off (and connects) the two stairways is a strange, long, 1.5-m-wide gallery, immediately above the West Door (Fig. 9.4:iii). It is lit by 12 small circular openings in the outer wall which look out across Cathedral Green through four quatrefoil niches in the facade (Fig. 9.5). Originally these niches held angel statues. Eight of the holes, in four pairs, are 4 feet (1.23 m) above ground level and the other four at 5 ft 6 inches (1.67 m). On its inner side the gallery is separated from the nave of the church by a solid screen of masonry (Fig. 9.4:iv), and so is independent of it acoustically. Sampson does not fully explain why seven junior choristers needed eight holes, or why four additional ports of adult-height (and slightly different form) needed to be provided. However he is convinced that this *is* the function of the gallery, and envisages the boys' voices emerging from it and wafting ethereally over the crowd. The singers' faces would have been effectively invisible behind the brilliantly painted angel sculptures — from which (to the medieval believer) the music would have appeared to emanate. Sampson draws further, practical support from the success of an experiment by Dean Mitchell (not otherwise detailed) in which the choir's voices could be heard right across the Green and 'the enclosed passageway acted as a resonance chamber'.

The gallery chamber does certainly present strongly resonant properties — naturally, since it is an enclosed rectangular space lined throughout with straight, flat, parallel walls, floor and ceiling of smoothly dressed stone, and has stone stairs rising *up-wards* at each end (the gallery is in effect a mezzanine).[2] However, such resonance may be less intentional — in terms of the practical musical and ceremonial purpose of the structure — than its acoustic separation from the nave, which is very pronounced. It may also be less significant than the acoustic properties of the ports themselves. If it is striking how these are located so as to present themselves precisely to standing singers, both adults and juveniles, their shapes also seem very precisely engineered — and precisely similar. At time of writing (2002) their acoustic properties have yet to be modelled by the present writer; however, several preliminary observations may already be made of an archaeological kind.

Firstly, their steeply conical longitudinal section and very smooth finish seem eminently consistent with sound-related use. Because they expand from a narrower external opening to a wider internal one they present the putative singer with a horn-mouth into which to sing, not so much like a megaphone as like an early mechanical recording microphone (Fig. 9.6). Secondly, it is notable that where the cone opens to the outside world it does so through a perfectly circular aperture, plainly and abruptly, without any decorative edging or rounding-off, and within a perfectly smooth, flat wall surface. Again this recalls recent acoustic devices: in particular the forms of some early public-address loudspeakers, such as those of old-fashioned school classroom radios, which were set in the centres of large, flat wooden boards. Such flat surfaces were employed to enhance forward projection of output sound within certain frequency ranges; and intriguingly they hark back to principles long employed in the manufacture of traditional musical instruments. A similar relationship, helpfully, characterizes the sound-holes of medieval wooden stringed instruments such as harps, where they are often circular and open out similarly from resonant chambers onto flat external surfaces. It is also a recurrent characteristic of many mouth-blown wind instruments whose bores, instead of flaring trumpet-like at their distal end, terminate in the centre of a flat disc. This is a familiar feature of the school recorder or block-flute, and of traditional Scottish and English bagpipe chanters. It is also found in shawms: reed-pipes of oboe kind current in Mediterranean and Asiatic cultures, which are well represented not only today but in the musical iconography of medieval Europe too.

One wonders whether this apparent convergence between instrument and architecture is entirely coincidental: whether practical experience with the sounds of medieval instruments could in any way have informed architectural engineering. Such transfer-

Figure 9.6. *Wells Cathedral, West Front, view from inside the gallery, showing the conical form of one of the eight ?chorister's ports (and eighteenth-century graffiti). The metal grille is a comparatively recent addition to exclude pigeons. Through the port can be seen the left-hand side-wall of the quatrefoil niche (this being the left port of a pair). (Photograph: Wendy Lawson, by kind permission of the Dean and Chapter.)*

ability between the small-scale and the large-scale, if extensive, could have implications for our understanding of prehistoric acoustic architectures. Significantly, disc-mounted apertures of closely similar kind are already a highly conspicuous feature of the cast metal horns of the Scandinavian Bronze Age (for which see Chapter 6 this volume, Figs. 6.8 & 6.9).

However this may be, it is at least encouraging from our immediate archaeoacoustical viewpoint that a sound-related function might thus be suspected from the form of the structure itself and its resemblances to other structures of known acoustic intention, even without the support of the documents. Indeed even a brief visit to the site and a cursory inspection of the compact little gallery are sufficient to suggest such a purpose. The importance attached to it by the builders of Wells is indicated by the extent of additional investment which its integration into the building's original design has clearly entailed. There are architectural parallels to consider too.

Elsewhere in England — in the west fronts of the cathedrals of Lichfield in Staffordshire and Salisbury in Wiltshire — Sampson identifies two closely-comparable galleries. Inspection of the vertical sections shown in Figure 9.7 reveals their resemblance to that at Wells. They are clearly not only related in purpose but connected in architectural tradition. There are also some interesting differences. Whereas Lichfield, like Wells, has its gallery separated acoustically from the

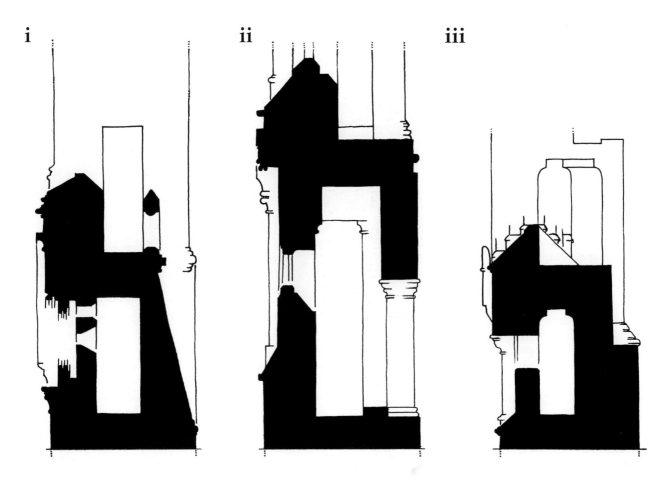

Figure 9.7. *English cathedral west fronts, vertical sections through ?singers' galleries and ports: i) Wells, Somerset; ii) Salisbury, Wiltshire; iii) Lichfield, Staffordshire. (After Sampson 1998, 172.)*

rest of the church, at Salisbury there are large openings (no fewer than four double arches) opening into the nave, which would clearly have allowed sound from the gallery to spill freely into the main body of the church. Perhaps the gallery at Salisbury was meant to serve more than one purpose. Sampson speculates that it may just be associated with performance inside the church of 'liturgical drama', a form of devotional expression which was becoming popular during the twelfth and thirteenth centuries. However, in other respects the correspondence seems close. When originally built the external ports at Salisbury were probably 11cm lower than those at Wells, relative to the putlog holes for a temporary platform there; but otherwise all dimensions are similar: indeed much too similar to have been independently conceived. Sampson playfully envisages the historical Nicholas of Ely, master mason at Salisbury, visiting his contemporary Thomas Norreys at Wells and taking measurements while being shown around — but then adapting the design to his own agenda. At Lichfield, by contrast, the overall dimensions differ markedly from Wells and

Salisbury, and the holes too are somewhat different in form: narrow vertical slits, in four pairs. Yet here also there is an element of correspondence to historical fact for, significantly, only seven of the holes are open and one has been deliberately blanked off. Sampson takes this to confirm their association with the seven choristers of the *Gloria laus* (1998, 172). A third parallel, meanwhile, shows a further, still more distant connexion. At the cathedral of Kilkenny, Ireland, above the west doorway (built — significantly — of Somerset limestone, probably around 1260) are three small openings into a small gallery. This structure is so small it could not have accommodated more than three or four small boys; and apart from music it is difficult to imagine what practical purpose it could possibly have served.

Remarkably we do not need to look as far as Kilkenny, or even Salisbury, to find close parallels for the Wells ports themselves; and this time support for an acoustic explanation is contextual rather than historical. High up in the same central part of the western edifice is a further row of eight circular holes

(Fig. 9.5:ii). This time they emerge not from a gallery but from the large loft space between the roof and the vault of the nave. No documentation refers to them in any way. However, several aspects seem consistent with an acoustical purpose. Firstly, they are conical and have each been treated, at least in part, with the same fine finish as those of the gallery below. There is a similar platform, albeit of rougher construction, at a suitable height inside (Fig. 9.8). But the walls here are of altogether greater thickness, resulting in cones of a much greater length; and only the part of the cone nearest the outer opening is smooth. No singer, unless a contortionist, could sing directly into this smoothed area. On the other hand, their lengths and external diameters are closely consistent with the lengths and distal diameters of trumpets which survive from the medieval period (for a fine archaeological example of which see Lawson & Egan 1988; Lawson 1991). Of particular interest in this respect are the locations of the external apertures within the sculptural iconography of the West Front, set along the top of the Nine Orders of angels. Flanking the Nine Orders Sampson is able to identify two trumpeting angels set in the inward-facing sides of the adjacent buttresses (Sampson 1998, 187–9). The first is a 1.34-m-high, severely damaged figure in the pose of a trumpeter, set in the South-facing side of the left buttress (i.e. immediately to the viewer's left, seen from the Green below). Its sinister hand once held the mouthpiece to its lips, the other

Figure 9.8. *Wells Cathedral, West Front, view from inside the roof space over the West end of the nave, showing seven of the eight conical ?trumpeter's ports beneath their stone lintels, and the rubble platform below them. The timber walk-way is modern. (Photograph: Wendy Lawson, by kind permission of the Dean and Chapter.)*

supporting the instrument at waist-height. The instrument is itself lost, but the mouthpiece and some of the proximal part of the trumpet was evidently present in 1903. The second trumpeter is better preserved: a 1.34-m-high figure visible in the North-facing side of the right buttress (i.e. immediately to viewer's right). The lower part of the trumpet has been anchored just below his crossed knee. Both this additional piece and some of the distal part of the stone are now missing (which, from the ground, makes the instrument appear misleadingly flute-like!) Thus the nine angels and their eight accompanying holes are bracketed by

two trumpeting figures. The effect of such a dramatic combination of image and sound upon a deeply religious (not to say superstitious) medieval observer can only be guessed at.

Conclusions

Clearly tradition of one kind or another, oral or documentary, is greatly beneficial to these three cases. However, interest here lies in the material factors present, or which may reasonably be predicted, that could independently indicate acoustic purpose.

The case for sound-related purpose in so-called 'acoustic vases' arises firstly from their observable acoustic properties. It is sustained, at least for the time being, by the absence of any other obvious explanation for their presence in such unusual locations and dispositions: mounted on their sides in unheated, unventilated air-spaces below floor-level. It is enhanced by their repeated association either with small buildings with little intrinsic resonance of their own or with particular locations in larger buildings. It helps that tradition tells us that these locations are and were choirs; but already we might well feel justified in proposing such attribution even without such knowledge. Analogous vessels are known from the architectures of a range of other cultures, and are represented in suggestive contexts (such as Greek theatres) in some of their archaeologies.

The case for acoustic adaptation in the forms of 'boat-shaped' stone-settings and halls rests at present on documents which link such assembly-spaces to acoustic behaviours such as speech and (in the case of halls) the accompaniment of lyres. It has to be admitted that no lyre has yet been found in either situation. However, since the lyre's association with what we might call 'warrior culture' is now very well attested by fifth- to eighth-century grave finds, it would require only a single identifiable *in situ* fragment to strengthen the archaeological connexion significantly. Such evidence may well come to light in future, and is being actively sought.[3]

The case, finally, for acoustic purpose in the gallery and loft at Wells Cathedral again benefits enormously from documentary tradition, but could stand scrutiny on purely archaeological grounds. In the lower gallery the ports stand at face-level. At Salisbury, where they do not, there is evidence of a temporary timber platform. The dimensions of the ports in the upper gable at Wells coincide with both the meaning of their associated iconography (angels with trumpets) and also with archaeological evidence, from excavations elsewhere, which reveals the forms of trumpets of the period and the manner in which they were played. The acoustic efficiencies of the various port structures, both loft and gallery, have yet to be modelled, but sound-projection of some sort seems so far the only interpretation that explains them convincingly. The external forms of the ports seem to reflect principles utilized in musical instrument technologies of several periods.

How far architects and builders of this or any other time might have shared practical acoustical experience and knowledge with makers of musical instruments we do not know for sure. However, the instruments themselves were evidently as common

in those days as radios and televisions are today, so it would be no surprise if craftsmen of other kinds were familiar with them. That, however, is another story.

Notes

1. I am much indebted to Martin Biddle, for access to his collected notes on acoustic devices in historical architecture, which were one of the starting-points of this study (see Lawson *et al.* 1998).

2. I should like to extend my especial thanks to Canon Melvin Matthews, Wells, for his generosity in granting me access to the hidden wonders of the singers' gallery and to the strange world above the vaults of the nave; also to Elsa van der Zee for so kindly showing me around the site.

3. Since this paper was read two further examples have been discovered. Both, alas, are again from graves; however, a panel of scratched decoration occupying the face of one of them clearly shows a scene of men with shields and spears standing inside — or perhaps immediately in front of — such a building.

References

Lawson, G., 1991. Medieval trumpet from the City of London II. *Galpin Society Journal* XLIV, 150–56 & pls. XXVII–XXVIII.

Lawson, G., 2001. The lyre remains from Grave 32, in *Snape Anglo-Saxon Cemetery: Excavations and Surveys 1884-1992*, eds. W. Filmer-Sankey & T. Pestell. (East Anglian Archaeology 95.) (Grave 32 plans and catalogue entry 77–8 and fig. 56.) Ipswich: Suffolk County Council Archaeology Service (Environment & Transport), 215–23.

Lawson, G., 2005. Music, intentionality and tradition: identifying purpose, and continuity of purpose, in the music-archaeological record, in *Studien zur Musikarchäologie IV*, eds. E. Hickmann & R. Eichmann. (Orient-Archäologie series.) Rahden, Westf.: Verlag Marie Leidorf, 61–97.

Lawson, G. & G. Egan, 1988. Medieval trumpet from the City of London: an interim report. *Galpin Society Journal* XLI, 63–6 & pls. VI–VII.

Lawson, G., C. Scarre, I. Cross & C. Hills, 1998. Mounds, megaliths, music and mind: some thoughts on the acoustical properties *and purposes* of archaeological spaces. *Archaeological Review from Cambridge* 15(1) ('Senses & Perception' issue, 1996), 111–34.

McKenny Hughes, T., 1915. Acoustic vases in churches. Cambridge Antiquarian Society *Communications* XIX, 63–90.

Megaw, J.V.S., 1968. The earliest musical instruments in Europe. *Archaeology* 231, 124–32.

Olsen, D. & H. Schmidt, 1977. *Fyrkat, en Jysk Vikingeborg.* (Nordiske Forntidsminder, Serie B, 3–4.) Copenhagen: Det Kgl. Nordiske Oldskriftselskab/Lynge & Søn.

Sampson, J., 1998. *Wells Cathedral West Front: Construction, Sculpture and Conservation.* Stroud: Sutton Publishing.

Chapter 10

Hunter-Gatherer Music and its Implications for Identifying Intentionality in the Use of Acoustic Space

Iain Morley

In attempting to identify human intention in the use of acoustic features of the environment, it is important that consideration be given to the potential forms and purposes of the activities that may have been carried out in the space under investigation. The significance of the acoustic properties of spaces, and their possible modification, may depend upon the activities practised there. This study describes the types of instruments used traditionally by four groups of modern hunter-gatherers from around the world, and the nature of the musical activities in which they are employed. Legitimate parallels to past auditory behaviours can be based on the pattern of shared constraints; the tools and materials available to these peoples for instrument manufacture often resemble those available to past human groups. Attention is drawn to the diversities and similarities of musical behaviours and instrumentation, and highlights some of the implications that these hold for the use of acoustical space in the past.

In attempting to identify the presence of human intention in the use of acoustic features of the environment, it is important that consideration is given to the potential forms of the activities that may have been carried out in the space under investigation. There are several issues regarding the potential use of sound-spaces which need to be considered. What is the purpose of the acoustic practice carried out in the space? What implications does this purpose hold for the acoustic properties of the space chosen for its execution? Reciprocally, will the acoustic properties of a space have any implications for the way in which an activity was carried out in that space?

Our conceptions of the possible forms of such activities may be broadened by a consideration of the diversity of forms that such behaviours can take in other societies. A sound-space might be actively chosen because its acoustic properties are an important component of the activities carried out there, and/or the activities might be shaped by the acoustic properties of the space in which they are executed. The space may have been chosen specifically for that purpose, or its auditory effects may be unanticipated by-prod-

ucts. Furthermore, we may be considering the use of a space which is a natural environmental feature, or conversely we may be dealing with a space that was constructed for a particular auditory activity.

To consider merely the 'raw' acoustical properties of a structure may fail to address the type of sound that is being created within it. The desirable acoustical property of a space will be determined by the type of sound that is being produced. This has been a major factor in the development of music venues in more recent western history (e.g. baroque music rooms, large halls, choral and resonant vaulted churches, etc.). The one influences the other — the building influences the composition, just as the construction is influenced by the sound to be produced there. So when considering whether human intention underlay the acoustic properties of a particular space, we must first ask about the types of sounds for which that space may have been used.

This paper describes the types of instruments used traditionally by four groups of modern hunter-gatherers from around the world, and the nature of the musical activities in which they are engaged. These groups are the Native Americans of the plains (Blackfoot and Sioux), the Aka and Mbuti African Pygmies, the Pintupi-speaking Australian Aborigines, and the Yupik Eskimos of Southwest Alaska. Between them, they include representatives from each of the continents still inhabited by hunter-gatherers. They also occupy four very different types of environments: rolling temperate grasslands, wet rainforest, arid desert, and Arctic tundra respectively. In each case, the ways in which music is employed within those cultures, the use of instruments and their materials of manufacture will be examined with a view to illuminating the possible nature and role of musical behaviours in auditory environments in the past.

Bearing in mind the limitations (and strengths) associated with drawing analogies between past societies and the present ethnographic record, the aims of this paper are quite specific. It does not seek to explain acoustical evidence in the archaeological record by drawing direct parallels with the present or recent history. Instead, it seeks to draw attention to the diversities and similarities of musical behaviours and instrumentation, and highlight a number of the implications which these hold for the use of acoustical space in the past. Legitimate parallels to past auditory behaviours can be based on the pattern of shared constraints. The tools and raw materials which these peoples have available to them for the creation of instruments often resemble those available to past human groups. Before contact with westerners, for example, the Plains Indians (Taylor 1991), Pygmies (Ichikawa 1999) and Australian Aborigines (Morton 1999) made no use of metal in the manufacture of their tools and artefacts, using only wood, stone and occasionally bone.

Native Americans of the Plains (Blackfoot and Sioux)

The first group of hunter-gatherers to be considered are the Native Americans of the plains of central North America. Although at least 32 tribes were occupying this region in the year 1800, some of the best documentation relates to the Sioux and the Blackfoot. Both tribes, the Blackfoot in the northern plains, and the Sioux in the east, lived in areas of relatively high humidity that produced rolling grasslands as the major habitat form (Taylor 1991). This plains environment may in fact be more reminiscent of the habitat occupied by ancestral hunter-gatherers in Africa than those habitats that are home to hunter-gatherers in Africa today. This is because hunter-gatherers in Africa today occupy areas either of very low rainfall (e.g. the !Kung San of the Kalahari desert) or of very high rainfall (e.g. the rainforest-dwelling Pygmies), with all of the temperate grassland now occupied by settled agriculturalists (Foley 1992).

The Blackfoot were traditionally nomadic hunters of antelope and bison (buffalo) and, until the introduction of horses by Europeans in the eighteenth century, hunted and travelled on foot. Interestingly, they used a hunting method which was also employed by Middle and Upper Palaeolithic hunters, both Neanderthal and modern human (Chase 1989). The men would drive a herd of the animals into a v-shaped drive leading over a cliff edge or ditch so that the animals fell to their deaths, ready to be collected and processed (Taylor 1991). Particularly relevant is the use of song amongst the Blackfoot in this procedure. The herd was initially enticed towards the drive area by a young man singing a spiritually potent song in the manner of a bleating calf (Kehoe 1999).

All able-bodied members of the group would help process such a kill. Blackfoot women also harvested plant foods from the surrounding environment, such as berries, bulbs and turnips, and engaged in some limited cultivation (Kehoe 1999). They followed the buffalo herds' annual movements, living in groups of 10–20 tipis, with around eight persons in each, moving to grasslands in the spring, meeting with other groups in the summer, and then to sheltered river-valleys in the autumn (Epp 1988).

The summer meeting between groups involved the resolution of disputes, policies and trade, as well as the performance of the 'Sun Dance' to bring prosperity and health. Groups had leaders, and certain families were seen as privileged, such that they did not have to participate in daily menial work, but were instead concerned with leadership activities. Leadership was subject, however, to the views of the members of the group (including children), and individual autonomy was also highly valued (Kehoe 1999). Although the nomadic nature of their existence is curtailed by the reservation system today, many of the other activities of the society, including music, are still practised (Nettl 1992).

The music of the Plains Indians resembles that of the majority of Native Americans, in that it is almost always *monophonic* (contains only one melody proceeding at any one time), and the melody is nearly always vocal rather than instrumental (Nettl 1992; McAllester 1996). Such instrumentation as there is consists predominantly of percussion in the form of drums or rattles, which are used to accompany the vocal melody. This limited variety of instruments is in fact typical of the whole of the North American continent, where the selection of musical instruments used by the native inhabitants is surprisingly small, considering the widespread use of music and the diversity of peoples.

Although almost all conform to basic types of idiophone (instruments whose bodies vibrate to produce their sound), the instruments within this category are very varied. There are rattles made from dried gourds (which rattle on account of the dry seeds or stones inside), tree bark and spiders' nests, as well as deer hooves and turtle shells, to quote only some examples (McAllester 1996). The deer hoof rattles consist of around twenty doe hooves suspended from a stick. Drums tend to be either frame-drums or barrel drums, made from wood and skin, some only a piece of rawhide suspended from a stake (Nettl 1992). Sometimes simply a plank of wood is beaten (Nettl 1956) and idiophones made from notched sticks are also used (Nettl 1992). Much less common, but also used, are aerophones such as bullroarers and whistles or flutes. The latter often have no finger holes and so produce a single tone, and are made of wood or bird-bone; others have up to six finger holes (Nettl 1956). It is noteworthy that all of the instruments used are manufactured from organic materials that occur naturally in the Plains Indians' environment, and that many require little if any modification before use.

It may seem that the associated music is rather simplistic, but amongst the Plains Indians the value of the music is not measured in terms of its complexity. Instead, it is its ability to integrate ceremonial and social events, to integrate society in general and represent it to outsiders, and to evoke supernatural influence that is important (Nettl 1992). The Plains Indians traditionally believed that music came to people through supernatural input in dreams, so little credit for agency in composition was given to individuals (Nettl 1956). The use of music to evoke supernatural power is particularly prevalent amongst the Blackfoot Indians, who have specific songs for each act in a ceremony. For example, in a ceremony to influence the weather, a bundle of objects is opened and the correct song must be sung for each, in the right order, to 'activate' each object. Some of these ceremonial bundles can contain over 160 items (Nettl 1992).

Such religious activities are very frequently accompanied by dancing as well as the music, and this is the most common use of music amongst the Plains Indians. The second most common use is to accompany *social* dancing. War dances and puberty rites are important social and ceremonial occasions accompanied by music and dance, and the aforementioned deer-hoof rattles accompany the latter in particular (Nettl 1956). In all these instances, the men perform the majority of the dancing and singing. In the religious activities involving the opening of bundles of

items, the performance is limited to the medicine man performing the ritual, but in the more social activities, the performance involves many members of the group. This includes the women, who join in certain of the men's songs, and walk around the periphery of the dancing area, rather than dancing themselves (Nettl 1992).

Both the vocal and the rhythmic elements of the Blackfoot and Sioux music involve a great deal of repetition, with very subtle variations on a theme (McAllester 1996). The vocal technique used in the Sioux 'Grass Dance' (a war dance) is of particular interest. It uses 'vocables' (non-lexical, meaningless syllables) with high emotive input rather than translatable words as the basis of the song (McAllester 1996). This is, in fact, a common feature of virtually all Plains Indian songs, with any words occupying only a tiny portion of the melody (Nettl 1992). The aforementioned Blackfoot Sun Dance ceremony, for example. contains only the words 'Sun says to sing', and a medicine bundle ceremony contains only the words 'It is spring, let others see you'; all the rest of the melody, although verbal, consists of vocables (Nettl 1989).

Although this vocable music is clearly used in close association with symbolic practices, and a particular song can relate very specifically to a particular activity, the music itself is said to have no symbolic content. According to Nettl, 'native informants are able to say almost nothing on the symbolic aspect of their [non-lexical] music' (Nettl 1956, 25). It would seem that the main purpose of this type of vocalization is to contribute to the emotional responses evoked by the music (McAllester 1996), and it has no (conscious) symbolism behind it. This is in contrast to lyrical music, or to instrumental pieces which deliberately attempt to evoke the various traits of their subjects, be they *Mars, the war-bringer*, *Winter*, or the sounds of the Australian bush, as is the case with the Pintupi described below. The only exception to this amongst the Plains Indians would appear to be the imitation of a bleating calf used in the hunting tactic described at the beginning of this section.

African Pygmies of the equatorial forest (Aka and Mbuti)

The second group of hunter-gatherers to be examined are the Pygmies of the Ituri forest of equatorial Africa, in particular the Aka (or BaAka) and Mbuti (or BaMbuti) communities. These two groups are particularly worthy of note as they still acquire the majority of their subsistence from wild foods, which they forage and hunt. This is in contrast to the majority of the other

Pygmy groups (such as the Efe and Baka) who now tend to live near to villages of farmers, and provide services in exchange for a diet of more cultivated food (Hitchcock 1999).

Both Aka and Mbuti live in dense humid forest near the equator in central Africa. Their principle habitation is a family dome made from bent branches and thatched with leaves, organized into communities of 30–100. These communities are nomadic, and tend to move on every month or two, following their quarry. The communities are egalitarian and co-operative, with no formalized hierarchy, although individuals may be acknowledged as experts in particular skills. Ownership of personal possessions is minimal, largely as a product of the nomadic lifestyle (Turino 1992), and they do not make any use of metal or earthenware in manufacturing their tools and containers (Ichikawa 1999), which tend to be made of wood or bark (Bahuchet 1999).

They hunt using nets, spears and poisoned darts (Bahuchet 1999; Ichikawa 1999). Amongst the Aka, subsistence from hunting accounts for about two-thirds of their diet. The other third is made up of foraged plants, fungi and animals, such as wild yam, leaves, nuts, snails, tortoises, weevils, beetles and caterpillars. Foraging is predominantly carried out by women, whereas the men collect honey and do most of the hunting of large game. The game are mainly elephants, antelope, river hogs, gorillas, monkeys and chimpanzees. Monkeys are hunted with bows and poisoned darts; large game is hunted with broad-bladed spears. During the dry season, when many Aka communities band together, communal hunting often occurs, when all the men, women and children get together to 'beat' duiker into rings of nets (Bahuchet 1999). This activity is also carried out by the Mbuti, although hunting among the Mbuti accounts for a smaller proprotion of their subsistence than among the Aka. The Mbuti also rely on the foraging of wild vegetables, honey, nuts and invertebrates as a portion of their diets, although in recent years more of their diet has been provided by nearby farmers (Ichikawa 1999).

The music of the Aka and Mbuti is, like most aspects of their culture, a communal activity, without specialist musicians. Like that of the Plains Indians, it is predominantly vocal, with little instrumentation; this is one of several features shared by Pygmy and Plains Indian music. Aka and Mbuti music is also considered to be of supernatural origin, told to individuals by their ancestors in their sleep, and is used as a way of communicating with the spirits of their surrounding environment (Ichikawa 1999). They believe the way to communicate with the divine is through

sound alone; as a result, song texts are minimal, often consisting of only one line such as 'the forest is good' among the Aka (Turino 1992) or 'we are the children of the forest' among the Mbuti (Turnbull 1962). The remainder of the vocal element of the music consists, as with Plains Indians, of *vocables* (non-lexical vocal syllables) (Locke 1996).

Some music is performed individually, such as lullabies, but communal singing for ceremonial activities is most important (Turino 1992). Such music is often related to specific subsistence activities, with particular songs being performed for each activity. Thus, there are songs for net-hunting, elephant-hunting, and honey-collecting. The *mabo* song and dance of the Aka, for example, is a net-hunting dance, and is used for the ritual administration of hunting medicine. It is also used as a method for instruction in dance, including between neighbouring settlements (Kisliuk 1991, cited in Locke 1996). In this respect, it acts both as a philological aid and a diplomatic mechanism. The *mobandi* ritual dance is related to honey-collecting, and is unusual in that it is the only one that is seasonal rather than taking place before or after the hunt. It is performed after the rains when the *mbaso* tree flowers, and is a purification ritual. The Aka believe that any misfortune that occurs in hunting and gathering is the result of human misconduct which jeopardizes the help of the spirits in that activity. During the *mobandi* all the members of the group gently hit themselves with branches to transfer any evil forces out of themselves and onto the branch (Bahuchet 1999), avoiding this risk.

Songs also mark formal 'rites of passage' ceremonies such as circumcision, girls' puberty, marriages and funerals (Ichikawa 1999). On these occasions the songs are usually performed by women, unlike the hunting-related songs, which are performed by men (Turino 1992). It is only in these ceremonies that gender or age distinctions structure the performance of music; in other performances, anyone may participate who wishes to (Turino 1992).

Instrumentation consists mainly of percussive accompaniment to the vocal tunes by hand-claps or drumming on skins which cover the end of cone-shaped logs and by rapping sticks on the drum body (Locke 1996). There are also a few rattles, as well as some end-blown flute pipes made from cane (Turino 1992). Along with all of the Pygmies' traditional artefacts, these instruments are made from organic materials occurring in the local environment. In that respect, the instrumentation is similar to that of the Plains Indians described above. Despite this general similarity, however, the music of the Pygmies differs from that of the Plains Indians in that it is *polyphonic*;

a performance consists of several different melodies sung simultaneously by different groups, which 'interlock' with each other to form a multi-layered piece of music (Turino 1992).

The majority of the music itself appears to lack any inherent symbolic content (in terms of lexical meaning or mimicry), although it is clearly associated with activities which do have symbolic content and associations. The melodies do not attempt to emulate or evoke any other thing, but follow particular structures for different activities and dances. The exception to this is the *molimo* music, which is performed specifically to wake the forest if hunting is bad. This ceremony is performed at night and can last several months, and is rooted in the belief that if hunting is poor, it is because the forest is sleeping. It uses the *molimo* trumpet, a single end-blown tube, which is supposed to mimic the sounds of the forest and answer the men's singing (Turino 1992). As such, the *molimo* sound does have a direct symbolic association.

Australian Aborigines of the Western Desert (Pintupi)

The Aboriginal population of Australia falls into two main language groups, with peoples being divided more by geographical features than by 'tribal' groupings (Peterson 1999). Communities exist within these categories, but widespread systems of exchange across the continent — of goods, ceremonies, social practices and some intermarriage — have led to an indigenous way of life which is fairly homogeneous throughout the continent. Archaeological evidence suggests that systems of long-distance exchange were in place at least 30,000 years ago (Mulvaney 1976); amongst historical populations at least, these exchanges were as much for the benefit of social relationships as for practical purposes (Peterson 1999).

Of particular note amongst the Aboriginal groups are the Pintupi-speaking people of the Western desert, because they were the last Aboriginal population to be in any way incorporated into settler society, during the 1960s (Myers 1999). Consequently, they were (until then) less severely influenced by Western lifestyle than many of the other groups, and recent records exist of their traditional way of life. The incorporation was short-lived. During the 1970s they started to create a few autonomous satellite communities around Papunya, and by the early 1980s, most had returned to their traditional territories of the Gibson desert (Myers 1999). The traditions outlined below are related in the past tense, as they describe the features of the Pintupi before their re-settlement. Since members of the culture have begun to return to their traditional territories

today, it is hoped that they will perpetuate many of these cultural elements and subsistence methods, as have other Aborigine groups in recent years.

The Gibson desert is an area of sandy dunes, plains and hills, with sparse vegetation. Rainfall is minimal, mostly falling only during January and February. The principal fauna are lizards, feral cats, kangaroos, wallabies and emu. These animals were traditionally hunted by the men using stone axes, spears and spear-throwers. Women collected seeds, fruit, vegetables, honey-ants and grubs using digging-sticks and containers made from tree-bark. The foods gathered by the women constituted the majority of the Pintupi diet (60–80 per cent) for most of the year (Gould 1969); most of the protein was provided by lizards, caught by both men and women (Myers 1999). Hunting was generally carried out alone or in small groups, and large game was shared amongst all the families of a residential group (10–30 members) (Myers 1999). As with the Plains Indians and the Pygmies, the dry season (dri*est* season, in the case of the Pintupi) was the time when many separate communities of the same group would gather together for social and ceremonial activities; amongst the Pintupi, up to ten such groups would gather on these occasions. Traditional shelters were made of brush and branches, and would house a nuclear family. Groups of unmarried men still undergoing initiation and widowed women sometimes had their own habitations (Myers 1999).

Ownership of the land was seen as dictated by the content of songs, stories and rituals pertaining to the Dreaming (see below), with each group being guardians of a particular set of this information (Breen 1994). Such 'ownership', however, did not relate strongly to the actual group boundaries, which were quite flexible (Myers 1999). Social organization was largely non-hierarchical, without designated leaders, but additional respect was given on the basis of age or the successful performance of rituals. Gender relations were predominantly egalitarian (Myers 1999).

Pintupi music, like that of the Arrernte (Morton 1999), Cape York (Martin 1999) and Ngarrindjeri Aborigines (Tonkinson 1999), was tied up closely with story and ritual describing their hereditary land (Myers 1999). These combined renditions acted out events from the *Tjukurrpa*, or 'The Dreaming'. During *Tjukurrpa*, ancestor spirits travelled the land leaving their marks on the landscape and the essence of people and animals on the land. Pintupi songs incorporate these mythologies into the performances, and describe the world around them (Myers 1999). The precise preservation of these songs was regarded by them as fundamental to their continued survival and the constant renewal of nature, and so was considered extremely powerful and valuable. As they possessed no written records or notation, oral tradition was the only way in which this information could be passed on and preserved, and the musical form brought important mnemonic benefits to this end (Jones 1983).

Unlike the music of the Plains Indians and the Pygmies, the music of the Pintupi was lyrically-dominated; in fact, the perpetuation and communication of lyrical information was central to the purpose of much of the singing. The music itself resembles that of the Plains Indians and Pygmies (and other Aboriginal groups), however, in that it was predominantly vocal, and featured little instrumentation (Breen 1994). In fact, much of the music relied on percussion produced without any instruments at all, but by means of clapping hands, slapping the body and stamping feet on the ground. When instrumentation was used, it was the same as that used by the majority of other Aboriginal groups (Nettl 1992). Percussion instrumentation consisted traditionally of two eucalyptus sticks that were struck together called *bilma* ((Nettl 1992; Breen 1994).

The only non-percussive instrument used was the *didjeridu*, a long pipe made from the limb of a eucalyptus tree hollowed out by termites (Breen 1994). This is played like a trumpet, creating a low single-tone droning sound, the 'colour' of which can be varied by changing the shape of the mouth (Nettl 1992). The didjeridu originated amongst the Aboriginals of the northern part of the continent, but is now used universally. Originally it was only played by men specially selected by elder members of the group, and in learning it, players were encouraged to listen to all of the sounds of the bush in order to be able to imitate the sounds of nature (Breen 1994).

The music of the Pintupi had explicit symbolic associations, as other Aboriginal music still does. This symbolism was very important, as it described the world and the history of the people, and its preservation was considered fundamental to the well-being of the group. The sound produced by the only non-percussive instrumentation, the didjeridu, also had symbolic meaning; players aimed to mimic the sounds of the surrounding environment, this adding to the symbolism of the song it accompanied (Breen 1994).

The Eskimo of southwest Alaska (Yupik) and Canada (Inuit)

The preceding sections have considered hunter-gatherers of the temperate plains, equatorial jungle and the desert; this section looks at hunter-gatherers living in sub-arctic tundra. This setting is a demanding one in which to subsist, with a limited range of resources and difficult environmental conditions.

The peoples inhabiting the area to the south of the Bering Strait and Norton Sound in southwest Alaska are known collectively as the Yupik. The vast majority of the specific research into the music of the Yupik has been carried out by Johnston, who provides the only comprehensive description of their musical traditions (Johnston 1989). Much of the following section draws upon this work. The climate here is milder than that further north, where the Inupiaq Eskimo live, and the landscape consists mainly of low marshy tracts close to sea-level. The area is largely treeless, although the Eskimo do move upstream to penetrate the forested inland areas too (Nelson 1899/1983). Although there are no fully-formed trees, there is a variety of other vegetation. This is found particularly in sheltered areas on hillsides and along the courses of river valleys, and includes willows and alders, as well as the grasses, sphagnum and flowering plants that occur in the rest of the landscape (Nelson 1899/1983).

The Yupik number around 17,000 today, and they subsist in the traditional manner on sea-mammal-hunting, salmon-fishing and reindeer-hunting, as well as on wild berries. These are gathered, mainly by women and older children, and are stored until needed in winter in underground chambers (Johnston 1989). They are divided into groups of up to 100 people, who associate themselves with particular tracts of land. This occupancy is not normally considered as ownership of the land or its resources, but simply that a given community are the 'traditional occupants' of that particular tract (Riches 1995). Socially the groups are best described as having a structure that is flexible, egalitarian and individualistic (Gardner 1991), with little ranking within the group, or between groups. Leadership tends to be attributed on the basis of exemplary behaviour in some aspect of life, and the security of the leaders' position rests purely with the fact that others have *chosen* to follow them (Riches 1995). The provision of food is a reciprocal system, with all members of a 'task-group' (up to 30 people) contributing to the total, and those contributing the most receiving some prestige as a consequence (Riches 1984, quoted in Riches 1995).

The music of the Yupik is predominantly vocal, with at most only two different instruments, if any. All melody is carried by the vocal parts, whilst the instruments provide percussion. The commonest instrument is a simple frame drum, made from a round wooden frame covered with a sea-mammal membrane; each village tends to have a specialist maker of traditional drums. The other instrument sometimes used is a rattle; this may consist, for example, of a hoop strung with puffin-bills which rattle against each other when shaken (Johnston 1989).

The Yupik themselves classify their songs and musical styles into thirteen categories; these are described in some detail by Johnston (1989), and his findings are summarized below. The first six are for adults: dance songs, shamans' songs, hunting songs, teasing songs, travelling songs and berry-picking songs. The remaining seven are for children (either to be performed by children, or by adults for children): story songs, juggling-game songs, jump-rope game songs, ghost-game songs, bird identification songs, fish identification songs and *inqum* 'cooing' songs (Johnston 1989).

Dance songs tend to feature drumming. This is performed by four to eight people simultaneously who drum in synchrony, whilst chanting the words of the song. Drummers do not participate in dancing, and dancers do not sing either, although the audience may sing along. The drummer-singers are almost always male, although there is no formal rule against women drumming (Johnston 1989). The subjects of Yupik dance songs fall into three main areas: relating the past adventures of cultural/community heroes, description of comic incidents; and the portrayal of animal or bird-life. Since the songs often form a repository of knowledge of past adventures and lore for the community, the singers are usually those who have most of interest to relate. The dance motions reflect the story-telling nature of the song, and mimic activities of daily life. Men's dance actions tend to resemble activities such as sledding and harpooning whilst the women's dance motions mimic activities such as carcass-cutting and feather-plucking.

The melody of the songs tends to be formed from only two or three notes, with the note changing with each syllable of the song. As well as the narrative words much use is made of *vocable* non-linguistic syllables. Many of these communal songs place an emphasis on comic occurrences and events, and have a strong bonding and socially lubricating effect on the community. As Johnston (1989) points out, this can be very important in communities of people confined to constricted living quarters in some of the harshest environmental conditions in the world.

Another way in which song is used as a social lubricant is in the so-called teasing songs. These are a form of legal mechanism and a way of avoiding direct conflict between two protagonists. The offended individual would compose a witty, chiding, song aimed at the offender, which they would perform in front of the community. This would embarrass the latter, and hopefully also act as a deterrent for future repetitions of the offending action (Johnston 1989).

Music and song are not only used as aids to social interaction, but also to influence the world around the Yupik. The shamans were traditionally the intermediaries between the hunters and the gods of hunting, who control the success of the hunt. It was thought that the shaman's soul could leave his body and travel to the moon, where the hunting gods resided, in order to commune with them; this process was aided by the shaman's drumming as he sang. These songs are still often used at important festivals, and composed for the event itself (Johnston 1989). The hunters themselves also employ music to influence the unpredictable environment in which they have to operate, using song to affect the hunt. The hunting songs are performed during the hunt itself and are thought to have the power to stop wounded game from escaping.

Songs may hold important knowledge, whilst being a source of entertainment; this is the case with the travelling songs and the berry-picking songs. Yupik frequently travel long distances for subsistence purposes and for the maintenance of alliances between different communities. Whilst they travel, they sing songs which often relate adventure narratives; the importance and significance of the Yupiks' awareness of their environment is reflected in that these songs frequently include highly detailed descriptions of prevailing weather conditions as the journey is described.

Environmental information is also contained within the berry-picking songs performed by the women and children as they travel to pick the cloud-berries and blueberries for storage for the winter. These songs are often concerned with the tundra and its features, particularly the descriptive names of features which aid in the location of the berries. In this respect, these songs closely parallel the content and use of the songs of the Pintupi (and other) Australian Aborigines (see above), specifically used as a mnemonic describing the surrounding environment.

The Yupik songs performed for or by children also seem to have educational purposes: as an aid to developing co-ordination skills (the juggling-game, string-figure-game and the jump-rope songs), as an educational medium concerning the natural world (bird-identification and fish-identification songs), encouraging creativity and interaction (the ghost-game songs) and as examples of triumph over adversity (the story songs).

The jump-rope songs take a question-and-answer form, with the rope-holders asking a question and the rope-jumper answering whilst avoiding getting caught in the skipping-rope. The juggling-game songs are performed both by adults and children, and are reported from communities throughout Greenland, Canada, Alaska and Siberia; it is thus likely that they are an extremely old form of song. The performer sings the song, which tends to have satirical or rather indelicate subject matter, whilst juggling stones in one hand. The string-figure game is a variation of cats-cradle, with a loop of string held between the hands and feet or forehead of the performer. As the song is performed, the individual winds extra twists and loops into the string in time with the rhythm and syllables of the song. This game develops dexterity and spatial-directional skills whilst the juggling game develops hand–eye co-ordination skills (Johnston 1989).

The bird- and fish-identification songs teach important information about the appearance and be-haviour of birds, small animals and fish. They are sung by elders to children and contain information about markings, nesting, courting, migrations and the way these relate to the environment and the weather. They also aid in the hunting and catching of these creatures for subsistence, which children are encouraged to do at a young age. The Yupik also aim in the context of these songs to mimic the sounds and behaviours of the animals they find in their surroundings. A seal-hunter may, for example, entice curious seals by accurately mimicking seal noises. Fish that are caught are often sung to in the hope that they will enjoy being caught and return the next year in their re-incarnated form to be caught again (Johnston 1989).

Like the jump-rope songs, the ghost-game songs are bipartite, consisting of question and answer between the participants; in this instance, however, the replies to the question (usually concerning the whereabouts of an undesirable spirit) are improvised. The children are thus required to be spontaneously creative; any participant who fails to come up with an answer becomes the ghost and has to chase and catch the other children (Johnston 1989). It is a game of physical activity too.

It will be seen that there is a very great variety of song and music amongst the Yupik of the sub-arctic tundra, and also that it serves a variety of purposes, at both an individual and community level. Music and song, for the Yupik, can be informative and edu-cational, a social lubricant, an aid to hunting, a way of learning physical and mental skills, or purely a pastime.

Very different but also worthy of note are the throat-games of the Inuit, which are known as 'Kataj-jait'. These games are found in eastern and central Canada, northern Quebec and South Baffin Land, and are performed by Igloolik, Caribou and Nelsilik Inuit (Nattiez 1983; Baghemil 1988). They are generally played by two women who face each other at close range (Baghemil 1988), sometimes even holding each other's shoulders (Nattiez 1983). Both participants

produce sequences of short repeated vocalizations. These are strung together into longer phrases and syn-copated into complex structures which are a mixture of droning and complex guttural sounds (Baghemil 1988). The game is a sort of endurance test, in that it ends when one participant runs out of energy or in-spiration, or starts to laugh (Baghemil 1988). The game is performed playfully, but the performance is valued for endurance, and for the virtuosity and aesthetics of sound — participants have to win with 'beautiful sounds' (Nattiez 1983).

The sounds themselves take the form of mor-phemes and vocables (Beaudry 1978) and create repeated motifs 'made up of a morpheme, a rhythm, an intonation contour and a pattern of voiced and voiceless, inspirated and expirated sounds' (Nattiez 1983). As a rule no more than three or four tone levels are used for the utterances (Baghemil 1988). This small number of elements is constantly re-combined in novel ways during the course of the competition. The sounds produced may have subject matter in the sense of us-ing real words, which may form a narrative, but most often there is no narrative at all. More frequently the sounds imitate animal noises such as the cries of geese, ducks, walruses, panting dogs or mosquitoes. Alter-natively they may simply be abstract sounds made for aesthetic effect (Baghemil 1988). Baghemil reports that the Inuit themselves consider the Katajjait to be the language spoken by the Tunnituaruit, or 'flying heads', mythical creatures that are half-woman, half-bird. The dead are also thought to communicate by this language, especially as manifested in the Aurora Borealis. Nattiez, however, reports to the contrary that the superstitious/spiritual language element is only rarely linked to the games and that there does not seem to be any consistent 'deep meaning' or symbol-ism to the games; they are usually performed for their own sake as entertainment (Nattiez 1983). This is also consistent with what Beaudry (1978) was told by the performers she observed. The degree of symbolism and perceived content may be something that has varied historically. According to Nattiez, the games used to be performed by up to four people at once, at any time of the day, month or year. The performers, although usually women, could also be men or boys. The games seemed to be multifunctional, and could be performed as entertainment, celebration or just to keep a baby quiet (Nattiez 1983).

These throat games are usually studied as a form of music, but Baghemil (1988) argues that they would be better analyzed as a form of language. They seem in some ways to straddle both music and language in the vocalizations they use. Baghemil observes that the voicing and airstream mechanisms used in the games have more in common with several languages, and only rarely occur in song. Interestingly, the system appears to be independent of the Inuktitut language — the features of vocalization that occur in the games have not been transferred across from the language as they would be in traditional song (Baghemil 1988).

Conclusions

These four groups of people occupy four very different environments on three separate continents. They are united only by their mode of subsistence and by their humanity; they are separated by, for the most part, thousands of miles and thousands of years since last contact. Thus similarities between their musical practices would suggest either convergent development (presumably influenced by subsistence factors or human characteristics) or a shared heritage.

Music and dance may have an important role in engendering group cohesion and altering mood, as an aid to teaching, or to facilitate group interaction and communality within and between groups. In the majority of instances studied here the music itself has no inherent symbolism, but it can be used to accompany symbolic activities. Amongst the Pintupi, as with the Yupik, song is a repository for knowledge of tribal history and legend, and is a mnemonic aid.

All four groups meet up with fellow communities during their most difficult subsistence season, and at this time there is increased performance of ceremonial and communal music and dance. In all four cultures, music has an important ceremonial and social use, and is a communal rather than solitary activity; the majority of music is accompanied by dancing, and so takes place in a designated space. Whether that space is inside or outside is obviously dependent upon prevailing environmental conditions. In all four cultures music is also performed as a communal activity purely for pleasure.

In considering the possible use of soundspaces in the past, we should therefore consider the likelihood that any space used for such activities would have had to accommodate a fairly large group of people. We should also consider whether the focus of the auditory activity carried out in a given space is likely to have been performer(s), other participants, or an audience. In the groups considered, a distinction is rarely drawn between the performer and other people present; instead, most musical activities are inclusive, albeit with differentiation of roles within the musical activity as a whole. With the exception of certain ritual activities focused on a solitary specialist, there is often little concept of an 'audience' — instead, a large proportion of those people present appear to have been participants.

All four groups have music which is predominantly vocal, and is accompanied mainly by percussion instruments. The use of melodic instruments is minimal and, when used, invariably consists of end-blown pipes. These are usually single-toned instruments. All the instruments, whether percussive or melodic, are made from naturally-occurring organic materials, so we should consider how these types of sounds in particular would be manifested in a given acoustic environment.

The music contains two main types of vocal melodic content — vocable (emotive vocal sounds) or lyrical vocalizations. Amongst the Blackfoot and Sioux Plains Indians and the Aka and Mbuti Pygmies, song has minimal lyrical content, vocalizations instead consisting of *vocables*, which are emotive sounds with no obvious symbolism. In these two cultures, music accompanies rites of passage and rituals relating to subsistence and hunting. The sounds being produced would not need to remain intelligible and discrete as they have no lexical content. Particular consideration should be given to how discrete vocables sound, and especially to how percussive sounds resonate in a given space as these are by far the most commonly recurring musical sounds across the cultures considered.

As regards the vocal content of their music, the Pintupi Aborigines stand in contrast to the Plains Indians and Pygmies, in that their music is almost exclusively lyrical and is a repository for community knowledge and mythologies. Inuit and Yupik music has both types of content. Much consists of non-lyrical vocables and animal sounds, or sounds made only for aesthetic purposes, but the greater proportion relates stories, descriptions of events, environments, journeys and subsistence sources, and so constitutes an important repository of knowledge for both adults and children. Obviously in these instances it would be very important that lyrical content remained intelligible, and the acoustic properties of the space chosen would have to reflect this.

How does the acoustic aid in replicating environmental sounds? This is an important consideration for the potency of the music among Pygmy and Australian Aborigine populations. Other evidence from the archaeological record should hence be considered alongside the acoustic space in order to determine the likely emphases placed on activities carried out there.

All four of the peoples considered above believe themselves to have come from the land, to be akin with the other fauna of their environment, and use music in an attempt to influence the world around them. This world view is clearly a very important common element, and must have implications for the ways in which they interact with and seek to alter their environment on a physical and auditory level. There is clearly often a belief that sound has a physical presence and influence in the world. In fact, in many cases no distinction between the auditory and natural environment would be made.

Summary

In attempting to identify which acoustic properties of a given place have human intention behind them, we need to consider very carefully what type of activity is likely to have been carried out there. Conversely, if we can identify a particular space as a likely focus of human activity, analysis of its acoustic properties should allow us to narrow down the types of activities which would have been possible or practical there. By implication, an unmodified natural feature used as a focus of activity (such as a cave or clearing) might be chosen because its particular acoustic properties suited the sounds to be made there. If other considerations weighed more heavily, the auditory performance would have to be tailored to fit the potential of the site. On the other hand, a manufactured location (stone circle, hut, barrow) might be built with particular acoustical properties in mind to suit an auditory behaviour to be replicated there. At the very least, if we can identify particularly striking acoustic properties in response to the types of sounds *that are likely to have been made there* (natural instruments, percussion, human voice) we are at once narrowing down the number of factors for which we are seeking intentionality.

References

Baghemeil, B., 1988. The morphology and phonology of Katajjait (Inuit throat-games). *Canadian Journal of Linguistics* 33, 1–58.

Bahuchet, S., 1999. Aka Pygmies, in *The Cambridge Encyclopedia of Hunters and Gatherers*, eds. R.B. Lee & R. Daly. Cambridge: Cambridge University Press, 190–94.

Beaudry, N., 1978. Towards transcription and analysis of Inuit throat-games: macro-structure. *Ethnomusicology* 22, 261–73.

Breen, M., 1994. I have a dreamtime: aboriginal music and black rights in Australia, in *World Music: the Rough Guide,* eds. S. Broughton S. Broughton, M. Ellingham, D Muddyman & R. Trillo. London: Rough Guides Limited, 655–62.

Chase, P., 1989. How different was Middle Palaeolithic subsistence? A zooarchaeological perspective on the Middle to Upper Palaeolithic transition, in *The Human Revolution: Behavioural and Biological Perspectives in the Origins of Modern Humans*, eds. P. Mellars & C.

Stringer. Edinburgh: Edinburgh University Press, 321–37.

Epp, H.T., 1988. Way of the migrant herds: dual dispersion strategy amongst bison. *Plains Anthropologist* 33, 95–111.

Foley, R., 1992. Studying human evolution by analogy, in *The Cambridge Encyclopedia of Hunters and Gatherers*, eds. R.B. Lee & R. Daly. Cambridge: Cambridge University Press, 335–40.

Gardner, P., 1991. Forager pursuit of individual autonomy. *Current Anthropology* 32, 543–72.

Gould, R.A., 1969. *Yiwara: Foragers of the Australian Western Desert*. New York (NY): Scribner's.

Hitchcock, R.K., 1999. Introduction: Africa, in *The Cambridge Encyclopedia of Hunters and Gatherers*, eds. R.B. Lee & R. Daly. Cambridge: Cambridge University Press, 175–84.

Ichikawa, M., 1999. The Mbuti of northern Congo, in *The Cambridge Encyclopedia of Hunters and Gatherers*, eds. R.B. Lee & R. Daly. Cambridge: Cambridge University Press, 210–14.

Johnston, T.F., 1989. Song categories and musical style of the Yupik Eskimo. *Anthropos* 84, 423–31.

Jones, T.A., 1983. Australia, in *The New Oxford Companion to Music*, vol. 1, ed. D. Arnold. Oxford: Oxford University Press, 117–19.

Kehoe, A.B., 1999. Blackfoot and other hunters of the North American Plains, in *The Cambridge Encyclopedia of Hunters and Gatherers*, eds. R.B. Lee & R. Daly. Cambridge: Cambridge University Press, 36–40.

Kisliuk, M., 1991. Confronting the Quintessential: Singing, Dancing and Everyday Life Among the Biaka Pygmies (Central African Republic). Unpublished PhD dissertation, New York University, New York.

Locke, D., 1996. Africa: Ewe, Mande, Dagbamba, Shona, BaAka, in *Worlds of Music: an Introduction to the Music of the World's People*, ed. J.T. Titon. 3rd edition. New York (NY): Schirmer, 71–143.

Martin, D.F., 1999. Cape York Peoples, North Queensland, Australia, in *The Cambridge Encyclopedia of Hunters and Gatherers*, eds. R.B. Lee & R. Daly. Cambridge: Cambridge University Press, 335–8.

McAllester, D.P., 1996. North America/Native America, in *Worlds of Music: an Introduction to the Music of the World's People*, ed. J.T. Titon. 3rd edition. New York (NY): Schirmer, 17–70.

Morton, J., 1999. The Arrernte of Central Australia, in *The Cambridge Encyclopedia of Hunters and Gatherers*, eds. R.B. Lee & R. Daly. Cambridge: Cambridge University Press, 329–35.

Mulvaney, J., 1976. The chain of connection: the material evidence, in *Tribes and Boundaries in Australia*, ed. N. Peterson. Canberra: Australian Institute of Aboriginal Studies, 72–94.

Myers, F.R., 1999. Pintupi-speaking Aboriginals of the Western Desert, in *The Cambridge Encyclopedia of Hunters and Gatherers*, eds. R.B. Lee & R. Daly. Cambridge: Cambridge University Press, 348–57.

Nattiez, J.J., 1983. Some aspects of Inuit vocal games. *Ethnomusicology* 27, 457–75.

Nelson, E.W., 1899/1983. *The Eskimo About Bering Strait.* Washington (DC): Smithsonian Institution.

Nettl, B., 1956. *Music in Primitive Culture.* Cambridge (MA): Harvard University Press.

Nettl, B., 1989. *Blackfoot Musical Thought: Comparative Perspectives.* Kent (OH): Kent State University Press.

Nettl, B., 1992. North American Indian music, in *Excursions in World Music*, eds. B. Nettl, C. Capwell, P. Bohlman, I. Wong & T. Turino. Englewood Cliffs (NJ): Prentice Hall, 260–77.

Peterson, N., 1999. Introduction: Australia, in *The Cambridge Encyclopedia of Hunters and Gatherers*, eds. R.B. Lee & R. Daly. Cambridge: Cambridge University Press, 317–23.

Riches, D., 1984. Hunters, herders and potlatchers: towards a sociological theory of prestige. *Man* 19, 234–51.

Riches, D., 1995. Hunter-gatherer structural transformations. *Journal of the Royal Anthropological Institute* 1, 679–701.

Taylor, C., 1991. The Plains, in *The Native Americans: the Indigenous People of North America*, ed. C.F. Taylor. London: Salamander Books (Tiger Books), 62–99.

Tonkinson, R., 1999. The Ngarrindjeri of Southeastern Australia, in *The Cambridge Encyclopedia of Hunters and Gatherers*, eds. R.B. Lee & R. Daly. Cambridge: Cambridge University Press, 343–7.

Turino, T., 1992. The music of Sub-Saharan Africa, in *Excursions in World Music*, eds. B. Nettl, C. Capwell, P. Bohlman, I. Wong & T. Turino. Englewood Cliffs (NJ): Prentice Hall, 165–95.

Turnbull, C., 1962. *The Forest People.* New York (NY): Simon & Schuster.

Chapter 11

Acoustics and the Human Experience
of Socially-organized Sound

Ian Cross & Aaron Watson

To what extent are 'standard' architectural and environmental acoustical measurements applicable to contexts outside those that are governed by nineteenth- and twentieth-century western preferences in speech and music performance? Can we apply those 'standard' measures to the practices of cultures other than those of the recent west? In other words, can we use the information represented in these measurements to understand the substance of social activities involving sound in cultures and periods other than our own? At the least, these measurements appear to relate to dimensions of the human experience of sound that might represent real uniformities in the human experience of social sound (though these may be valued positively or negatively by members of different cultures). At a first approximation we can treat the data that these measurements afford as reflecting constraints on the human experience of socially-organized and directed sound. Hence they might allow the assessment of the feasibility of highly-specific types of sound-producing behaviours, both speech and musical, group and individual, as well as allowing inferences to be made about the degree to which acoustically-functional characteristics of archaeological sites and spaces might have been intentionally incorporated in their design and construction.

The role and effect of sound and the human experience of sound in archaeological environments is severely under-researched. Sound is a primary source of information about the world, and the human experience of sound shapes many of the ways in which we interact with the world and with each other. Yet sound has generally been a missing dimension in archaeological research, an omission that has only recently been challenged (e.g. Dams 1984; Reznikoff & Dauvois 1988; Devereux & Jahn 1996; Watson & Keating 1999). As a modern discipline, archaeology is predicated upon the sensory domination of vision in our own society (see Pocock 1981; Porteous 1990; Rodaway 1994), and there has been a tendency to project this bias into the past. Furthermore, sound is evanescent, and for most of human history (never mind prehistory) its basic nature has been poorly understood. Indeed, it was not until the end of the nineteenth century that accounts of sound enabled its physical basis to be predictively understood and the

perception of sound to be explored productively (e.g. Sabine 1921; Rayleigh 1945).

This paper is primarily concerned with outlining a methodology by which the acoustics of ancient buildings and spaces might be further elucidated. Pilot studies at Neolithic monuments in the British Isles (*c.* 3800–2000 BC) have suggested that these places were conducive to the creation of dynamic multisensory experiences, affording acoustic effects such as echoes, resonance and standing waves (Watson & Keating 1999; 2000; Watson 2001a,b). While it could be argued that these effects are simply a fortuitous by-product of architecture that was originally intended to serve quite different purposes, it seems unlikely that acoustic effects would have gone unnoticed in prehistory. The application of a detailed research methodology could reveal further evidence to support this possibility. For example, might those sites that can be identified as having had ritual or specialized roles (for instance, the presence of 'art' or evidence for the symbolic treatment

Effects of Indirect Sound

(i) Increase in intensity of sound

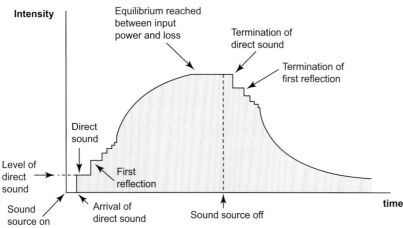

Figure 11.1a. *Increase in sound levels arising from summation of indirect (reflected) sound energy and direct sound energy from source.*

(ii) Increase in duration of sound

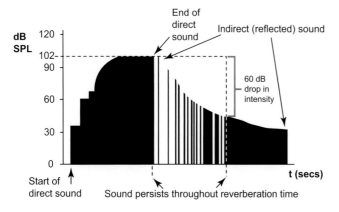

Figure 11.1b. *Extension of apparent duration of sound because of longer path length (hence later arrival) of indirect sound relative to direct sound.*

(iii) Changes in direction of sound

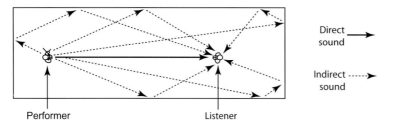

Figure 11.1c. *Potential apparent changes in direction of sound arising from reflections distant from source.*

of the dead) privilege certain types of sound-producing behaviours? Contrasted against the experience of sound in the wider landscape or within structures that display entirely different evidence (for instance, places of industry or habitation), this has the potential to enrich interpretations of how ancient buildings or spaces were used. There is also a possibility of gaining an insight into the extent to which acoustical considerations contributed to the design and construction of ancient sites.

In this paper we shall review the effects of spaces on the behaviour and experience of sound before considering the utility of 'standard' measures of sounds in architectural spaces for an understanding of sound in archaeological contexts.

Concepts and methods

Over the last century a range of methods have been developed for quantifying the acoustics of different physical environments and interpreting their appropriateness for different types of sound production and reception. These methods have been applied with increasing success to predict the behaviour and the experience of sound in situations where it is 'foregrounded' (as in the alleviation of environmental sound intrusion, or in the specification of designs of spaces for speech and music performance).

When a sound is encountered in the open air in a horizontal plane landscape, the sound that reaches a listener proceeds by a direct path from the sound source. For sounds in an enclosed space a listener will receive not only the direct sound but also the sound energy that is reflected from the surfaces of the enclosed space. The boundaries of the space will have three principal effects on the experience of sound; sound intensity is likely to increase, sound duration is likely to increase, and apparent sound direction may be altered (see Rasch &

Plomp 1982). This occurs in part because the our auditory systems integrate sound energy over small but finite time windows (thus summing a fraction of the reflected sound energy with that received direct from the source) and in part because of the complex nature of the cues that the ear relies on in ascribing location to a sound source. In a semi-enclosed space (e.g. with no roof and only partial walls or other obstructions), to these effects one must add the likelihood that the boundary elements will attenuate sounds external to the site and may change their frequency spectrum.

Current approaches to the acoustics of architectural spaces measure a range of parameters that correlate with the three principal effects outlined above and that can be employed to extend our understanding of how such sites and spaces might be used. The value of applying such standard measures lies largely in the fact that their application allows current knowledge of acoustically-centred uses of spaces to be brought to bear on the interpretation of sound in archaeological contexts. The huge reservoir of acoustical measurements of contemporary and historical built structures that exists provides a very secure foundation for making inferences about the usability of archaeological spaces for different sound-producing behaviours, and should afford insight into the contemporaneous perception of such spaces as acoustical environments.

However, a couple of caveats must be entered here. Current acoustical measures are largely predicated on particular uses of spaces that involve a collective focus of auditory attention, as in concert halls or lecture theatres. As far as we know, there is little that appears to be known about the acoustics of spaces that is related to, for instance, collective sound-producing and perceiving behaviours. Moreover, there may be acoustical features of archaeological spaces and sites that current approaches would tend to treat as undesirable (such as the presence of flutter echoes, or resonances). When such features are quantified in current measurements that quantification tends to be carried out with a view to minimizing their effect rather than to exploring how they might impact positively on the experience of sound in the spaces that give rise to them. It seems very likely that these features could have been regarded as desirable by the builders or users of these sites and spaces, yet current measurement techniques offer little guidance as to how they should be assessed and interpreted.

Some 'standard' architectural-acoustical measures

The 'standard' measures that may be applied provide information about specific dimensions of the experience of sound in enclosed spaces (specifically, loudness, duration and spatial impression). Note that loudness, duration and spatial impression are all psychological attributes of sound in enclosed spaces. Standard 'objective' measures address the physical aspects of sounds in spaces that correlate with these psychological attributes; hence loudness would be assessed by means of measurements of intensity, duration in terms of measurements of temporal extension and spatial impression by measurements of the directions from which reflected sound reaches a listener. These objective measures include: total sound level; objective clarity (C_{50} [speech] or C_{80} [music]; reverberation time; early decay time; and objective envelopment (Barron 1993).

Intensity

Total sound level is a measure of the increased intensity of the acoustic signal that occurs in any enclosed space with reflective surfaces. This corresponds to the total sound level at the measurement position minus the sound level of the direct sound measured at 10 m from the sound source. It is expected that different locations in any given site are likely to yield different total sound level values, and on each site a range of measurements would have to be taken.

Temporal effects

Objective clarity is a measure of the ratio of direct sound to indirect sound in an enclosed space; high levels of clarity indicate high levels of direct sound relative to indirect sound. It can be measured so as to correlate with perceived speech intelligibility (C_{50}, where the direct sound is defined as including all indirect sound occurring within 50 msec of the direct sound) or with the perceived 'distinctness' of music's structure in time (C_{80}, where the direct sound incorporates all indirect sound occurring within 80 msec of the direct sound). Again, clarity can be expected to vary across a space so multiple measurements will be taken at each site.

Reverberation time is the classical measure of the effect of an enclosed space on the perceived duration of a sound, and is defined as the time taken for the acoustic signal to decay by 60 dB from the cessation of the direct sound. Though similar to clarity, it provides an index of the 'liveness' of a space, and hence its suitability for types of activities involving sound that proceed at different paces. Measurements of *Reverberation time* should be supplemented by measurements of *Early decay time*, which provides an index similar to reverberation time but one that appears to correspond more directly to the subjective judgments of reverberation when the decay in a space is not completely linear (a feature that is likely to vary between sites).

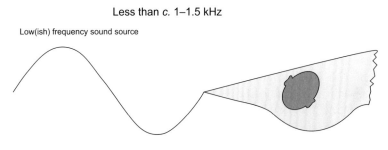

Less than *c.* 1–1.5 kHz

Low(ish) frequency sound source

Lower frequency sound 'bends' round head or DIFFRACTS

Figure 11.2a. *Low frequency sound (below c. 1.5 kHz) from lateral directions may 'bend' (diffract) round head, hence there is no significant difference in sound energy level reaching each ear.*

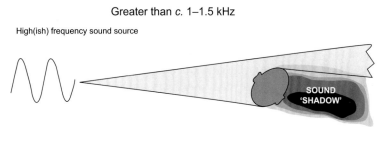

Greater than *c.* 1–1.5 kHz

High(ish) frequency sound source

SOUND 'SHADOW'

Figure 11.2b. *High(ish) frequency sound (above c. 1.5 kHz) from lateral directions allows formation of 'sound shadow' (inter-aural sound energy level difference) as sounds with wavelengths that are short relative to inter-ear distance round head (hence higher frequency sounds) will not diffract round head.*

Spatial effects

Objective envelopment, or *early lateral energy fraction*, is a measure of the ratio of early energy arriving at a point from lateral directions to total early energy arriving at that point (early energy being defined as within 80 msec of the direct sound). This gives an index of the perceived spatial configuration of a space on the basis of acoustical cues and is likely to relate to the degree to which a listener can, or cannot, orient themselves in that space on the basis of sound alone.

The measurements derived in respect of the above parameters must be interpreted relatively, to some extent. While they rely on certain 'absolute' levels (for example, a decay by 60 dB from the end of the direct sound in defining reverberation time), it is very likely that the inhabitants of the pre-modern world encountered everyday soundscapes (a term coined by the Canadian composer R. Murray Schafer as an auditory analogue of the term landscape) that were very different from those of the modern urban world. They were thus likely to have been sensitized to features of those everyday soundscapes (see McFadden & Callaway 1999) in ways that may have shaped

their responses to sound in special, sacred or monumental sites. Hence it would seem important at least to obtain measurements of sound levels that are likely to be representative of the sonic environments of the users and inhabitants of the archaeological sites in question, perhaps in the form of measures such as LA*eq*. LA*eq* is a standard measure of the loudness (L) of environmental sound averaged over a time period, with different frequency bands weighted according to the dB(A) scale (hence A*eq*) so as to relate to the sensitivity of the human auditory system; this provides an index of averaged and perceptually normalized environmental sound level.

Assuming that this can be done, it should be possible (in conjunction with other types of archaeological information) to use these standard measures to derive information about the probable temporal textures of sound used in spaces and sites, as well as about the disposition of participants. From *Total sound level* one can obtain an index of the 'strength' of the acoustic signal in a space, which could be compared to measurements in local contemporary domestic structures (either measured or estimated) as well as to measurements of environmental sound levels (LA*eq*) in each locale. It is likely that the total sound level within a completely enclosed site (whether constructed, such as the chambers of Newgrange or Maeshowe, see Watson & Keating 1999, or naturally occurring, such as Pech-Merle or Escoural, see Dams 1985) will be very significantly greater than at any other point in the locale, suggesting that it would have been an appropriate location for communal activities involving sound. In contrast, total sound levels in semi-enclosed sites (e.g. stone circles such as Stonehenge, Avebury or the Ring of Brodgar: see Watson & Keating 2000; Watson 2001b) tends to be highly variable according to measurement position, suggesting possible loci and disposition of participants for activities involving sound.

From measurement of *Clarity* in its two forms one can legitimately make inferences about the suitability of a space or site for speech, or for activities involving 'heightened speech' (as in declamation) or music. Such inferences can be buttressed by measures of *Reverberation time*, as a long *RT* (or long *Early decay time*) will seem to 'smear' or 'blend' sounds over time, making it more suitable for sound sequences that are either slow in pace or that require a degree of blending it time to achieve their efficacy (typically found in a range of ritual and liturgical contexts in the present day), while a short reverberation time is likely to enhance the experience of rapid sound sequences and of speech intelligibility.

It is somewhat more difficult to understand how measures of *Objective envelopment* might be interpreted. While this will provide an index of the perceived spatial configuration of a space on the basis of acoustical cues, and perhaps indicate the degree to which a listener may be able to orient themselves in that space on the basis of sound alone, the irregular configuration of most archaeological sites and spaces is likely to mean that this measure will be extremely variable in any given site, and perhaps of less importance than measurement of other features that might impact on the impression, or on the 'localizability', of sounds in such spaces. These other features include echoes, flutter-echoes, resonances, 'filter' and partial sound occlusion phenomena, and while these may be measured their interpretation may be less securely grounded in current architectural-acoustical data than are measures relating to intensity and temporal effects.

Echoes, flutter-echoes, resonances, 'filter' and partial sound occlusion phenomena tend to be viewed as 'undesirable' phenomena in current architectural-acoustical contexts, and research that bears on these focuses on their suppression rather than on their exploration or exploitation. However, it is highly likely that these types of phenomena which are likely to give rise of 'aural illusions' would have been highly valued in some pre-modern contexts and hence would have been exploited. In order to interpret measurements of these phenomena it seems necessary to consider not only the acoustics but also the psychoacoustics of spaces, and in particular the psychoacoustics of sound localization. As we shall see, this is a complex area involving the interaction of at least two perceptual mechanisms and it may well be that each instance of such phenomena would have to be interpreted in part on its own terms.

The psychoacoustics of space and location

The human experience of the location of a sound is governed by mechanisms that compare inter-aural time difference (ITD) and inter-aural intensity level difference (ILD) — see Grantham (1995); in effect, we

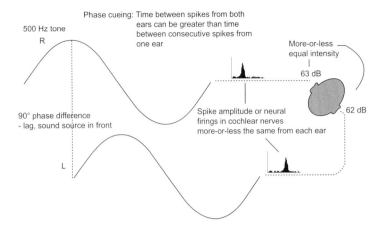

Figure 11.3a. *For low-frequency sounds from lateral directions, there may be no significant inter-aural intensity level difference although there is a difference in the time of arrival of the sound energy at each ear. Detection of the neural response to this inter-aural time difference may be used by a perceiver to localize the sound source.*

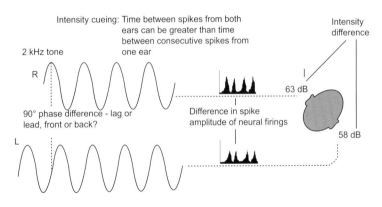

Figure 11.3b. *For higher frequency sounds from lateral directions inter-aural time differences provide ambiguous cues as to location, and inter-aural intensity level differences may be used to localize sound.*

localize sound in our perceptions by using as cues the differences in loudness, or the differences in time of arrival, of sound waves at each ear to infer the location of the source from which the sound waves originate. In the horizontal plane, ITDs are dominant cues for localization of low-frequency and broadband sounds while ILDs are dominant cues for localizing high-frequency sounds. In the vertical plane, localization cues derive from the interferences in the incoming sound waves that arise from reflections from the folds of the pinna, the external ear, which will differentially affect different frequency bands, boosting some and reducing others; these pinna-based spectral cues

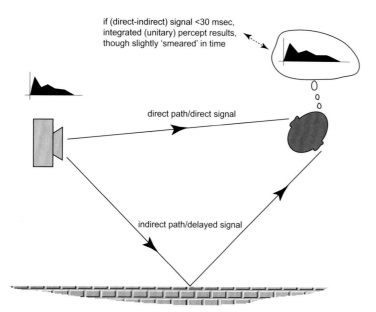

if (direct-indirect) signal <30 msec, integrated (unitary) percept results, though slightly 'smeared' in time

direct path/direct signal

indirect path/delayed signal

Figure 11.4a. *When indirect (reflected) sound energy reaches the perceiver within 30–35 msec of direct sound, both inputs are likely to be integrated into a single percept.*

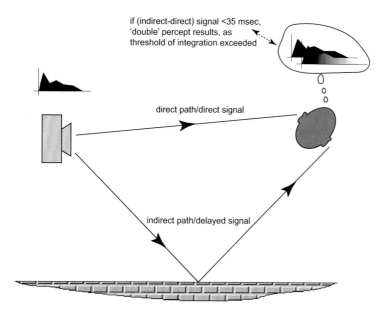

if (indirect-direct) signal <35 msec, 'double' percept results, as threshold of integration exceeded

direct path/direct signal

indirect path/delayed signal

Figure 11.4b. *When indirect (reflected) sound energy reaches the perceiver later than 30–35 msec after the direct sound, the inputs will not be integrated and a double percept is likely to result.*

(peaks and notches) are only really effective for sounds containing a significant energy component above 7 kHz. At present it appears that the most parsimonious explanation of detection of a moving sound source (or of the impression that a sound source is moving) seems likely to be based on comparison between successive applications of processing of the 'static' soundfield (the 'snapshot' hypothesis), limited by the localization resolution (the MMA, Minimum Auditory Angle).

Even in a free field, where a listener experiences only the sound arriving direct from the source, the operation of these processes of localization may sometimes result in ambiguous percepts; understanding how these psychoacoustical processes operate in the localization of sound sources becomes yet more complex when the influence of indirect, reflected sound is taken into account. In part this arises because of the need to consider the effect of the temporal grain of the human auditory system on the experience of sound in reflecting environments.

When sound is encountered in a space with reflective surfaces, if the time delay between the direct and indirect sound is less than *c.* 30 msec, the sound energy is integrated and a single unitary percept results. If the time delay is greater that *c.* 30–35 msec, then a double percept will be experienced; if the time delay is significantly greater than 35 msec and the first reflection to arrive is substantially more intense than any subsequent reflections, a clear echo will be experienced. The 30 msec integration threshold is effectively the threshold of generic perceptual event integration at the neural level (Pöppel & Wittmann 1999); in other words, 30 msec appears to be the limit of temporal resolution, or the basic 'grain', of human temporal perception.

In general one can say that when the time interval between successive reflections is much less than 30 msec a space's reflections will contribute to the experience of the sound in a synthetic rather than analytic manner. Hence, when a resonance is encountered in the audio range (having a frequency of greater than 20–30 Hz), frequencies in a signal at and around integer multiples of the resonance frequency will be enhanced relative to the other frequencies in that signal. This will, at the least, 'colour' the sound significantly, altering its perceptual characteristics, and this is a phenomenon that could certainly have been exploited in certain sites and spaces (as suggested in Reznikoff 1988). However, when a flutter-echo is encountered, the time delay between successive reflected signals is usually greater than 30 msec, corresponding to a more-or-less sub-audio or infrasonic 'resonance'. In these instances the perceived behaviour of sound may be more complex, depending on the signal that elicits the flutter-echo; the rapid and decaying succession of flutter-echoes that are produced may be interpretable as the movement of a single sound source, as a 'coloration' of the original signal, or conceivably as a 'fractionation' of the original sound into a succession of discrete sounds with a motion component. Similarly, the 'filter' or partial sound-occlusion effects that may arise in a partially enclosed site such as a henge or stone circle may be experienced differently according to the perceiver's location and according to the eliciting signal; it may be that some diffraction effects give rise to apparent sound-source motion, or colour sound in perceptual significant ways.

Seemingly anomalous behaviours of indirect sound such as resonance, echoes, flutter-echo or filter effects can give rise to auditory illusions because of the ambiguity of the cues afforded to a listener by the behaviour of sound waves in particular auditory environments. So for example, a resonance at a particular location in an enclosed or semi-enclosed space might lead to a sound produced at a particular pitch being startlingly louder than sounds produced at other pitches, this increase in amplitude being achieved with no extra effort on the part of the sound's producer. In the case of an echo, a sound produced in a particular location appears to be 'answered' from another location (see Waller this volume). In spaces that give rise to flutter-echoes, on occasion a sound may appear to elicit another, quite different sound that seems to move in space.

Here, the standard measures seem to fail; as far as we are aware the 'effects' in question have received little attention from acousticians other than as undesirable phenomena to be suppressed in any architectural design. However, as suggested above, it is very likely that such effects may have been viewed positively in pre-modern times, being exploited in the use of certain acoustical spaces, particularly those that can be interpreted as having ritual or liminal attributes and uses. Accordingly it seems that a case-by-case approach is necessary here, taking account of all the conceivable sound-producing practices and that might have been employed and exploring each site's acoustical particularities in the light of an understanding of human perceptual processes. For example, it seems likely that any sub-audio frequencies elicited as flutter echoes by brief, sharp-onset acoustic signals in reflective environments will be experienced as modulations of the original signal, although how that will impact on the overall perception of the signal remains to be elucidated. One can suggest that a viable approach might involve the exploration of any differential behaviour of sub-audio (less than 20 Hz), low-frequency (less than 1.5 kHz) and high frequency (greater than 1.5 kHz)

sounds in different acoustical environments, as well as the exploration of the ways in which complex sounds with significant and discrete components in each frequency region are consequently experienced.

The discussion so far has remained at a theoretical level, being confined to outlining some acoustic measures and features in respect of which the acoustics of ancient spaces might be elucidated. To put some flesh on these theoretical bones, and to give an instance of how acoustical effects that are difficult to quantify using standard measures might have impacted on the perceptions of people in the past, we will now cite an example of a subtle acoustical effect discovered accidentally in the course of a project which the first author undertook with Ezra Zubrow and Frank Cowan in which the potential of Upper Palaeolithic flint blades as sound-producing objects was being explored (see Cross *et al.* 2002).

A case study: lithophones and the numinous

For safety reasons, flint knapping was conducted out of doors, in a courtyard in the Music School in Cambridge. As the knapper, Frank Cowan, was producing the blades another member of the team, the present first author, was informally testing each new blade by suspending it by a nodal point between thumb and middle finger and tapping it with a flint percussor. While tapping he happened to turn round so that he was not directly between the sound source (the blade) and the two parallel walls constituting the long sides of the rectangular courtyard. Suddenly, a single tap on the blade was followed by a high pitched flutter — an animate sound seemingly located some distance from the sound source — that appeared to recede into the distance. The effect was quite unearthly; though out of doors and in the full afternoon sun, it seemed that the tapping had suddenly awoken some real yet invisible entity — perhaps a bird, or at least an avian spirit? — that evanesced, disappearing somehow into the (brick) boundary walls.

A few more taps and flutters and some hard thinking and what was happening became evident. The reflected sound from the two parallel walls (about 7.2 metres apart) was setting up a standing wave in the form of a 'flutter echo' which gradually died away. The source of the standing wave was the sound produced by tapping the blade, a high pitched tone (the mean frequency of all blades tested was about 6.2 kHz) with a sudden onset, hence the 'flutter echo' took the form of a fluttering sound with repeated sharp onsets and a high though unclear pitch, the flutter itself having a periodicity of around 42 msec (or 1/24th of a second). The apparent difference in location of the flutter echo from the sound source, and its apparent fading into the distance are likely to have derived from the complex cues that the phenomenon affords to the human auditory system.

In this situation it is conceivable that the flutter echo initiated by a rapid-onset and high-pitched sound afforded a complex signal with periodic modulations of amplitude. The location of the listener closer to one reflective surface than the other might have afforded a decrease in signal level with each increase and decrease of the overall amplitude envelope that was different at each ear (i.e. significantly greater decrease with each periodic change in amplitude envelope at one ear relative to the other). Alternatively, differences in the absorptive or diffusing characteristics of the two parallel reflective surfaces sustaining the flutter-echo (one was a plane brick wall, the opposite wall being partially brick and partially glass) might have afforded such regular laterally-biased intensity decrements. Either of these two possibilities could have led to the sound appearing to have a motion component. Indeed, it is likely that this 'illusion' is likely to occur only forparticular types of initiating sound in quite specific auditory environments; here, contingently, the sharp-onset high-frequency lithic-percussive sound produced in an environment with a strong flutter-echo would be the ideal 'fit' for such an effect. Notwithstanding these hypotheses, elucidating these issues fully would require considerable experimental research.

The fact that we were able to account for the effect in hard scientific terms did nothing to dispel the 'magical' qualities of the sound; much of the rest of the day was devoted to exploring the slight differences in apparent location, and in apparent direction of disappearance, of the flutter echoes produced by a range of blades tapped in different locations in the courtyard. By standing at a specific orientation in a given location with a given blade one could reliably repeat the effect, continually 'evoking' the same 'entity' that reliably 'disappeared' into the walls in a specific direction. While this effect was elicited in a modern architectural space bounded by (mainly) brick walls, it can in theory occur in *any* space bounded by parallel hard surfaces; all that is required is that the initial sharp sound — and the listener — be placed between two parallel, sound-reflecting surfaces, which need not by large in area. Indeed, it is likely that even in a bounded space of which the surfaces are noticeably irregular (such as a naturally formed cave), one or two points in that space will fall on a line between two surfaces that are both plane and parallel and hence afford the elicitation of a flutter-echo.

It was notable that even when fully in possession of a viable scientific explanation for the phenomenon, the effect was numinous. In the absence of any conceptual framework within which to articulate such an explanation, the phenomenon must appear self-evidently super-natural; an invisible, perhaps avian, entity, its presence warranted in sound, suddenly appears when evoked by a tap on the flint blade, then journeys off rapidly into the distance, always seemingly in the same direction but never in a direction that one could quite securely identify or follow. The resonances with many recent and extant ritual practices, where birds may constitute the mediators between living and dying (e.g. Feld 1982) or a bird may constitute the form in which a shaman journeys in a spirit quest (e.g. Balzer 1996), and the appearance of bird-headed human figures in some early rock art (see e.g. Clottes & Lewis-Williams 1998) appear noteworthy, and lead us to speculate that 'shamanistic' practices, conducted in appropriate acoustical environments, might have constituted a situation within which flutter-echoes — possibly generated by sharp high-frequency impulses of the type produced by flint percussors — could have been exploited. Indeed, this speculation fits well with the suggestions by Reznikoff (1988) and by Waller (1993) that there is a close relationship between the locations of at least some Upper Palaeolithic rock art and the acoustical properties of those locations, in particular, their resonance and echo characteristics, though further research and experiment is certainly required before any formal hypothesis can be developed.

It has been suggested (Devereux 2001) that this close relationship was motivated by the 'disorienting' effects of the low frequencies of at least some of the resonances, certain of which are infrasonic (below *c.* 20 Hz), though the experimental evidence in the literature that would support this is at best contentious.[1] It would seem that the exploitation of the complexities of the human response to complex acoustical phenomena such as flutter echoes may constitute a more viable explanation of this relationship, particularly in view of the illusions of sound displacement that appear to be associated with these types of resonances. It should be noted that acoustic illusions may appear to be especially powerful as the acoustical cues that give rise to these have no visible correlates; in effect, acoustic phenomena such as echoes, resonances and flutter-echoes — all of which are deemed 'undesirable' in terms of contemporary architectural acoustics — can be powerful mediators of a sense of mystery simply because their sources lie *solely* in the acoustical domain.

Conclusions

In this paper, we have sketched out some possible methods for acoustic research in archaeological contexts and have outlined a case study to emphasize how, once acquired, technical data requires interpretation. The application of objective acoustical research will not in itself reveal the perceptions of people in the past. Although we can make an educated guess about the physical and psychophysical basis for numinous phenomena, exemplified by the flint lithophone example, clarification of its perceptual basis would take a considerable amount of empirical and multidisciplinary research. The moral of the story is perhaps that although we are in a position to make considerable progress in identifying and defining the pre-modern experience of sounds in archaeological sites and spaces through the application of 'standard' acoustical measures, rather more work remains to be done to further elucidate the meanings, emotions or powers that ancient soundscapes embodied for the people who encountered them. It is critical that, alongside the application of rigorous methods, acoustical investigations acknowledge the social contexts within which sound may have been experienced, and remain aware that it is easy to impose modern cultural understandings and experiences onto past societies. In conclusion, an archaeology of sound will necessitate the application of detailed research techniques applied *in conjunction* with active and informed interpretation; the alternative is to risk hearing only echoes of ourselves.

Notes

1. Negative effects of infrasound appear to be reported by Mohr *et al.* (1965). However, this finding is contradicted by the later report of Harris *et al.* (1976), who note that the previous study had conflated negative effects of extremely high levels of low-frequency sound (between 20 and 100 Hz) with putative effects of infrasound (vibration energy at less than 20 Hz); the latter study found no deleterious effects of very high levels of infrasound on human performance. In addition, the impact of infrasound may vary significantly between individuals (see Nussbaum & Reinis 1985).

References

Barron, M., 1993. *Auditorium Acoustics and Architectural Design*. London: E. & F. N. Spon.

Balzer, M.M., 1996. Flights of the sacred — symbolism and theory in Siberian shamanism. *American Anthropologist* 98(2), 305–18.

Clottes, J. & D. Lewis-Williams, 1998. *The Shamans of Prehistory: Trance and Magic in the Painted Caves*. trans. S.

Hawkes. New York (NY): Abrams.

Cross, I., E. Zubrow & F. Cowan, 2002. Musical behaviours and the archaeological record: a preliminary study, in *Experimental Archaeology*, ed. J. Mathieu. (British Archaeological Reports International Series 1035.) Oxford: BAR, 25–34.

Dams, L., 1984. Preliminary findings at the 'Organ' Sanctuary in the cave of Nerja, Malaga, Spain. *Oxford Journal of Archaeology* 3(1), 1–14.

Dams, L., 1985 Palaeolithic lithophones: descriptions and comparisons. *Oxford Journal of Archaeology* 4(1), 31–46.

Devereux, P., 2001. *Stone Age Soundtracks: the Acoustic Archaeology of Ancient Sites*. London: Vega.

Devereux, P. & R.G. Jahn, 1996. Preliminary investigations and cognitive considerations of the acoustical resonances of selected archaeological sites. *Antiquity* 70, 665–6.

Feld, S., 1982. *Sound and Sentiment: Birds, Weeping, Poetics, and Song in Kaluli Expression*. Philadelphia (PA): University of Pennsylvania Press.

Grantham, D.W., 1995. Spatial hearing and related phenomena, in *Hearing*, ed. B.C.J. Moore. London: Academic Press, 297–345.

Harris, C.S., H.C. Sommer & D.L. Johnson, 1976. Review of the effects of infrasound on man. *Aviation, Space, and Environmental Medicine* 47, 430–34.

McFadden, D. & N.L. Callaway, 1999. Better discrimination of small changes in commonly encountered than in less commonly encountered auditory stimuli. *Journal of Experimental Psychology: Human Perception And Performance* 25(2), 543–60.

Mohr, G.C., J.N. Cole, E. Guild & H.E. Von-Gierke, 1965. Effects of low frequency and infrasonic noise on man. *Aerospace Medicine* 36(9), 817–24.

Nussbaum, D.S. & S. Reinis, 1985. *Some Individual Differences in Human Response to Infrasound*. (Report 282.) Toronto: University of Toronto Institute for Aerospace Studies.

Pocock, D., 1981. Sight and knowledge. *Transactions, Institute of British Geographers (New Series)* 6, 385–93.

Pöppel, E. & M. Wittmann, 1999. Time in the mind, in *The MIT Encyclopedia of the Cognitive Sciences*, eds. R.A. Wilson & F.C. Keil. Cambridge (MA): MIT Press, 841–3.

Porteous, J.D., 1990. *Landscapes of the Mind: Worlds of Sense and Metaphor*. Toronto: University of Toronto Press.

Rasch, R. & R. Plomp, 1982. The listener and the auditory environment, in *The Psychology of Music*, ed. D. Deutsch. 1st edition. London: Academic Press, 135–47.

Rayleigh, J.W.S., 1945. *The Theory of Sound*. New York (NY): Dover Publications.

Reznikoff, I., 1988. On the sound dimension of prehistoric caves and rocks, in *Musical Signification: Essays in the Semiotic Theory and Analysis of Music*, ed. E. Tarasti. Berlin: Mouton de Gruyter, 541–57.

Reznikoff, I. & M. Dauvois, 1988. La dimension sonore des grottes ornées. *Bulletin de la Société Préhistorique Française* 85(8), 238–46.

Rodaway, P., 1994. *Sensuous Geographies*. London: Routledge.

Sabine, W.C., 1921. *Collected Papers on Acoustics*. New York (NY): Dover Publications.

Waller, S.J., 1993. Sound and rock art. *Nature* 363(6429), 501.

Watson, A., 2001a. The sounds of transformation: acoustics, monuments and ritual in the British Neolithic, in *The Archaeology of Shamanism*, ed. N. Price. London: Routledge, 178–92.

Watson, A., 2001b. Composing Avebury. *World Archaeology* 33(2), 296–314.

Watson, A. & D. Keating, 1999. Architecture and sound: an acoustic analysis of megalithic monuments in prehistoric Britain. *Antiquity* 73, 325–36.

Watson, A. & D. Keating, 2000. The architecture of sound in Neolithic Orkney, in *Neolithic Orkney in its European Context*, ed. A. Ritchie. (McDonald Institute Monographs.) Cambridge: McDonald Institute for Archaeological Research, pp. 259-63.

Chapter 12

The Origin of Music and Rhythm

Ezra B.W. Zubrow & E.C. Blake

This paper explores the origin of music and rhythm. By 'origin' is meant the very earliest evidence of intentional music by humans. A brief discussion of the ethnographic analogues in the 'shamanistic' music of northern arctic groups, whose subsistence patterns are similar to late Upper Palaeolithic cultures, is followed by consideration of the relationship between the origin of music and prehistoric instruments. At some point in the Upper Palaeolithic there was a transition from 'non-music' to 'music' that was accompanied by shifts in intent, instrumentality, religion, cognition, education, perception, and causality. New evidence is presented for the existence of Upper Palaeolithic lithophones made of flint, in addition to the remains of prehistoric bone flutes. Experimental evidence on the origin of rhythm through the heart monitoring of modern flint knappers suggests that the origin of rhythm was related to heartbeat rates during the knapping process. Finally, the paper concludes that studies of the origin of music will benefit from a classification of models of prehistoric sound and music — from stages where ancient music is played on modern instruments; to those where ancient music is played on modern replicas of ancient instruments; to those where ancient music is played on ancient instruments; to stages where ancient music is played with ancient instruments in their ancient surroundings.

This is a volume on prehistoric sounds and their 'intentionality'. Our interest is the origin of music and the origin of rhythm. We are factually interested in when it was that music began and how. Or, to put it in a different way, was there a time and a place when our ancestors did not have music? If so, the transition from non-music to music is a fundamental question impacting culture, language, art, warfare, economics and other areas of life.[1] Thus, the determination and verification of the 'intentionality' of prehistoric sound is a very relevant issue for us. It is not the only question, however, since whether unintentional sound may be music is a separate and may be equally central concern pertaining to the origins of music. Of course, these are not new questions. As early as the thirteenth century, enquiries regarding the measurement of musical sounds, the physiological functioning of the auditory system, and the effects that music produces in the sentient being were thought to be fundamental (Crombie 1994).

We propose in this paper is to provide a brief background to our research and then develop its relevance to both the methodological and the substantive issues regarding the intentionality of prehistoric sounds.

Background

From even the most conservative perspective, the Upper Palaeolithic and early Mesolithic were characterized by a well-known fluorescence of technical and artistic development. The famous cave art of roughly contemporaneous sites, exemplified by Lascaux, is matched by the development of highly-stylized lithic technologies in Aurignacian, Solutrean and Perigordian. These were in turn replaced by the innovative compound tools of the Mesolithic and the new settlement patterns represented by such open-air campsites or settlements of Pincevent and Verberie.

Presently, Zubrow is analyzing with the excavator (Françoise Audouze) the Magdalenian site of

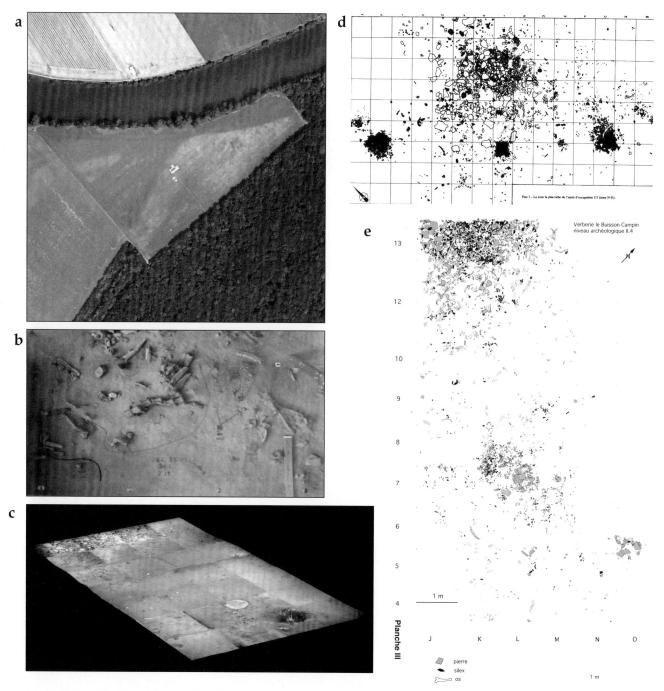

Figure 12.1. *The Magdalenian site of Verberie, France: a) aerial photo showing site including the present and palaeo-river; b) detail photo of bone and flint* in situ; *c) photo montage level IV with hearth and dump; d) detailed artefact scatter unit diagram; e) map of part of level IV showing hearth and part of dump.*

Verberie (see Fig. 12.1 where a, b, and c are site photos and artefact distributions are d and e). Located in the Paris basin, it was a frequently reoccupied reindeer-hunting and butchering camp dating to approximately 15,000 years ago. Close to the migratory route of the reindeer, Verberie was a localized killing zone with open-air structures, hearths, and work areas. At this time Paris was part of the French steppe and weather conditions were similar to those of northern Sweden, Finland and Siberia today.

In seeking ethnographic materials from similar environments, attention is drawn to the long tradition of analysis of the North American Inuit (Eskimo), Aleut, Athapaskan, and Cree as well as the

European and Asian Sami (Lapp), Tlingit, Chukchee, Even (Tungus), and Koryak (Fitzhugh & Crowell 1988). There one sees similar reindeer-hunting societies adapting to similar northern steppe and arctic environments.

Other evidence for early music are the two 'bone flutes' — one from Württemberg dated to 36,000 years ago, and the more controversial 'Neanderthal flute' from Divje Babe, Slovenia dating to 43,000 years ago (Fig. 12.2). A joint project conducted by Zubrow (archaeology), Cross (music), and Cowan (flint knapping) has hypothesized that since, however, it is lithic technology that has the longest material history of any hominin technology, early musicians would have made use of this technology during the millions of years of tool-making from *Homo habilis* to *Homo sapiens*. Non-western lithophones include African ringing stones (Grove & Sadie 1980) ancient Chinese *pien ch'ing* (Grove & Sadie 1980) and Peruvian Potosian ringing stones (Stobart & Howard 2002) while Western uses include the Victorian stone piano (the stone dulcimer, rock harmonicon or geological piano), Karl Orff's compositions, and stone marimbas (Fig. 12.3).

The research design comprised five successive steps:

- simulating prehistoric tool-making by modern expert flint-knappers and the making of potential tools and lithophones;
- playing of these lithophones by music graduate students;
- analyzing the lithophones for use-wear patterns that were unique both before and after playing;
- modelling the sound structure; and
- finding prehistoric examples.

Over 200 blades and cores were played according to specific protocols. More than 1300 percussions were recorded and then analyzed using modern acoustic equipment. Acoustically, the sounds can be predicted by the same equations as those used for a marimba, provided the differences in materials are taken into account. Most importantly, a unique form of use-wear was found, located on the acoustically nodal areas of

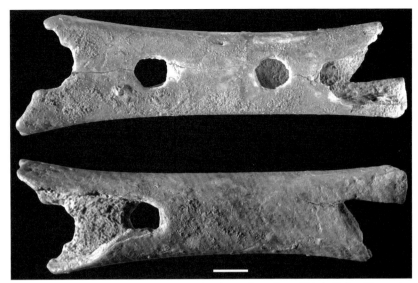

Figure 12.2. *Controversial Mousterian bone flute from Divje Babe, Slovenia. (Scale: 1 cm. Photo: F. d'Errico.)*

Figure 12.3. *Stone marimba (modern).*

the blades under a microscope. Figure 12.4 shows the position of the nodal areas and use-wear on the blade, along with pre-and post surface damage created by musical play. For the independent test, some 2600 hundred blades from the Cambridge University Museum of Archaeology and Anthropology were examined for this type of 'musically unique' surface damage. Six blades from the site of Cro-Magnon produced similar evidence.

Over thirty years ago, Rodney Needham put the question 'why is noise that is produced by striking or shaking so widely used in order to communicate with the other world?' (Needham 1967) Somewhat conversely, Martin Clayton (1996) summarizing eth-

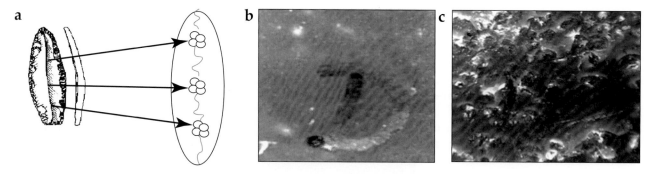

Figure 12.4. *Unique use-wear patterns caused by playing a flint lithophone: a) location of use-wear (three locations for three tones); b) low magnification microscopic photograph of the flint prior to playing, marked with 'D' for spatial reference; c) low magnification microscopic photograph after playing, marked with 'D' for spatial reference showing use-wear.*

Table 12.1. *Comparison of 'pre-music' and 'post-music' stages*

	Intent	Instrumentality
Pre-music	Sounds without musical intent	Vocal
Post-music	Sounds with musical intent	Vocal and instruments

	Religion	Cognition
Pre-music	Pre-shamanistic	Pre-abstraction
Post-music	Shamanistic and Post-shamanistic	Post-abstraction

	Hominins	Education
Pre-music	Pre-*Homo sapiens*	No cross-generational music
Post-music	Post-*Homo sapiens*	Cross-generational music

	Construction	Modelling
Pre-music	Non-constructive perception	Non-causal
Post-music	Construction	Causal

	Sounds	Senses
Pre-music	Sound generation from voice and objects	Listening, watching
Post-music	Sound generation from voice and objects	Listening, watching, hearing, touching, feeling

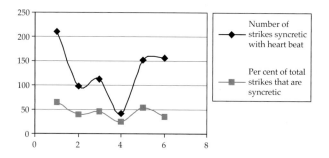

Figure 12.5. *Number and percentage of flint-knapper strikes that are synchronous with the flint-knapper's heart beat.*

rates of manufacture of a variety of products, including sound. Early heart rates — those of *Homo habilis*, *Australopithecus africanus*, and *Australopithecus robustus* — were probably more rapid than present ones. The rate is generally inversely proportional to body size (C. Begum pers. comm.; D. Berman pers. comm.), but there is considerable new evidence that the number of beats in a lifetime is fixed across species (Scherrmann pers. comm.).

In an attempt to begin to understand the origins of rhythm[2] a study was undertaken by the present authors with a three-step blind-test research design:
- simulating prehistoric tool and flint music making by flint-knappers who had no idea of the rationale for the experiment,
- recording both naïve and expert lithophone players while monitoring their heart rates,
- analyzing the relationships between the rhythms produced and the players' heartbeats throughout the immediately before, during, and after playing.

The preliminary results based upon six persons show that sound-stroke and heartbeat are exactly syncretic for between 1 in 2 to 1 in 3 beats. It would appear that approximately 50 per cent are exactly syncretic,

nographic music, notes 'that from a global perspective … unmetered or free rhythm is a widespread and important phenomenon'. One line of research has suggested that the human heart rate is related to

120

although heartbeats are short events separated by longer intervals (Fig. 12.5).

The musical transition: non-music to music

We believe that many of the methodological issues about prehistoric sound systems and music are clearer when one considers the 'origin of music'. The definitional and processual questions should be clearer for earlier periods because at the beginning of a phenomenon they are simpler and fewer exogenous forces are usually in operation. The difference between 'non-existence' and 'existence' stands out in stronger contrast than do differences of degree within the same phenomenon.

Contrasts between likely 'pre-music' and 'post-music' stages can be proposed (see Table 12.1). There are a variety of possibilities depending upon the parameter contrasted. Given the present state of research, their validity is open to debate, but they provide a valuable heuristic to generate questions.

Was the origin of music marked by a transition from non-intentional sound-systems to intentional sound-systems? May there be music without intent? May there be music that is partially intentional and partially non-intentional? We might, for example, assume that the earliest forms of percussion are an offshoot of the tool-making process of flint knapping. The flint-knapping process is clearly intentional, but the knapping rate may derive from the heartbeat. Since humans are not usually aware of their heartbeat, such music would be partially intentional (sound production) and partially non-intentional (rhythm). A related but separate question is whether the process by which sound systems become music is intentional. Could it be simply an advantageous accident (Glymour 2001)? Furthermore, it could be a self-engendering process. In other words, the very recognition of music, its labelling as such by our prehistoric ancestors, may have induced the generation of more music. It would be a type of 'feed-forward' looping process — a snowball effect.

Finally, we suggest that the transition probably involved the senses. Zubrow & Daly (1998) have suggested that the senses relate and combine to generate specific geographical experiences and perceptions. This can be extended to musical experience. When experiencing music the senses operate together in many combinations and the sum of their partnership exceeds the effectiveness of each sense alone. Thus the transition may have been not a change in the sounds but the adding-on of additional senses — first listening, then watching, then hearing, then touching, etc.

What is intent? Intent and chance; issues definitional and methodological

We suggest that intent is the mental purpose needed to accomplish a specific act — in our case music. Having noted that, we are aware that intent is a Pandora's box of definitions and methodological quagmires. Malle & Knobe have shown empirically, however, that people have a remarkable folk consistency with regard to intentionality.

> An action is considered intentional if the agent has (a) a desire for an outcome, (b) a belief that the action will lead to the outcome, (c) an intention to perform the action, (d) skill to perform the action, and (e) awareness while performing it (Malle & Knobe 1997).

These may be considered reasonable criteria for music. Sounds become music when the person: a) desires music; b) believes that by making the sounds he or she is making music; c) intends to make the sounds; d) has the skill to make the sounds; and e) is aware that he or she is performing these sounds. Such a scenario clearly shows intent. One might note that this does not mean that one has to be satisfied with the resulting sounds.

For archaeologists who are working with later sites, there are further issues pertaining to the musical environment. One question might be whether the site was used for the composition of music. Another is whether the site was created for the playing of music; still another, whether the site was created for the listening to music and finally whether it was intended for something else and was intentionally readapted for the production or appreciation of music.

Archaeologists working on the origin of music are not only faced with the same questions as the above but also by another and perhaps more troubling set. What are the relationships between hominin evolution, cognitive evolution, intent, language and music? Is intent a hallmark of humanity? If so, do these barriers have to be crossed before there is music? Does music precede language? Are the two contemporaneous or does one appear later than the other? Are there differences in the levels of 'intentionality' in communicating information between language and music?

For these scholars, intent is woven with 'consciousness' and the recognition of the 'self'. It is a special mental element that is required, that goes beyond any necessary mental state. In legal parlance, this would be the 'actus reus'; for us, it should be the 'actus musicus'. There are three further considerations. First, it is not sufficient simply to produce the music; it must be demonstrable that the sounds that are produced were desired, whether or not they are musical. This implies the intention to change the 'musicscape' from 'before the music' to 'during the music' and possibly even 'after the music. Second, one should be able to show the mechanism that forms the link between desire and reaction. Third, intent is temporally and spatially context-dependent. The 'whispering gallery' may be accidental when constructed, but when one places an orchestra there because of its acoustics, it is being used intentionally. What is intended in one society may be an accidental in the next — although we believe that, given diffusion, the converse is more probable.

There are several difficulties with the concept of 'intent'. The boundary between noise and music may be a matter of intent. That is not only culturally-specific but also may be individual-specific. Noise for you may be music to our ears. In a more general sense, however, one may consider whether music comes through the harnessing of chance sounds into meaningful compositions. We might want to argue that the evolution of music has been from 'noises and more random sounds' to 'increasingly organized and intentionally restricted sound patterns'. Later, there may be times and places where music takes a step backwards, towards a less organized and more chance-oriented form. This suggests that the development of music would not be a smooth evolutionary development but rather a process of 'starts and stops' and 'forwards and backwards'. In Western classical music, for example, composers such as Cage (Nyman 1999) and Devine (2003) have attempted to demonstrate methods of composition that are based on chance, not only in the process of composition but also in the performance.

Similarly, the boundaries between listener and performer and the boundaries between stage, or 'performance place', and environment need not follow our present understandings. There is a general pattern over time of increasingly specialized 'performance places' with greater and greater dedication and construction of specialized environments for music.

The importance not only of location but the identification of location by the listener has been an issue of some interest to Ian Cross and Eleonora Rocconi (Cross & Watson this volume; Rocconi this volume). Moreover, some modern composers have made a point of location. For example, Stockhausen's compositions (Kohl 1981; Kurtz 1992) use the directions of sounds and their movements through space. Prehistoric soundscapes are analyzed according to the sounds that may be heard or generated from particular performance places. GIS can be used to discern and model prehistoric soundscapes in the same way as one analyzes a natural or cultural landscape. Performance place and listening environ-

ments are connected by location.

There are other issues. How do we demonstrate intent when objects intended for music are accidentally used for non-functional purposes; or alternatively, when an object made for another purpose, such as a comb, is accidentally played first, and then later intentionally played? Conversely, non-functional objects have sometimes been found to have functional uses.

In short, intent is a slippery slope. Cultures may create and label as intentional what other societies would claim are non-intentional phenomena. In one such example, the wind becomes the 'Devil's music' in the mountains of Greece.

> Bands of male demons ... with their leader, the black-faced limping Devil, sometimes surround and torment a lonely shepherd. The female demons are referred to as the 'ladies who bring good luck' ... a propitiatory euphemism which indicates their power. Like their masculine counterparts, these ladies prefer the mountaintops and forests or a lonely meadow in the plain. Very often, they join the male demons in an orgiastic feast, the ladies of good luck wearing long white dresses, the men in kilts of the same colour. On a night when there is wind, one often hears the Devil's music in the high crags. Otherwise, when they are not feasting or provoking humans, they pass their time eternally spinning and very occasionally one comes across a spindle-weight which one of them has dropped. (Campbell 1964)

The wind becomes the intentional music of the devil and, furthermore, a connection is made between unconnected phenomena such as the absence of music (wind), the action of spinning, and the prehistoric spindle weight.

The distance between intent and improvisation, both intentional and unintentional, is a fine line. As improvisation becomes increasingly spontaneous and increasingly abstracted from the melody, it crosses over a boundary and becomes chance. As remarked earlier, the Saami may exemplify those kinds of societies operating in conditions environmentally (arctic and sub-arctic) and economically (reindeer-hunting) similar to those of the Magdalenian and late Upper Palaeolithic. While recognizing that there are significant problems in such distant analogies that transcend the generations of time, their music may still provide information about intent.

> Then he howls like this
> when he eats a reindeer,
> and when he has finished eating
> he starts to howl
> uuooaa uuooaa uuooaa.
> When he has howled so
> then he trots off to the forest
> and makes for the marshes.

Juoigos is very much a matter of improvisation. Often it is merely the expression of a passing whim, and is soon forgotten, but it is also, as the Lapp writer Turi says, 'an art to remember'. Once a song is impressed on the memory, it is sung again and again and learned by others. In this way it becomes traditional and is passed on from generation to generation' (Vorren 1962).

Intent and evolution

Along with bipedal locomotion, use of the hands, and numerous other traits, 'intentionality' has been conceived of as a trait that sets humans apart from animals and as something exclusively human. Two groups of scholars have suggested, however, that this is not the case. Both base their arguments on the idea that other species have intentionality. On the one hand, evolutionary biologists have suggested that intelligent animals might posses a kind of intentionality and on the other, certain cognitive scientists have claimed that, in principle, computers might exhibit intentionality.

More importantly, when considering the origin of music and the origin of rhythm, evolution may play a trick. These scholars point out that what appears to be related or intentional may not in fact be so. If we consider rhythm to be derived from the heartbeat, for example, we should note Dennett's comment 13 years ago:

> To me the most fascinating property of the process of evolution is its uncanny capacity to mirror some properties of the human mind (the intelligent Artificer) while being bereft of others. While it can never be stressed enough that natural selection operates with no foresight and no purpose, we should not lose sight of the fact that the process of natural selection has proven itself to be exquisitely sensitive to rationales, making myriads of discriminating 'choices', and 'recognizing' and 'appreciating' many subtle relationships. To put it even more provocatively, when natural selection selects, it can 'choose' a particular design for one reason rather than another — without ever consciously — or unconsciously! — 'representing' either the choice or the reasons. (Hearts were chosen for their excellence as blood circulators, not for the captivating rhythm of their beating — though that might have been the reason something was 'chosen' by natural selection.) (Dennett 1990)

Evaluation, demonstration, validation and verification

Ideally, to evaluate intentionality at the time of the 'origin of music' one would need to be there to discuss with the bone flute player or stone gong player their motivations. Second best, but far better than what one

may do today, would be to watch their demonstration of making music. Unfortunately, for today's scholar thousands of generations later, the best is far more limited. The main activities involved in the testing are:

1. generation of test cases (test inputs, such as bringing appropriate instruments and people to an Aurignacian site to play;
2. execution of the programme using the test cases (playing music at the site);
3. evaluation of the test results (comparing them with the expected results, to ascertain whether, for example, the sound that was expected to travel across the site is totally muffled.

Testing is more, however, than just the selection of test inputs and the execution of the programme test on those inputs. With any testing, two fundamental questions arises: first, how good is the testing; and second, are the tests that have been performed adequate? The quality of the testing should be measured.

Ultimately, one is creating models of prehistoric music. Some are real models, such as the modern reproductions that Graham Lawson and Peter Holmes play; others are more theoretical. Michael McIntyre (1997) suggests that the process of making and appreciating music is in itself the fitting of a model to disconnected points of sound and that it is the organization of the models that one should emphasize.

The stages of demonstration: a problem in frustration

In attempting to study the origin of music and rhythm using simulation and experimentation, or to recreate prehistoric music, real world demonstrations should be created that demonstrate empirically what is expected to have occurred. This is especially the case where there are questions about the intent of the sound producers. Demonstration reinforces the arguments for the validity of the ideas. It must be emphasized, however, that a demonstration does not confirm or prove any outcome. What is a sufficient demonstration? There is no answer. Rather, a demonstration lends strength to the interpretation of a phenomenon. For studies in this volume, one may divide the types of demonstration into the following stages: Engineering, Baroque, Pro-Musica, Stradivarius, and Asklepieion.

In archaeoacoustics, it is important but not sufficient to show that sounds have interesting characteristics and correlations in particular environments. Thus, if one takes a 'pulse' or 'standardized sound' and plays it in caves, echo areas, archaeological sites or near prehistoric rock art, that does not mean that those were places where music was performed, even if there is a particular acoustic response. This *engineer-*

ing or correlative stage is, however, a significant step in the right direction. Moreover, the strength of the argument is increased if there is not only a positive but also a negative demonstration; namely, that in other areas (non-caves, non-echo areas, areas without prehistoric art) there is no correlation between sound and archaeology.

The next stage does not produce simply a controlled set of frequencies or auditory sounds, as in the previous demonstration, but involves the creation of sounds that one believes are similar to the prehistoric sounds. In this, the attempt is being made to recreate the sounds that were actually played prehistorically on modern instruments in a modern environment. This may be called the *Baroque* or *early music* step. It is equivalent to attending a concert of music by Jan Pieterszoon Sweelinck (1562–1621), Claudio Monteverdi (1567–1643), Girolamo Frescobaldi (1583–1643), and Heinrich Schutz (1585–1672) played by members of the Boston Symphony Orchestra at Symphony Hall in Boston.

The fact that ancient music is produced on modern instruments does not mean that the music would have sounded the same nor that the original players would have played their instruments in a similar manner. Such demonstrations are useful and provide an insight into prehistoric music, but they raise many questions. Did the ancient musician intend the music to be played *forte*, for example? How can one know?

The next stage in demonstration is what we call the *Pro-Musica* step after the New York Pro-Musica. For this demonstration, the prehistoric music is played on reproductions of prehistoric instruments. Peter Holmes and Graeme Lawson have provided good examples in their work. Zubrow, Cross, and Cowan have done likewise with the flint lithophones, playing what are effectively modern reproductions of ancient instruments (Zubrow *et al.* 2002). In these studies, some aspects of the methodology are clearly correct. One needs to understand the ancient technology and the ancient techniques of the ancient musician in order to play the reproduction. Again, it is a step in the right direction and lends strength to the argument. This does not demonstrate, however, that one is using the same techniques. The mere production of replica ancient instruments and their use does not necessarily mean that prehistoric individuals made or played their instruments similarly.

For the fourth stage, original ancient instruments are used to create the music. We might call this the *Stradivarius approach*. For example, Menuhin played the 'Soil' Stradivarius for years and now it is being played by Perlman (Foxhale 2003). Frequently, the instrument to be played is taken out of a museum collection, such as the Smithsonian collection or a specialized borrowing collection such as that of the Stradivari society (Fonoroff & Kondziolka 2003). Zubrow's musicians should properly have played the original blades from the site of Cro-Magnon, though this was not done. In reality, the Stradivarius stage frequently is combined with the previous stage. Promusica Rara, for example, plays both original instruments and reproductions (Rara 2003). This is also a step in the right direction. It is not, however, sufficient. The fact that one may play ancient instruments with present knowledge of their properties and present knowledge of music does not mean that prehistoric individuals had the same knowledge nor that they used the same techniques. Nor, does it mean that the original instruments sound the same today as they did when they were originally constructed. As an acoustic engineer (Woodhouse pers. comm.) reminds us 'The instruments have changed over time'.

Fifth, it is not sufficient to play the music in the original surroundings. One might call this the *Asklepeion* or the *ancient amphitheatre* approach. Scholars are carefully analyzing when and where ancient music was played (Rocconi this volume). It is clearly possible to reconstruct ancient music with ancient instruments and to play it in an ancient environment, such as theatre at Taormina (Felix 2003). The fact that Rampal played his wooded flute in one of the French prehistoric caves or that Jelle Atema (Miller 2000) played a replica of the Slovenian flute made of cave-bear bone does not demonstrate that they actually were played in caves, no matter how wonderfully they may sound. Of course, Woodhouse's criticism applies to the musical environment as it does to the instrument; that the environment probably did not sound the same when instruments were being played. For the environment has changed — architecturally, geologically, and in landscape features. Most environments are as dynamic temporally as they are spatially; and surely must also have been acoustically different. It is almost impossible for a modern listener to imagine a world in which there are no mechanical devices making noise somewhere in the acoustical background.

Perhaps the most that may be said about the 'intentionality' of prehistoric music and sound systems is that one may build an argument. This argument is augmented by playing music in the form that one thinks it would have been played, on replica and original instruments and in the environment in which it was originally played. Even if each of these is done successfully, one has not proved intent. Such an approach may, however, take us a long way down the road of acceptance and allow us to claim that the probability value of the evidence exceeds the prejudice against it. Perhaps that is the best for which one may hope.

Conclusions

In archaeology, interpretation is difficult because observations are fragmentary or poorly preserved. It is even more difficult where the behaviour under scrutiny does not leave direct physical traces. Music frequently falls into this latter category. In fact, in the case of prehistoric sound systems, we may be obliged to recognize that some types of music will never be discoverable and some types of data will be impossible to measure. How will one find evidence of prehistoric song?

We believe that the earlier the music, the earlier the prehistoric sound systems, and the earlier the environments in which they were played, the more difficult it will be to demonstrate the intentionality behind those sound systems and music. The material presented in this study has suggested that we may draw the following conclusions about the intentionality of prehistoric sound systems:
- that the origin of music may be traced through prehistoric instruments;
- that new evidence exists for prehistoric flint lithophones in addition to extant evidence for prehistoric bone flutes;
- that the origin of music has ethnographic analogues in the 'shamanistic' music of northern arctic groups such as Chuckchee, Tungus, Yakuts, Even, and Saami who are similar in their subsistence patterns to late Upper Palaeolithic and Magdalenian sites (such as Verberie);
- that new evidence, through heart monitoring of modern flint knapping, suggests that the origin of rhythm was related to heartbeat;
- that at some point in time there must have been a transition from 'non-music' to 'music' and that will have been accompanied by shifts in intent, instrumentality, religion, cognition, speciation, education, perception, and causality in some combination
- that the definition of 'intent' is difficult when applied to prehistoric sound systems and music and is complicated by problem of defining the boundaries between noise and music, improvisation and chance, nature and culture are both unclear and culturally variable;
- that 'intent' has both determinants and consequences in evolutionary terms;
- that in order to determine 'intent' for prehistoric sound systems one needs to create adequacy criteria and that there will be difficulties when these

criteria do not agree given the same models;
- that one may attempt to demonstrate (simulate) the models of prehistoric sound and music systems through a series of stages that we have labelled Engineering, Baroque, Pro-Musica, Stradivarius, and Asklepeion.

In the 1960s, Paul Martin, Mark Leone and Ezra Zubrow invited Thomas Kuhn, the philosopher and historian of science, to spend a week with them at an archaeological field site in the Southwestern United States where problems of economy and social organization were being explored. Kuhn noted that 'archaeology is such a frustrating human endeavour both in terms of its subject matter and its methodology.' It is even more so when trying to understand prehistoric sound systems and prehistoric music. Today, if we could, we would invite the modern philosopher of science and social contructionist Ian Hacking, who suggests perhaps more optimistically that 'two alien peoples can get to know each other remarkably quickly on a vast range of matters that are for both of them practical and pragmatic'. We think that sound and music are both practical and pragmatic.

Notes

1. Traditionally there have been three major views about the origin of music: it may have been 'coincidence based on the structure of a related phenomenon', 'motivated by a non-musical need' or 'inevitable through some process of evolution in a given direction' (Nettl 1958).
2.. Rhythm exists somewhat fluidly between discrete events and vibrations or tone. It is a regularly repeating sound event although accelerating and decelerating rhythms are easily recognized. Many scholars suggest that stimuli occur within a range of 0.5 events to eight events per second with durations of 120 to 1800 milliseconds. More events create tone, fewer discrete events (Devine & Stephens 1993).

References

Campbell, J.K., 1964. *Honour, Family and Patronage: a Study of Institutions and Moral Values in a Greek Mountain Community.* Oxford: Clarendon Press

Clayton, M., 1996. Free rhythm: ethnomusicology and the study of music without metre. *Bulletin of the School of Oriental and African Studies* 59, 323–32.

Crombie, A.C., 1994. *Styles of Scientific Thinking in the European Tradition: the History of Argument and Explanation Especially in the Mathematical and Biomedical Sciences and Arts.* London: Duckworth.

Dennett, D.D., 1990. Evolution, error and intentionality, in *The Foundations of Artificial Intelligence,* eds. Y. Wilks & D. Partridge. Cambridge: Cambridge University Press.

Devine, R., 2003 *Intention and Music*. http://www.apple.com/pro/music/devine/index2.html.

Devine, A.M. & L.D.Stephens, 1993. Evidence from experimental psychology for the rhythm and metre of Greek verse. *Transactions of the American Philological Association* 123, 379–403.

Felix, C., 2003. *Greek and Roman Taormina*. http://www.taormina-network.it/english/theater.htm.

Fitzhugh, W.W. & A. Crowell, 1988. *Crossroads of Continents: Cultures of Siberia and Alaska*. Washington (DC): Smithsonian Institution.

Fonoroff, E. & G. Kondziolka, 2003. *The Stradivari Society*. http://www.stradivarisociety.com.

Foxhale, M., 2003. *The Most Beautiful Violins*. http://www.leviolonmagique.net/strad/violins.htm.

Glaser, B.G. & A.L. Strauss, 1967. *The Discovery of Grounded Theory: Strategies for Qualitative Research*. Chicago (IL): Aldine.

Glymour, B., 2001. Selection, indeterminism, and evolutionary theory. *Philosophy of Science* 68, 518–35.

Grove, G. & S. Sadie, 1980. *The New Grove Dictionary of Music and Musicians*. Washington (DC): Grove's Dictionaries of Music.

Kohl, J.J., 1981. *Serial and Non-serial Techniques in the Music of Karlheinz Stockhausen from 1962–1968*. PhD thesis, University of Washington. Ann Arbor (MI): University Microfilms International, 1983.

Kurtz, M., 1992. *Stockhausen: a Biography*. London: Faber.

Malle, B.F. & J. Knobe, 1997. The folk concept of intentionality. *Journal of Experimental Social Psychology* 33, 101–21.

McIntyre, M.E., 1997. Lucidity and science II. From acausality, illusions and free will to final theories, mathematics and music. *Interdisciplinary Science Reviews* 22, 285–303.

Miller, M.K., 2000. *Music of the Neanderthals Dispatches From the Field*. AAAS 2000 Annual Meeting. http://www.exploratorium.edu/aaas-2000/0221_dispatch_flutes.html.

Needham, R., 1967. Percussion and transition. *Man* 2, 606–14.

Nettl, B., 1958. Historical aspects of ethnomusicology. *American Anthropologist* 60, 518–32.

Nyman, M., 1999. *Experimental Music: Cage and Beyond*. 2nd edition. Cambridge & New York (NY): Cambridge University Press.

Rara, Pro-Musica, 2003. *Pro Musica Rara*. http://www.promusicarara.org/.

Stobart, H. & R. Howard (eds.), 2002. *Knowledge and Learning in the Andes: Ethnographic Perspectives*. Liverpool: Liverpool University Press.

Thagard, P., 1992. *Conceptual Revolutions*. Princeton (NJ): Princeton University Press.

Thagard, P., 2000. *Coherence in Thought and Action*. Cambridge (MA): MIT Press.

Vorren, O., 1962. *Lapp Life and Customs: a Survey*. London: Oxford University Press.

Zubrow, E., 1973. Adequacy criteria and prediction in archaeological models, in *Research Theory in Current Anthropology*, ed. C. Redman. New York (NY): Wiley, 239–55.

Zubrow, E. & P.T. Daly, 1998. Symbolic behaviour: the origin of a spatial perspective, in *Cognition and Material Culture: the Archaeology of Symbolic Storage*, eds. C. Renfrew & C. Scarre. (McDonald Institute Monographs.) Cambridge: McDonald Institute for Archaeological Research, 157–74.

Zubrow, E., I. Cross & F. Cowan, 2002. Musical behaviors and the archaeological record: a preliminary study, in *Experimental Archaeology Replicating Past Objects, Behaviors, and Processes*, ed. J.R. Mathieu. Oxford: Archaeopress, 25–36.